Frommer's

Cyprus

with your family

915.69

From the best family beaches to mountain villages

WILEY

A John Wiley and Sons, Ltd, Publication

Contents

About the Author

Sue Bryant is an award-winning writer and editor, specialising in family travel and Mediterranean resorts. She writes for various national newspapers in the UK and magazines and websites worldwide, and has written, edited or contributed to 21 guidebooks.

Sue has been visiting Cyprus and writing about the island for 21 years in many capacities, from tourism to family travel, spas and golf, and remains captivated by its beauty and friendliness. She lives in London with her two children, Lauren and Joel.

Acknowledgements

My thanks to all the hoteliers who have offered me hospitality and insights into Cypriot life over the years, and all the tour operators I've visited on the island annually, bombarding them with questions. I'd also like to thank Lillian Panayi and Orestis Rossides of the Cyprus Tourism Organisation's London office for their continuing support.

My friends in Cyprus, Lucy and Zenon Zenonas and their children, Timothy and Dorothea, have provided a bed on countless occasions and shown me many fabulous places for families, providing an invaluable insider's view of life on the island as well as many happy evenings enjoying the local produce.

Thanks, too, to Liam, my partner, for helping me with the research on this book, doing all the driving so I could take notes and trying the weirdest things on the menus . . . and then putting up with me during the more pressurised phases of writing!

Finally, no acknowledgement would be complete without a mention of Lauren and Joel, young but expert travel critics and the best companions.

An Additional Note

Please be advised that travel information is subject to change at any time and this is especially true of prices. We therefore suggest that you write or call ahead for confirmation when making your travel plans. The authors, editors and publisher cannot be held responsible for experiences of readers while travelling. Your safety is important to us however, so we encourage you to stay alert and be aware of your surroundings.

Star Ratings, Icons & Abbreviations

Hotels, restaurants and attraction listings in this guide have been ranked for quality, value, service, amenities and special features using a star-rating system. Hotels, restaurants, attractions, shopping and nightlife are rated on a scale of zero stars (recommended) to three (exceptional). In addition to the star rating system, we also use 5 feature icons that point you to the great deals, in-the-know advice and unique experiences. Throughout the book, look for:

FIND	Special finds – those places only insiders know about
MOMENT	Special moments – those experiences that memories are made of
VALUE	Great values – where to get the best deals
OVERRATED	Places or experiences not worth your time or money
GREEN	Attractions employing responsible tourism policies

The following **abbreviations** are used for credit cards:

AE	American Express
MC	MasterCard
V	Visa

A Note on Prices

Frommer's provides exact prices in each destination's local currency. As this book went to press, the rate of exchange was €1 = £ 0.79. Rates of exchange are constantly in flux; for up-to-the minute information, consult a currency-conversion website such as www.oanda.com/convert/classic.

In the Family-friendly Accommodation section of this book we have used a price category system.

An Invitation to the Reader

In researching this book, we discovered many wonderful places –
hotels, restaurants, shops and more. We're sure you'll find others.
Please tell us about them, so we can share the information with
your fellow travellers in upcoming editions. If you were disappointed
with a recommendation, we'd love to know that too. Please email
frommers@wiley.co.uk or write to:

Frommer's Cyprus with Your Family, 1st Edition
John Wiley & Sons, Ltd
The Atrium
Southern Gate
Chichester
West Sussex, PO19 8SQ

Photo Credits

Inside Images

1 Family Highlights of Cyprus

Cyprus is an unusual island in that it is far greater than the sum of its parts. Everybody who visits loves it but first-time visitors may wonder initially what all the fuss is about. After all, the beaches are nothing special. The resorts are certainly far from beauteous. The countryside is fairly arid. The political situation of the impasse between Turkish and Greek, North and South, dominates conversation.

And yet... The smell of wild herbs the very minute you drive out of the airport. The mellow evening sun reflecting off the Rock of Aphrodite. The wind in the pines, high up in the Troodos Mountains. The joy of sitting with your toes in the sand, tucking into a vast meze of salads, dips and fresh, grilled sardines, washed down with delicious local wines.

On a more practical note, for families, it's the fact that you wouldn't dream of pitching up at a restaurant and saying 'Is this a child-friendly establishment?' Of course it is. Pretty much everywhere in Cyprus is child-friendly and all Cypriots appear to adore children. I've lost count of the times when I've seen a tired mother struggling with a grizzly baby at the breakfast buffet and some beaming waitress comes up and bears the child away, cooing, leaving the mother gaping in happy amazement.

Cypriots are genuinely hospitable and always find time to chat. It's true that their wonderful service ethic is being eroded somewhat by the influx of untrained workers from the new EU countries – but in most places, families receive a warm and effusive welcome. Cypriots enjoy money as much as anybody else but they have not been 'spoiled' by tourism; they're not cynical, or grasping, and pretty well every meal in a taverna ends in a conversation with the proprietor and a few brandies on the house.

Why else do I love Cyprus? Because it's genuinely beautiful; mountainous, forested, remote in places – and even after visiting for 25 years, first without my children, then with a newborn and now with preteens, I'm still finding new walks, new hidden coves and tiny hamlets of stone houses, tucked away in the mountains. I've made friends whom I visit year after year, and I envy the carefree outdoor lifestyle their children enjoy.

Although Cyprus is certainly an upmarket kind of destination, made more expensive by the fact that it's a little beyond the range of most low-cost airlines, it genuinely caters to all tastes. For those who care about nightlife, which you may well if you're travelling with teenagers, there's everything from chill-out beach bars to bouzouki clubs. If you're looking for luxury, you're in the right place. The island has what I consider to be the best overall standard of accommodation in the Mediterranean, ranging from the most chic boutiques imaginable, to ultra-deluxe five-star family resorts, to beautiful stone houses, carefully restored, affordable to all and offering an insight into village life.

Tourism in Cyprus has come full circle. Having visited so many times and over such a long period, I have watched the island evolve, from the hotel-building boom of the 1980s to the rise (and fall) of the Ayia Napa club scene, to the property gold rush of the early 21st century.

The latest trend, to me, is the most exciting, as Cyprus rediscovers its roots. Agrotourism – a government-funded tourism initiative to preserve the traditional rural lifestyle – has been around for years but suddenly it's really fashionable. In addition to choosing the big beach resorts, holidaymakers are opting for gorgeous old stone houses and village tavernas serving organic food. The Vakhis movement – the Cypriot answer to slow food – means the country's wonderful variety of native dishes is being celebrated once more. EU money means the sleepy hilltop villages that had become so neglected as young people migrated to the coast suddenly have a new lease of life. New walking trails are being developed in the mountains, and new 'experiences' that families can enjoy together are on offer, like staying on a farm and learning how to make halloumi cheese, or following a nature trail and studying the indigenous plants, birds and lizards. Whatever age your children, these are genuinely special activities to enjoy while doing your bit to preserve the authenticity of this most rewarding corner of the Mediterranean.

CYPRUS FAMILY HIGHLIGHTS

Best Family Events Cyprus has a lively calendar of celebrations, the best known of which is probably the **Limassol Wine Festival** (see p. 96) in September. While this sounds like a rather Bacchinalian event in which to involve children, like everything else in Cyprus, it welcomes families and the festivities include 10 days of music, folklore, dance and, of course, flowing wine as the growers around the town bring their newest vintages and set up shop near the beach, where the main festival takes place.

Another event of great interest to small boys (and probably petrolhead dads) is the **Cyprus Rally** (see p. 96), a nail-biting race, which is well established on the international circuit. The best fun is the night before the race starts, when all the cars are displayed along the seafront in Limassol and you can walk along and chat to the teams.

Best Natural Attractions Cyprus has natural attractions in spades, although some are hidden away deep in the countryside. The **Avakas Gorge** (see p. 81), a chasm in the rocks to the west of the Akamas Peninsula, is just about manageable with children of about eight and over as there's a fair bit of scrambling (and lots of hooting to make echoes off the walls, and wildlife spotting, and striking silly poses for photos that make you appear to be propping up the sides). It's astonishingly beautiful, although the stench from a dead sheep that had obviously toppled in put a bit of a damper on my last visit.

The pine-clad **Troodos mountain** range (see chapter 6) that forms the spine of the island is another great attraction, criss-crossed with walking trails and dotted with picnic spots. The views from the top are amazing – you can see right down into the Turkish-occupied north of the island and on a clear day, across the sea to the Turkish mainland.

Best Animal Attractions Lara Beach (see p. 78) on Akamas isn't an attraction in the traditional sense but few animal experiences can be as exciting for a child as holding a one-day-old sea turtle in the palm of their hand. Every summer, during the egg-laying season, conservationists set up camp in this heavily protected area to guard the nests and live a hippie lifestyle on the beach until all the eggs are hatched. It's pretty rough and ready but you can visit their camp, learn about the turtles and their perilous journey to adulthood, hold a baby and see the metal cages protecting the nests. I found it deeply moving and any child is guaranteed to come away full of righteous indignation about the importance of conservation.

A more formal attraction, which is very well done, is the

Resident of the Camel Park near Larnaca

Camel Park (see p. 159) outside Larnaca, beautifully laid out and populated by the friendliest, sleekest camels I've ever seen, possibly thanks to the bags of carob seeds you can buy at the entrance as offerings. There are rides, longer family treks on the beach, a petting zoo, an indoor games area and best of all, a rather good swimming pool and restaurant, so you can make a day trip out of it.

Best Beaches Beaches are not the strong point of Cyprus but plenty of them have EU Blue Flag status and there are decent sandy spots if you know where to look. **Coral Beach** (see p. 52), west of Paphos, is one such lovely place, with soft, yellow sand forming a wide arc between white stone cliffs at either end. There's a vast array of water toys to hire, from banana boats to pedalos with slides on them, and a decent café which serves food all day and cocktails to chill-out sounds at sunset.

Otherwise, if you're looking for a pure beach holiday, **Ayia Napa** (see p. 178) at the eastern end of the island is the place to be – or rather, its quieter neighbour, Protaras (see p. 181). Some of the little coves like Konnas Beach here are spectacularly beautiful – you could be in the Caribbean, the sea is so dazzlingly turquoise and clear. Needless to say, all the beaches attract huge crowds, which is a good reason to come off season. This end of the island, though, is a perfect place to come with toddlers who are just finding their feet and like splashing around in the shallows.

Best Outdoor Activities If you're travelling off-season, which is recommended with small children as summer is just too hot, there are loads of outdoor activities from horse riding to family cycle rides. Two of my favourites are to pack a picnic and do one of the marked hiking trails in the **Troodos** (see p. 142), or to take a boat trip around the tip of **Akamas** (see p. 84) and stop for swimming (skinny dipping, even) in a deserted bay. You can drive across the dirt tracks of Akamas, too, if you rent a four-wheel drive vehicle. It's quite an adventure for older children although too bumpy for a baby in a car seat. The whole area is wonderfully remote, with a few rutted trails leading down to deserted beaches.

Best Indoor Attractions One of the most unusual museums is the **Oleastro Olive Park** (see p. 57) at the unspoilt village of Anogyra. The park, set in a grove of organic olive trees, tells the story of 60,000 years of olive cultivation, bringing the healthy Mediterranean diet into the story, as well as mythology, cultivation techniques, recipes and products for sale, from high-grade organic oil to soaps and wood products. There are also ponies for riding, an ecological olive mill, a playground, an

View over Coral Bay, west of Paphos

artists' corner and an organic café.

Another unmissable visit is to some of the **mountain monasteries** in the Troodos. It may be hard to persuade children that a monastery is fun but Kykkos (see p. 139), one of the biggest, is such an eye-opener that even the most recalcitrant visitor (over the age of about six) should be impressed. The monastery is absolutely dripping with gold – gold walls, gold images, gold chandeliers, gold icons, gold candlesticks – and gives you a real idea of just how incredibly wealthy the church in Cyprus is. The visit is fairly swift but you may find children enjoy picking out biblical stories and scenes from the gleaming gold walls and tiled murals.

Best Hike One of the prettiest and most exciting hiking trails is the **Caledonia Falls** (see p. 137) in the Troodos Mountains. In the cool half-light of the forest,

Olive harvest

you feel as though you're in another world, light years from the hustle and bustle of the coast and the blazing heat. The walk is an easy scramble downhill, with a path all the way, and the most fun part for children is the fact that the trail crosses the river at several points via stepping stones. Six or seven years and upwards is the best age group for this walk, or you could do it with a baby in a backpack. The impressive waterfall cascades into a cool rock pool near the end of the trail and you can finish off the whole happy adventure in the restaurant at the bottom, which will serve freshly grilled mountain trout and order a taxi to take you back to your car, which you will have parked at the top of the mountain.

Best Waterpark There are several waterparks on the island but I like the **Paphos Aphrodite Water Park** (see p. 60) best – it has the added advantage that you can spot it on Google Earth before you leave home. These waterparks are a blessing in high season as Cyprus gets incredibly hot and with children, you can't really stray too far from anywhere with swimming opportunities. The Paphos Aphrodite Water Park has a good mix of rides for all ages, from the usual twisty water slides to fun things like the Water Bubble, a giant cushion that you scramble up and slide down.

Best History Lessons There's plenty to see in Cyprus, some of which has been around for couple

Roman Amphitheatre at Curium

will enjoy the thrill of the jeep suddenly veering off the road and down a bumpy track at a rather exciting speed. Plenty of companies offer safaris and each one has its own special routes. My favourite wound its way through the Troodos, stopping to look at cascading waterfalls, tiny villages and best of all if you're with children, little points of interest like wild herbs growing by the roadside, or lizards and snakes. An experienced guide will have an eye for this kind of detail as well as being a mine of information of Cypriot trivia.

of thousand years. The island cashes in unashamedly on its connection with the goddess Aphrodite, who allegedly emerged from the foam somewhere near **Pissouri**. The more solid historical reality, though, is perhaps of greater interest to children: the impressive Roman amphitheatre at **Curium** (see p. 98), where there are ballet performances under the stars in summer, or the solid bulk of **Kolossi Castle** (see p. 105), where Richard the Lionheart married, or the spectacular Roman **mosaics** in Paphos (see p. 56).

Best Day Trip There are two advantages to a **guided jeep safari** (see p. 58 and 111). First you won't have to navigate and get lost and bad-tempered, and second, you'll go even further off the beaten track than you might have thought possible. These days out are perfect for children of about seven and upwards who

Best for Teenagers Limassol (see p. 95) is the best resort if you're happy to let your teenagers out by themselves. The tourist area is one long strip running parallel to the beach and there are some cheap and cheerful places for teens to hang out within walking distance of a lot of the hotels, as well as hundreds of shops selling the kind of tourist tat that teenage girls love browsing. Walking along the beach is safe as there are always so many people out and about. **Ayia Napa** (see p. 178) has even more nightlife but Limassol somehow has a less decadent feel about it – and better family hotels, too.

BEST ACCOMMODATION

Best Resort Hotel Aphrodite Hills (see p. 67), tucked away in the hills behind the town of Pissouri, is the only resort of its

The stylish Londa, Limassol

kind in Cyprus, completely self-contained with everything from luxury accommodation to a 'village square' with numerous restaurants. The spa is simply heaven on earth and there's an excellent children's club. The resort's *raison d'être* is really its golf course but don't let that put you off – there is a lot for families to do here, including guided nature walks through the ravine that divides the front nine from the back. There's also a beach club with a shuttle bus service.

Most Stylish Hotel The **Londa** in Limassol is like nothing Cyprus has ever seen. Transformed from what was a boring business hotel to a haven of designer chic, it's breathtaking from the minute you enter the all-white lobby with its floor-to-ceiling glass walls overlooking the sea. The Londa isn't right for families with toddlers but it's a fantastic place for posing if you have a small baby and are still in denial about being a parent, or if

you want to score massive brownie points with your style-conscious teenagers.

Best Self-Catering Some of the agrotourism developments on the island are absolutely gorgeous. The village of **Tochni** (see p. 157), hidden in the hills between Limassol and Larnaca, is one such discovery, where some stone village houses have been renovated by a green-minded developer called Filokypros and are now set around a private pool and courtyard with olive trees. The apartments manage to combine rustic chic with contemporary fittings and some have an open gallery where you sleep, and an airy living room downstairs. There are several other stone houses in the village, too, also renovated with agrotourism grants.

Cyprus is featured by a huge number of specialist villa tour operators. Pretty much the very best of them is **Sunvil** (see p. 29), which specialises in off-the-beaten-track accommodation.

Provided you've got a car, there are many advantages to staying up in the hills as opposed to on the coast, the blissful quiet and the cooler temperature being two of them. Sunvil's accommodation is all sympathetically designed and most of the villas have a private pool, perfect for a house party or a quiet family holiday where you don't have to be on parade for anybody.

Best Beach Hotels Cyprus has an astonishingly high concentration of five-star beach hotels. My favourites include the very stylish **Columbia Beach Resort** (see p. 67), which has amazing double-height studio rooms overlooking one of the longest swimming pools I've ever seen and a small, secluded beach. One typical guest book comment says it all: "We are awaiting the birth of our first child and are sure we will return as a family." There's a children's club and the food is excellent. Book a babysitter and eat under the stars down by the beach; it's incredibly romantic.

More in the middle of the action is **Le Meridien** (see p. 118) in Limassol, which has the advantage of huge, grassy grounds leading down to the beach. The children's club here is a whole separate building with playground, a little café in the shade and a huge indoor play area with air conditioning. Other good things? The very authentic taverna in the grounds and the enormous, lagoon-shaped pool. If you can get time to yourself, check out the spa, which has been voted best in the world.

In Paphos, you can't beat the **Paphos Amathus Beach Hotel** (see p. 64) for friendliness and service. Many of the guests return, some every year, and the hotel has a real family feel about it, despite being one of the posher five stars. Like Le Meridien, it has extensive grounds stretching down to the beach, so there's never any sense of being crowded.

Best Guest House Small guest houses are relatively hard to find;

View from Amathus Beach Hotel, Paphos

Cyprus tends to be a mix of very classy, five-star hotels, unattractive blocks that make up three- and four-star properties, and self-catering villas. One exception is the gorgeous **Stou Kir Yianni** (see p. 148) in the vine-growing village of Omodhos. Stou Kir Yianni is a stone village house the opens onto a pretty central courtyard serving organic food and vegetables grown by owner Stavros and his family. Accommodation is in just a handful of suites in bright, contemporary colours with four-poster beds and spaces for children's beds in the sitting rooms. You get all the advantages of being in a busy village community by day (Omodhos attracts a lot of day trippers) and a real sense of tranquillity at night, with just a bit of bouzouki music for entertainment.

BEST EATING OPTIONS

Best Sunday Lunch Eat where the locals eat at **Panayotis** (see p. 125), a taverna with blue and white checked table cloths overlooking Governor's Beach, a stretch of gritty sand bordered by steep white cliffs off the main road between Limassol and Larnaca. The restaurant, which has been here for decades, offers a huge fish meze and a children's menu. After lunch, you can walk down the cliff path to the beach for a swim.

Best Educational Dining If you really want to learn about Cypriot food, take your family to the **Seven St Georges Taverna** (see p. 69) outside Paphos. Proprietor George is absolutely passionate about food and even makes his own wine. There's no set menu and everything is at the very least locally produced and mostly organic into the bargain, all flavoured with freshly picked island herbs. George is a mine of knowledge about Cypriot snakes, insects, flowers and vegetables and loves sharing this with children. The day passes in a wonderfully leisurely fashion as more and more meze dishes appear, everything freshly cooked.

Best View **Viklari Taverna** (see p. 71), also known as The Last Castle for its crusader origins, is right on the edge of the Akamas wilderness. It's completely eccentric, the exterior strewn with rusting farming equipment, partially enveloped by a small banana plantation. The taverna itself has the most incredible views across the peninsula and on a breezy day, you can actually feel the warm wind whistling up here. A raised seating area on a platform looks out over the entrance to the Avakas Gorge. Sitting on this perch inspires a feeling of being on top of the world. Like everywhere, the taverna is family-friendly. Come at lunchtime for the inevitable meze and spend the afternoon on Lara Beach, or drive up here after hiking the gorge for a beer at sunset. As the whole side of the tavern faces due west, you'll have uninterrupted views.

Best Picnic Spot The **Akamas Peninsula** and the **Troodos** are dotted with ready-made picnic spots, one of the prettiest of which is the weirdly named **Smigies Picnic Site**, on the edge of the national park, just off a dirt track. When we arrived, the only sound was the wind whistling in the pine trees; there's absolutely no other noise (unless there's a loud family party going on, of course). You can grill your *souvlakia* in the big barbecue pits and tuck into your picnic sitting at wooden benches and tables, while children play on the slide, swings and climbing frame.

Best Coffee Stop The quirky **Art Café** (see p. 92), tucked away in a corner of the sleepy town of Polis in the island's north-west has a vaguely alternative feel about it. Adults can sit and read the paper at stone tables in a shady garden, full of arty *objets,* while children play

with books, board games, swings and assorted baby toys scattered around. Local artists exhibit their work here and in summer, children's films are shown indoors, which makes a great siesta for all.

Best Traditional Experience Wednesday nights in the hilltop village of **Pissouri** (see p. 48) are slightly less touristy than the tavernas along the coast. A row of restaurants on one pretty, pedestrianised street at the heart of the village all share a group of roving musicians and Cypriot dancers, creating a very jolly atmosphere. All the restaurants are independent of one another but offer essentially typical Cypriot fare – salads and *souvlaki* as well as fresh fish, rabbit, *kleftiko* and *stifado*, at tables under the grapevines with scrawny cats weaving around your feet.

Best Atmosphere It's amazing how many people stay in their beach hotels when they could be

Visit Pissouri for less touristy tavernas

dining on a balmy summer's night in front of a floodlit medieval castle in the heart of **Limassol** (see p. 105), the whole area buzzing with life. The castle grounds are encircled by restaurants, from hip Italian to designer Cypriot, to more modest cafés and tavernas.

Another very atmospheric place is **Laiki Yitonia** (which actually means 'popular neighbourhood'), the ancient maze of alleys and shaded tavernas at the heart of Nicosia, the capital (see p. 201). You're only likely to be in Nicosia for a day trip and much of that will be spent sightseeing, so a long lunch outdoors is a welcome break. Most of the tavernas have terraces shaded by vines and the meze in this area is especially good; Nicosia's restaurants tend to serve locals and expatriate business people rather than tourists and the standard is higher than elsewhere. Children will enjoy the artisans' workshops in the old streets, as well as spending their holiday euros in the many souvenir shops.

Best for a Break from Meze

Personally, I could eat meze six days out of seven but there comes a point where even the most dedicated lover of hummous and *souvlaki* needs a rest, for the sake of the waistline as much as anything else.

Luckily, there are family-friendly places everywhere, from old staples like Pizza Express and TGI Fridays to more imaginative establishments. **Stretto** (see p. 123) at the old Carob Mill by Limassol Castle is a fashionable bar with a Mediterranean theme, serving waffles and crêpes. In Larnaca, **Momo Fusion** is ultra-hip but has outside seating on a wooden deck where families will be happiest. The food is Mediterranean and Asian. Also good for Asian, although probably better for a night out for two than with children in tow, is **Asiachi** (see p. 69) at the Paphos Amathus Beach Hotel, a very sophisticated venue serving Southeast Asian and Japanese cuisine with a delicious twist on wasabi prawns and a fine line in noodles.

The atmospheric Laiki Yitonia

2 Planning a Family Trip to Cyprus

CYPRUS

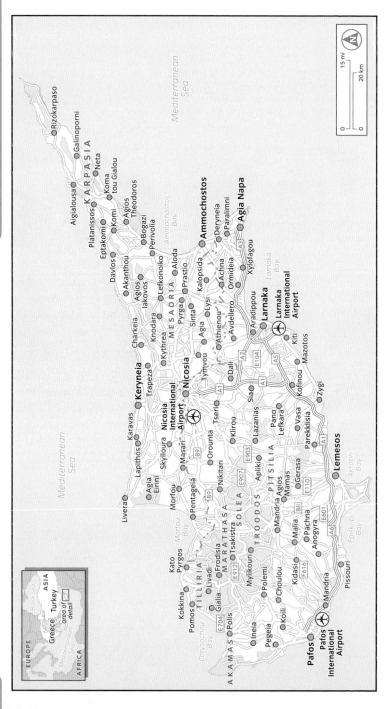

A little insider knowledge about Cyprus goes a long way. Yet many families barely stray from their hotel, which is a shame, as they miss out on 90% of what this wonderful island has to offer.

All the main tourist centres – Paphos, Limassol, Larnaca and Ayia Napa – and the subsidiary ones, the Pissouri region and the Troodos, are easily accessible and part of an excellent infrastructure. Driving is easy and convenient. If you get lost, finding an English-speaker to help won't be difficult. Best of all, the island is completely child-friendly, so planning a series of excursions, or even a touring holiday, is easy as there isn't really anywhere or anything to avoid.

In the heat of summer, I'd suggest excursions early in the morning or late afternoon, with swimming built in wherever possible. The Troodos region is always a couple of degrees cooler than the coast and Nicosia in summer is hotter, so plan accordingly. Outside the main summer months, you'll have more flexibility.

This book is arranged in a west-to-east direction, starting with Paphos and the Akamas region; moving eastwards to Pissouri, Limassol and the Troodos; onwards to Larnaca; and to the other end of the island, Ayia Napa and Protaras. Finally, there's a chapter on Nicosia, the capital, which for most families, is really a day trip rather than a place to stay.

I've used anglicised spellings of Cypriot place names throughout, although you will see variations of these on the island.

VISITOR INFORMATION

Child-Specific Websites

I haven't discovered any good websites covering family travel in Cyprus specifically but there are plenty of general travel websites with useful advice for travelling with children.

For general travel tips, *www.babygoes2.com* and *www.takethefamily.com* are both good. The Cyprus Tourism Organisation's website, *www.visitcyprus.com* is comprehensive but frustrating to navigate. For a good insider's guide, check out *www.cyprus-travel-secrets.com* and for general gossip and British forums, *http://cyprus.angloinfo.com* is worth trawling through.

A must for children before you go and when you come back is Google Earth (*www.googleearth.com*) which has excellent, close-range aerial views of the island.

Entry Requirements, Customs & Bringing Pets

Passports & Visas

Holders of passports from EU countries, Australia, New Zealand, Canada and the USA (among many others) do not require a visa if they are bona fide tourists and stay for less than 90 days. If you decide to stay longer, you need to apply for a Temporary Residence Permit. Dependants – spouses and children – enjoy the same rights as the European citizen they accompany, but a dependant who is not a national of an EU country must have a visa.

Passports issued by the Turkish Republic of Northern Cyprus (TRNC), an entity not recognised by the Republic of Cyprus or the United Nations, are not considered valid. If you have a TRNC stamp in your passport, the immigration authorities will cancel it but should let you in. The reality is that when you cross into the north, a stamp is given on a separate piece of paper to avoid this hassle.

The legal points of entry are: Paphos and Larnaca airports; and Limassol, Larnaca, Latchi and Paphos ports. The north is not considered a legal point of entry. The Government of the Republic of Cyprus reserves the right to fine EU (including British) citizens for illegal entry if they cross into the south. In practice, their current policy is not to do so.

Bringing Pets

I certainly wouldn't recommend bringing a pet to Cyprus for a short holiday but if you're moving here, there are systems in place to make it easier. If you are coming from an EU member state, you are allowed to bring your pets to Cyprus provided they possess either a passport or an Animal Health Certificate. But, if you are coming from a non-EU country, you will also need a Vaccination Certificate (especially showing vaccination against rabies).

If you're bringing a long-haired dog, consider seriously getting it clipped before departure, as dogs can have trouble adjusting to the intense heat of summer.

Useful contacts are:

For transporting pets: Animals By Air Ltd, Second Floor, Unit 1, Building 307, Freight Terminal, Manchester Airport M90 5PL, 0870 833 8020, *www.animalsby air.co.uk*.

Also see *www.defra.gov.uk* for up-to-date information on taking animals abroad or back to the UK.

Tax-Free Allowances

The Republic of Cyprus is a member of the European Union. Every adult entering Cyprus from within the EU is entitled to import the following duty-paid articles (not intended for commercial purposes), provided they are carried in the passengers' hand luggage or accompanying baggage:

Tobacco
800 cigarettes
400 cigarillos
200 cigars
1 kg of tobacco

Alcohol

10 litres of spirits
20 litres fortified wine (such as
    port or sherry)
90 litres of wine (of which, a
    maximum of 60 litres of
    sparkling wine)
110 litres of beer

Travellers under the age of 17 are not entitled to duty-free tobacco products and alcohol.

Forbidden Items

You must not import agricultural products or propagating stock such as fruit, vegetables, cut flowers, dry nuts, seeds, bulbs, bulb-wood sticks, cuttings, etc., without prior approval of the Cypriot authorities. There is zero tolerance of drugs. The import of fire arms, ammunition, explosives, flick knives, daggers, swords, obscene books, photographs, films and articles as well as goods bearing a forged trademark or false trade description is prohibited or restricted. Also prohibited or restricted are pirated or counterfeit goods, animals, birds, uncooked meat and fish, milk and dairy products.

Coming Home

Duty-paid allowances on re-entering the UK from another EU country are up to:

3,200 cigarettes
400 cigarillos
200 cigars
3 kg smoking tobacco
10 litres of spirits
20 litres of fortified wine

90 litres of wine
110 litres of beer

You can claim a VAT refund on goods exported from Cyprus in your hand luggage if you are the holder of a passport from outside the EU.

To do this, you need to have made your purchases from shops that display a tax-free shopping sign and collected a tax-free document at the time of purchase – important if you're buying something valuable like jewellery.

When leaving Cyprus show your purchases and passport to customs officials and have your tax-free document stamped.

For more information, visit the website of the Customs & Excise department in Nicosia (*www.mof.gov.cy/ce*).

Single Parents Travelling with Children

If you are a single parent travelling with your children, as a precaution, I recommend having a letter signed by the children's other parent giving you permission to take them out of the UK. This isn't a legal requirement but I have been stopped travelling alone with my children and questioned by a (friendly) immigration officer.

The advice of the UK Foreign and Commonwealth Office (*www.fco.gov.uk*) for Cyprus at the time of going to press is that any adults travelling alone with children should be aware that they may need to bring documentary evidence of parental responsibility; for further information contact the High Commission of the Republic of Cyprus in London.

Money

At the beginning of 2008, Cyprus bid farewell to the Cyprus pound and said hello to the euro. Needless to say, a lot of prices went up but to make things easier, there is an official fixed exchange rate of €1 to CY£0.585274. This is why you'll see such strange euro prices in this book; at the time of writing, Cypriots were making straight conversions using this rate. Over time, prices are likely to be adjusted and rounded up or down to something more manageable.

There are seven denominations in euro banknotes: 5, 10, 20, 50, 100, 200 and 500 euros. They all have different colour and size, the higher the denomination, the bigger the size. One euro is divided into 100 cents. There are eight euro coins: 1, 2, 5, 10, 20 and 50 cents, €1 and €2. The designs on one side of the coins are common to all the countries of the euro area, while the other side reflects national identities. All euro coins can be used in all euro area countries, irrespective of their national side.

If you visit the Turkish occupied side of Cyprus, the currency is Turkish lire, although euros are widely accepted.

Credit & Debit Cards

Credit and debit cards are widely accepted in Cyprus and you can even pay for petrol with a card that plugs straight into the petrol pump.

You should have cash for the obvious things – taxis and buses, shopping in markets, beach vendors like watersports operators and deckchair attendants, and enough for drinks and snacks on a trip to the mountains in the event you stumble upon some fantastic village taverna that hasn't yet entered the 21st century.

ATMs are available in all the resorts and in Nicosia. The same rules apply as they do in other countries: keep an eye out for anything unusual about the machine and check your statements as soon as you get home in case of credit card fraud.

There's a number in Cyprus you can dial if you lose your cards and can't remember the emergency number at home: JCC Payment Systems Ltd, ℓ *22 868 100*.

Traveller's Cheques

Traveller's cheques can be cashed at the main banks in the resorts but are an increasingly rare phenomenon.

Tipping

Since a 10% service charge is levied in hotels and restaurants, tipping is not obligatory but is always welcome and appreciated. Taxi drivers don't expect a tip

What Things Cost in Cyprus	
Single bus ticket	around €1
Large beer	€3.50–5 – more in the resorts, less in the mountain villages
Cinema ticket	around €7 for adults and €5 for children
Theatre ticket	€17–25
Concert or opera ticket	€25–77
Continental breakfast in a café	€3.40–6
Lunch	€10–13.50
Dinner at a taverna (meze, including beer or cold drink)	around €20
Wine	much cheaper if you stick to Cypriot wines, which are worth trying; about €17 a bottle in a five-star hotel and about €3 in a supermarket

but you can round up the fare if you like.

When to Go & What to Pack

Cyprus is a year-round destination. November, December, January and February are cooler, with some rain and in January and February, snow in the Troodos Mountains. If you're going in winter, choose a hotel with an indoor pool.

March, April and May are wonderful for children, as are late September and October, it's warm enough to swim but still cool enough to do lots of activities. June, July, August and early September can be stiflingly hot – but this is the peak season. Sunshine is guaranteed but you may find the whole family too lethargic during the day to venture out much. The island is also at its busiest and most expensive because of European school holidays.

If you want to explore and are hiring a car in high summer, get one with air conditioning, especially if you have a baby.

Clothing requirements vary, depending on the length and the period of your visit. During April and May, days are pleasantly warm, but temperatures may drop at night. Spring and summer gear and long-sleeved tops or light jackets for the evenings are recommended. From June to the end of August, very light summer clothing is a must; you won't need anything smart unless you're staying in a five-star hotel or planning to visit the few restaurants with a dress code (in which case, no shorts at dinner and a decent shirt for men). September to October see quite a few warm days and cooler evenings. Light clothing for the day and long sleeves for the evenings in October is recommended. November has pleasantly warm days that can be enjoyed in jumpers and light jackets.

Other things to pack include: walking shoes if you intend to hike on Akamas or in the Troodos; snorkelling gear (although you can buy it in Cyprus); masses of strong sunblock for children (I prefer the high-protection UV swimsuits for mine so you don't have to keep reapplying – see *www.kids-kaper.co.uk* for a wide range of Sposh gear, the UK name for the brilliant Ozone brand from New Zealand.

Things you can easily buy in Cyprus include nappies, baby food, batteries, English newspapers, books and magazines, sunglasses, beach wear, water inflatables, all normal cosmetics and children's clothing.

Several services exist to make travelling with a baby easier. At the Almyra and the Anassa hotels, you can pre-order all your baby kit online (*www.thanoshotels. com*). If you're staying anywhere else, you can do the same on *www.tinytotsaway.com*. There's a service in Limassol, *www.cyprus withbabies.blogspot.com*, run by a British lady, which will obtain baby gear too, and deliver it to your hotel.

Public & School Holidays

1st January: New Year's Day

New Year, rather than Christmas, is when families exchange gifts. On New Year's Eve, a traditional cake, Vasilopitta, is baked, with a coin hidden in it. Children go out carol singing and some families play a fortune-telling game with olive leaves. The cake is cut the following day, with one slice for Jesus, one for the house and one for any family members who are absent. The person who gets the coin is considered lucky for a whole year.

6th January: Epiphany Day

Epiphany is one of the most important Greek Orthodox religious celebrations of the year. It is also known as the Feast of the Light, since it commemorates Christ's baptism in the River Jordan, symbolic of the spiritual rebirth of man. It is celebrated in a number of seaside towns in Cyprus (Larnaca hosts a dramatic service by the sea).

On the eve of Epiphany, known as **kalanda**, people gather in church for the blessing of the waters, which are supposed to have held evil spirits for the past 12 days. After mass, the priest visits all houses to cleanse them from the demons, or evil spirits, known as **kalikandjiari**. According to Cypriot tradition, these demons appear on Christmas Day, and for the next 12 days play evil tricks on people. On the eve of their departure, housewives throw pancakes and sausages on their roofs, where the demons are believed to dwell, in order to please them, so that they will leave contented without causing any trouble.

On Epiphany Day, a special celebration takes place at all seaside towns. After the Epiphany mass the Archbishop, or one of the Bishops, leads a procession down to the sea, where a ceremonial baptism is performed. During the ceremony the leading priest throws the holy cross into the sea. Young men dive into the water to retrieve the cross, and return it to the priest. Doves are released and at the same time, boats sound their horns.

Carnival

Carnival is a two-week period of festivity, before the 50 days preceding Easter.

The first week is called the Meat Week (**Kreatini**), as it is the last week for eating meat before Lent. The second week is known as the cheese week (**Tyrini**), when cheese and other dairy products may be consumed. Carnival festivities begin on the Thursday of the Meat Week. The last Sunday of the Cheese Week is the highlight of the Carnival, when parties are held all over the island. Limassol is the centre of the festivities, with fancy-dress parades and balls.

Variable: Green Monday (50 days before Greek Orthodox Easter)

Although this is the first day of Lent, Green Monday is a day of celebration and vegetarian picnics in the countryside. This is followed by 50 days of fast, during which strict Christians prepare themselves to receive the Redeemer. Some people follow a **vegetarian diet**, but not many nowadays, although Green Monday itself is a big event.

25th March: Greek National Day

Celebrated all over the island with parades, dancing and sporting events.

1st April: Greek Cypriot National Day

The anniversary of the start of the liberation struggle of the Greek Cypriots against British colonial rule in 1955.

Variable: Good Friday (Greek Orthodox Church)

Variable: Easter Monday (Greek Orthodox Church)

Easter is the biggest feast of the Greek Orthodox calendar and is a wonderful time to be in Cyprus. On Thursday before Easter, after morning mass, people bake Easter breads, pastries and cheese pies known as **flaounes**. Eggs are dyed red.

On Thursday evening, a representation of Christ's crucifixion takes place in church, where icons are draped in black. Good Friday is again a day of mourning, in which the village sepulchre is decorated with flowers and paraded around the parish during evening mass. On Saturday, during morning mass, as the priest announces Jesus' resurrection, the black drapes drop from the icons and the members of the congregation rap their seats to express their joy. At midnight, there is another mass, followed by a bonfire on which an imaginary Judas is burned, known as **lampradjia**. Traditional Easter fare is lemon and rice soup (**avgolemono**) with the red-dyed eggs.

1st May: Labour Day

A May day holiday.

Variable: Pentecost-Kataklysmos (Festival of the Flood)

A uniquely Cypriot celebration. Kataklysmos refers to the

destruction by flood of all living creatures on earth, apart from Noah and his family, and later, Deukalion and his wife, who were saved in order to give birth to a new and moral generation. The ceremonies for Kataklysmos last for a few days and take place in all seaside towns and resorts. Singing, dancing, folk festivals, boat races and water fights (to symbolise purification of body and soul) take place everywhere.

15th August: Assumption
Public holiday.

1st October: Cyprus Independence Day
Cyprus Independence Day is celebrated with a military parade in Nicosia and a reception at the Presidential Palace in the evening.

28th October: Greek National Day (Ochi Day)
Celebrated with student parades all over the island.

24th December: Christmas Eve
On Christmas Eve, special bread (**koulouria**) and pastries (**kourapiedes**) are baked while children go carol singing. Traditionally, children bring good health and fortune, so the householders always reward them with a small sum of money.

25th December: Christmas Day
Most people attend mass on Christmas Day, followed by egg-and-lemon rice soup for breakfast. This is traditionally a day of visiting friends and relatives.

26th December: Boxing Day

Special Events

In addition to the public holidays listed above, Cyprus has a lively calendar of cultural events and festivals. Finding out when these are can be frustrating and local municipalities' websites are often way out of date. If you want to time your visit to coincide with a particular event, like a village wine festival or a saint's day, you're really better off researching it by phone (see the tourist office details in every chapter of this book).

Each village has an annual saint's day festival and it's always worth taking children to see one of these – visitors are welcome and you'll see the role Cypriot children play in village life, too.

Insurance & Health

Medical treatment and assistance in Cyprus is offered free of charge to international tourists in cases of emergency at the Accident and Emergency Department of Government Hospitals and Health Institutions. EU citizens must produce an EHIC form issued by their country's healthcare authorities (*www.ehic.org.uk*). You can also claim any medical expenses on your holiday insurance with the agreement of your insurer but remember to phone them before spending any money – making a retroactive claim is harder.

Vaccinations

Cyprus has no dangerous infectious diseases. Visitors do not require any vaccinations to travel to Cyprus although make sure the routine vaccinations of babies and toddlers are up to date.

Staying Healthy

The most common problems in Cyprus are over-exposure to the sun and accidents among tourists falling off motorbikes and quad bikes. The latter is unlikely to apply to a family but the former is a real risk, so make sure the whole family is covered with sunblock, suitably hydrated and wearing sunhats.

If You Fall Ill

The local press (*Cyprus Mail* and *Cyprus Weekly* in English) has details of pharmacies and their opening hours. If you need a doctor for anybody in the family, your hotel can usually call one for you. Almost all doctors speak English and standards of care are high.

If your child suffers from a condition that may require swift emergency treatment like epilepsy, diabetes or asthma, consider getting a Medicalert bracelet, which is engraved with the details and comes with an emergency number through which the child's medical details can be accessed at any time in more than 100 languages (*www.medicalert.org.uk*).

Hospitals

There are two types of hospital: Government General Hospitals, all of which have an A&E department; and private clinics, only some of which take A&E cases.

Kyperounta Hospital ☎ *25 532 021.*

Larnaca General Hospital ☎ *24 800 500*, ☎ *24 800 369.*

Lefkosia General Hospital ☎ *22 801 400*, ☎ *22 801 475* (Accidents & Emergency).

Lemesos General Hospital ☎ *25 801 100*, ☎ *25 305 770.*

Pafos General Hospital ☎ *26 803 260*, ☎ *26 306 100.*

Paralimni Hospital ☎ *23 821 211.*

Polis Hospital ☎ *26 321 431.*

Travelling Safely with Children in Cyprus

Cyprus is a very safe country but the usual rules apply about keeping hold of children's hands in crowded places and never letting your eyes stray from them on the beach or by the pool. Cyprus's beaches are unpredictable and some have strong currents offshore, so be absolutely vigilant.

As soon as your children are old enough, have them memorise your mobile phone number in case of absolute emergency, and make sure they know where you are staying in the dire event that they get separated from you.

The Family in Cyprus

In Cyprus, family is more important than anything else. Families are extended and close-knit at the same time. Many Cypriot women do not work once they have children, and the role of homemaker is a valued one. Grandparents and other relatives help with childcare. Children stay at home for many years, usually until they marry, and are not likely to move very far away from the family residence. Family members are very protective of one another and in business, nepotism is rife, with parents often encouraging their children to follow in their footsteps and promoting them within the company once they have done so.

Cypriots, both men and women, love to talk about their children – a great conversation topic, or an ice-breaker! If you have Cypriot friends, or make friends while you're on the island, you are also likely to be invited to family gatherings, with your children.

In hotels, check out the children's club before depositing a young child in it. Ask what they'll be doing, how qualified the staff are, ratios for carers and babies or toddlers, and facilities for napping or staying out of the sun. Many of the children's clubs are run by local girls; it's up to you whether you consider the care of a suitable standard.

My biggest fear in Cyprus is the way people, both locals and tourists, drive around the resorts. You'll see people renting motorbikes who have never ridden one in their life, and taking to unfamiliar roads on it. Locals drive cars too fast and tourists drive them too nervously! You can spot the rental cars easily because they have red numberplates. On the motorways, Cypriots are fond of tailgating so just pull over and let them past.

Specialised Resources

For Single Parents

There are some tour operators specialising in single-parent travel to Cyprus. Olympic Holidays and Argo Holidays (see details below) also do special rates for single parents.

Single Parents on Holiday
℡ 0871 550 4053, *www.single parentsonholiday.co.uk*.

Small Families ℡ 01763 226 567, *www.smallfamilies.co.uk*.

Mango ℡ 01902 373 410, *www. mangokids.co.uk*.

For Grandparents

Cyprus is an ideal place for a group holiday spanning several generations – multigenerational groups are part of everyday life in Cypriot society, where grandparents are very much involved in the upbringing of their grand-children. You'll see big groups of Cypriots dining in tavernas all over the island.

If you are a big party, consider renting a villa or maybe taking a suite in a hotel so everybody has some privacy. This is entirely based on personal experience, but I'd also recommend two hire cars for a big family group as it's often the case that people want to do different things, particularly if you are working around a baby's schedule.

For Families with Special Needs

Cyprus is better than you might expect for disabled access, relative to some Mediterranean destinations. Many of the hotels and some self-catering accommodation are equipped with wheelchair ramps, and Larnaca and Paphos airports both have wheelchair hoists. Wheelchairs and scooters can be rented in Limassol and there are several tour companies that are happy to take wheelchair passengers, with advance notice. There is even a walking trail in the Troodos Mountains which is suitable for wheelchairs. The towns are all fairly flat, although pavements are generally uneven or crowded with chairs and tables of outdoor cafés.

For detailed information on equipment hire and accommodation, visit **www.paraquip.com.cy**, a very helpful website run by a disabled Cypriot and packed

with information on everything from wheelchair ramps on the beaches to where to try parascending. The Cyprus Tourism Organisation also has a useful section on its website, **www.visit cyprus.org.cy,** containing information about driving, taxis adapted for the disabled, tour operators and accommodation.

The 21st-Century Traveller

Mobile Phones

Mobile phones work all over Cyprus and you'll see Cypriots happily glued to them. There are several service providers and most work for voice and data.

Landline Phones

There are three numbers for directory enquiries: ℂ *11892*, ℂ *11822* and ℂ *11888*. Cyprus has coin-operated payphones and card phones but barely anybody uses them as everybody has a mobile now. You can dial home from your hotel room by placing 0044 in front of the UK number and leaving off the first 0.

The Internet

Most hotels provide Internet access via their business centres and some have WiFi from the bedrooms. In my experience, this is very expensive; if you only plan to check your email once or twice, you'd be better off popping into one of the many cyber cafés in the big resorts.

ESSENTIALS

Getting There

By Plane There are two international airports, Larnaca and Paphos. Larnaca International Airport, the main one, is 5 km from Larnaka town, 49 km from Lefkosia, 70 km from Lemesos, 46 km from Ayia Napa, and 139 km from Paphos.

For flight information (24 hours) dial ☎ 778 833). The tourist information booth is open 8.15am–11pm and is worth calling at to pick up a selection of maps. Other facilities include foreign exchange, hotel reservations (Cyprus Hotel Association, in the unlikely event that you have turned up on spec), duty-free, cafés and shops. It's not a place of beauty so don't turn up any earlier than you have to for your return flight. Private, metered taxis wait outside and all the car rental companies have offices here. Renting a car is easy – the car parks are right opposite the terminal entrance so it's simple to collect and drop off when you have a family in tow.

Paphos International Airport is 15 km from Paphos town and 63 km from Limassol. It has all the same facilities as Larnaca, most of which stay open until 11pm when the last flights arrive. I find Paphos slightly less manic than Larnaca; if you're staying in the west, I would definitely advise flying into here if possible.

Airlines serving Cyprus include: **Cyprus Airways** ☎ *020 8359 1333, www.cyprusairways. com*; **British Airways** ☎ *0844 493 0787, www.ba.com*; EuroCypria ☎ *22 365 750 www.eurocypria.com*; **easyJet** *www.easyjet.com*; **First Choice** ☎ *0871 200 7799* (premium rate line; phone bookings incur a £10 fee), *www.firstchoice. co.uk*; **Xcel Airways** ☎ *0871 911 4220, www.xl.com*; **Thomas Cook** ☎ *0901 576 0576* (premium rate), *www.flythomascook.com*; **Monarch** ☎ *08700 405 040, www. flymonarch.com*; **Thomsonfly** ☎ *0871 231 4691, www.thomson. co.uk*.

By Road You're unlikely to arrive in Cyprus by road unless you are moving here to live, in which case most people ship their car by container. Some summers there is a car ferry from Rhodes but its schedule doesn't become available until spring and it doesn't operate every year. One of the most reliable sites to check is *www.varianostravel.com*.

The partial lifting of restrictions on crossing the 'Green Line' allows Cypriots and visitors to cross in both directions at designated crossing points. It is possible to travel to the north of Cyprus from the south by crossing at several checkpoints, including the Ledra Palace checkpoint in central Nicosia. Cyprus immigration authorities have confirmed that EU passport holders with a 'TRNC ' stamp in their passport will not experience difficulties when entering the Republic of Cyprus. You may take a hired car through the checkpoints, except at Ledra Palace, which is for pedestrians only. You are strongly advised, however, to check the insurance implications with your car hire company before doing so. It is possible to hire a car once you have crossed into the north and to purchase appropriate insurance.

At present, there are five crossing points: the Ledra Palace border gate in Nicosia (pedestrians only); the new Lidra Street crossing in Nicosia; the Metehan (Kermia) border gate in Nicosia; Beyarmudu (Pile) near the British Sovereign bases at Dhekelia; and the Akyar border gates near Famagusta on the Larnaca–Famagusta road.

Before your visit, check out the UK Foreign Office website at *www.fco.gov.uk* for the latest update on the north–south situation. Talks are being held all the time to resolve the issue and more crossing points may well open without notice as the negotiations progress. At some point, all Cypriots hope the two sides of the island will be reunified.

By Rail Cyprus has no rail services.

By Sea Ferries are few and far between – there is one a week, summer only, from Greece, but it doesn't always operate and schedules are not announced until the spring each year. Weekly ferries also operate between Limassol and Haifa, Port Said and Latakia in Syria, although this service is sometimes suspended when the security situation becomes an issue. Check for schedules and prices on *www.varianostravel.com*.

Arriving by private yacht is possible. Larnaca, Limassol and Latchi all have customs and immigration. Larnaca Marina is situated in the bay of Larnaca and lies 110 nautical miles from Beirut and Tripoli, 145 n.m. from Tel-Aviv, 230 n.m. from Port Said and 250 n.m. from Rhodes. The position of the Marina is 34 deg. 55 min. North – 33 deg. 38 min. East. There are berths for 450 yachts but you must book in advance, especially in summer. Telex: 4500 CYT-MAR, ℡ *24 653 110*, ℡ *24 653 113*, [fax] *24 624 110*, *E: larnaca. marina@cytanet.com.cy*

St Raphael Marina, at the St Raphael Hotel outside Limassol, is smaller. The Marina, located at longitude 33 deg. 11 min. latitude 34 deg. 42 min, has 227 berths and again, you must book in advance. Telex: 3229, ℡ *25 635 800*, [fax] *25 635 208*, *E: raphael@ spidernet.com.cy*.

Package Deals & Activity Holidays

There are plenty of tour operators offering packages to Cyprus. If you want to stay in a hotel, this is still generally the most convenient way to book, especially with a young family. There is a full listing on the ABTA

National Parks in Cyprus

Cyprus has a few areas of designated National Park, which protects them from building. These are very popular at weekends, for hiking, picnicking and in some cases, visiting unspoilt beaches.

Troodos National Forest Park, with an area of 9,307 hectares; was declared as such in 1992, while four areas within the main park were declared as Nature Reserves. Troodos National Forest Park hosts not only the largest number of plants compared to any other area of Cyprus, but also the largest number of endemic plants. It has been designated as one of only 13 'Plant Diversity Hot Spots' in the Mediterranean.

There are several, much smaller National Forest Parks, including Cape Greco, in the south-east part of the island; Athalassa National Forest Park near Nicosia; Paedagogical Academy National Forest Park, also near Nicosia; Polemidia National Forest Park near Limassol; and Rizoelia National Forest Park near Larnaca. Tripylos Natural Reserve, with an area of 823 hectares, including the famous Cedar valley, is the first declared Nature Reserve. The Akamas peninsula in the north west is probably the most famous National Forest Park. It's a spacious 155 square kilometres of scrubland, dramatic cliffs, gorges, beaches and rocky shores, and is home to several unique species of flora and fauna. There are no roads as such, just dirt tracks, and a four-wheel drive is advisable if you're planning to go deep into the park.

Lara-Toxeftra, a particular area of Akamas, is a marine reserve, and green and loggerhead turtles lay their eggs every year on Lara Beach (see p. 78).

website (*www.abta.co.uk*). Here is a selection of specialists:

Amathus Holidays ☏ *020 7611 0901, www.amathusholidays.co. uk*; General Greece and Cyprus specialist.

Argo Holidays ☏ *020 7331 7070, www.argoholidays.com*; Cyprus specialist with good cross-section of hotels and apartments.

Cyplon Travel ☏ *020 8348 9142, www.cyplon.com*.

First Choice Holidays ☏ *01293 560 777, www.firstchoice.co.uk*;

Mainstream tour operator with large Cyprus programme.

Olympic Holidays ☏ *0870 429 4141, www.olympicholidays.co.uk*; Long-standing Cyprus specialist.

Planet Holidays ☏ *0870 066 0909, www.planet-holidays.net*; Good selection of hotels and self-catering.

Rent Cyprus Villas ☏ *08701 999 966, www.rentcyprusvillas.com*; Villa specialist, as the name suggests.

Seasons in Style ☏ *01244 202 000, www.seasonsinstyle.co.uk*;

Upmarket specialist featuring all of the island's top hotels and spas.

Sunvil Holidays ☏ *020 8758 4747, www.sunvil.co.uk/cyprus.* The best for villas with pools and agrotourism properties.

Getting Around

By Car Cyprus is officially divided into six districts: Famagusta, Kyrenia, Larnaca, Limassol, Nicosia and Paphos. The Turkish Cypriot area's administrative divisions include Kyrenia, all but a small part of Famagusta, and small parts of Nicosia and Larnaca.

> **INSIDER TIP** ≫
> One thing you'll notice straight away on the island is the use of alternative place names. In recent years, using an official system of transliteration from the Greek alphabet, names have changed as follows:
> Nicosia becomes Lefkosia
> Limassol becomes Lemesos
> Paphos becomes Pafos
> Ayia Napa becomes Agia Napa
> Larnaca becomes Larnaka
> Famagusta becomes Ammochostos

> **INSIDER TIP** ≫
> If you see a driver flashing their lights in daylight, that probably means that police radar is near and you should be aware of the speed limit.

Driving in Cyprus can be enjoyable thanks to the empty roads and good road network and the fact that driving is on the left. In some cases, a hire car is essential as regular transport services to remote areas of interest are not always available. The minimum driving age is 18. To rent a car, drivers must be in possession of a driving licence for at least three years or be aged over 25.

You can also rent mopeds, motorbikes and quad bikes but personally, I would not recommend any of these as they are a common cause of accidents.

Pre-book child and baby seats if you need them and inspect them yourself when you pick up your rental car. Consider upgrading to a car with air conditioning if you're travelling with children in the middle of summer. If you plan to drive on the Akamas peninsula, you will need a four-wheel drive, or you risk punctures, a shattered windscreen, damaged undercarriage and a very bumpy ride!

Roads in Cyprus are good. Motorways connect the capital, Nicosia with the coastal cities of Limmasol, Larnaca and Paphos and the motorway now extends to Ayia Napa at the eastern end of the island. Minor roads and forest roads are often unsurfaced, but in good condition (except when they run out and become dirt tracks!). Distances and speed limits are posted in kilometres and kilometre per hour (km/h), respectively. The maximum speed limit on motorways is 100 km/h and the minimum is 65 km/h. Seatbelts are compulsory both in the front and back, and the use of mobile phones is strictly prohibited while driving.

A word of warning about petrol stations: there are not as many as you might imagine. If you're driving between two major towns and need to refuel, do so before leaving the urban area.

Some car rental companies in Cyprus have the annoying policy of asking you to return the car empty (you pick it up full) so if you're only renting for a day, be warned. This also means you spend your last day madly trying to use up all the petrol and guessing exactly right so you return the car to the airport running on petrol fumes only... it's not a good system.

Speed limits in Cyprus are 50 km/h in urban areas and 100 km/h on open roads. Traffic travels on the left and headlights must be used from half-an-hour before sunset and half-an-hour before sunrise.

The legal alcohol limit in breath is 22 micrograms per 100 millilitres of breath. The legal limit in blood is 50 milligrams of alcohol per 100 millilitres of blood. You will be breathalysed if you are involved in an accident.

Car Rental Companies
Larnaca Airport
Andreas Petsas & Sons ℓ 24 643 350
Budget Car Rental ℓ 24 643 293
E: budgcar@cytanet.com.cy
Hertz Rent-a-Car ℓ 24 643 388, www.hertz.com.cy
Thrifty Car Rental ℓ 24 643 375

Paphos Airport
Andreas Petsas & Sons ℓ 26 423 046
Budget Car Rental ℓ 26 953 824

Hertz Rent-a-Car ℓ 26 933 985, www.hertz.com.cy
Sixt Rent a Car ℓ 26 422 910, www.sixt.com.cy

INSIDER TIP »

If you're driving west in the late afternoon, you will need a decent pair of sunglasses. The main roads all run in an east–west direction and the setting sun can be absolutely dazzling!

By Bus Cyprus has several bus companies offering three different types of service. Inter-urban buses link all towns on a daily basis and with frequent routes. Rural buses link villages and towns to the larger bus network, often with only one or two services a day. Urban buses operate within the main towns and resorts. There is no one helpful website offering all the bus timetables.

The main inter-urban bus companies are:

ALEPA Ltd ℓ 99 625 027. Operates: Nicosia–Limassol–Paphos.

Clarios Bus Co ℓ 23 721 321, ℓ 22 753 234. Operates: Nicosia–Troodos–Kakopetria.

EMAN Buses ℓ 24 643 492/3. Operates: Nicosia–Ayia Napa.

Intercity Buses (Green Buses) ℓ 22 665 814. Operates: Nicosia–Larnaca–Limassol.

Nea Amoroza Transport Co Ltd ℓ 26 936 822, ℓ 26 936 740. Operates: Nicosia–Paphos.

PEAL Bus Co 📞 *23 821 318.*
Operates: Nicosia–Paralimni–
Deryneia

Pedoulas–Platres Bus 📞 *99 618 865/22 952 437.*

For timetable information, telephone the following:

Nicosia 📞 *22 665 814.*
Limassol 📞 *25 370 592.*
Larnaca 📞 *24 650 477.*
Paphos 📞 *26 934 410.*
Paralimni 📞 *23 821 318.*
Ayia Napa 📞 *23 721 321.*
Polis 📞 *26 321 113.*

By Bike The island is too big to get around by bike unless you're a candidate for the Tour de France, but there is cycle hire in most resorts and you can plan a few simple family bike rides with the help of the Cyprus Tourist Organisation's booklet, Cyprus Cycling Routes. For information on bicycle hire from reliable suppliers, and on routes for families, contact Bike Cyprus on 📞 *99 666 200, www.bikecyprus.com.*

By Taxi Confusingly, there are three types of taxi in Cyprus. Shared taxis are minibuses that split the cost between four and eight people, and pick up from agreed points (usually your hotel). They connect major urban centres from Monday to Friday between 6am and 6pm, weekends between 7am and 5pm, and don't operate on public holidays. They also don't serve the airports or connect towns and villages. Book in advance by phone on 📞 *77 777 474.*

Rural taxis can only be hired from and to their base station. These taxis are not equipped with meters and charging is based on kilometre/tariff rate. You'll also be charged per piece of luggage over 12 kg and for waiting time.

If you're in a rural area and need a taxi, your best bet is to enquire at the local taverna, which will usually call one for you.

Urban taxis provide a 24-hour service and can be booked or hired on the street. They are equipped with meters. There are extra charges for heavy luggage, waiting time, night time, public holidays and pets.

ACCOMMODATION & EATING OUT

Accommodation

Campsites

Cyprus has five official campsites licensed by the Cyprus Tourist Organisation, each one with washrooms and some kind of snack bar. I wouldn't, however, recommend camping with children unless you are really keen; these sites really are as basic as they come (the official booklet says the one in Polis is 'in a pleasant eucalyptus grove,' which it is, but you'll also find it is littered with rusting caravans and abandoned old tents) and besides, it's just too hot in summer for children to be in a tent.

Hotels

Cyprus has a fine array of hotels and its four- and five-star properties are among the very best in the Mediterranean. Each of the main resorts (apart from Polis/Latchi, which only has one) has a wide choice of superb hotels with world-class spas, restaurants, several pools, children's clubs and beautiful gardens. Because the hotels are so affordable, you won't see any one- or two-star properties in tour operators' brochures, although they do exist.

Apartments

There's also a huge choice of apartments and self-catering 'holiday villages', some of which are very good. All of them are licensed by the Cyprus Hotel Association and are graded Luxury, A, B and C class instead of with stars. Tourist villages and the five campsites are graded A or B class.

Villas

Cyprus has literally hundreds of villas for rental, either through tour operators or websites. Many have private pools.

Village Houses and Agrotourism

A lot of village houses have been developed through **agrotourism** grants for tourist accommodation. I highly recommend a few

nights in one of these – waking up in an old stone house to the sounds of donkeys braying and cockerels crowing is completely different to the bustle of a big holiday resort! Book through the Cyprus Agrotourism Association (**www.agrotourism.com.cy**).

Eating Out

Eating out is one of the great pleasures in Cyprus and there are thousands of restaurants ranging from traditional Cypriot to Lebanese, French, Thai and Indian.

Cypriot tavernas specialise in meze – a vast array of food in one meal, starting with dips, nibbles like sausages and prawns, salads, a fish course, a selection of meats, then desserts. You need time and a large appetite for meze – I've never finished one myself. Tavernas by the sea specialise in fish meze, which is truly spectacular. Local fish include sea bream and sea bass but more exotic types will be imported and frozen.

Stick to Cypriot wines if you want to save money. They always taste better in Cyprus than they do when you bring them home but have improved beyond recognition in recent years and are much cheaper than imported wines.

Beers include KEO, which is brewed on the island and is extremely pleasant and refreshing on a hot day. For children, the usual array of soft drinks is available, although freshly-squeezed orange juice is

Why the Republic of Cyprus?

Despite the fact that travel between the north and the south is becoming easier, most people, particularly families, choose to limit their holiday to one side of the island.

This book only covers the Republic of Cyprus for a number of reasons. For the first time visitor, it is the more obvious place to go as it is served by direct flights from the UK. In order to reach Northern (Turkish-occupied) Cyprus by air, you still have to fly via the Turkish mainland. The airport in the north is not recognised as a legal point of entry into the Republic of Cyprus.

Although many people take a day trip into the north from the south, the concept of two centre holidays has not yet taken off. It's much better to base yourself in one of the resorts on the south and maybe take a couple of guided excursions into the Turkish-occupied north.

Another factor is time. For most families, Cyprus is essentially a beach holiday and even on a two-week trip, you'll find plenty to see in the south. Then there's the cost; as tour operators don't offer two centre holidays, a week in each part of the island could be expensive.

This is not to say the north is not worth considering. It's exceptionally beautiful and cheaper than the south in the current economic climate of the strong Euro (the currency is the Turkish lira). But the infrastructure is less developed and you won't find the same levels of luxury or the facilities for children as you do in resorts like Limassol and Paphos. Perhaps one day, when both sides of the island are reunified, the two-centre holiday will become more commonplace.

something not to be missed. Milk may be long-life from cartons in some establishments.

Restaurants should include all taxes and service charges in their prices; if you want to tip, 10% is adequate.

Cypriots usually eat lunch at around 1pm and dinner at around 8.30pm, taking time over a meal. You can eat earlier with children but it's typical in a taverna to have children sitting at the table (or asleep in baby seats beside it) until late. The only place you'll find restrictions on where you can take children is in

the poshest restaurants in the five-star hotels. They're welcome everywhere else and all local restaurants have high chairs.

GETTING CHILDREN INTERESTED IN CYPRUS

Show children on a map and on Google Earth where Cyprus is and how long it will take to get there. Explain to them about the island's wildlife and conservation issues – most children nowadays are mini-environmentalists and they'll love stories of turtles on the beach (see p. 86) and mouflon (see p. 138) roaming the hills.

For reading material, I love Marcia Williams' books on Greek mythology – enchanting illustrations and funny interpretations of the classic stories. You could teach your children a bit of Greek, which will charm the Cypriots; either use this book or invest in something simple like *Collins' Easy Greek*, a photo phrase book which will teach you the alphabet and some useful travel phrases.

Encourage children to keep a holiday scrapbook. Buy the scrapbook before you leave and spend the holiday collecting everything from museum tickets to little souvenirs that can be glued into a book. Mixing these mementoes with photos when you get back is a great way to tell the story of the holiday.

FAST FACTS: CYPRUS

Alcohol The legal drinking age in Cyprus is 17. See p. 30 for drinking and driving regulations.

Baby Equipment Hotels will supply high chairs and if you request it in advance, a travel cot. Car rental companies have child and baby seats. All major baby supplies can be bought from any of the big supermarkets in the major towns, or through pharmacies, so don't fill a suitcase with nappies before

you travel. Do, however, keep enough in your hand luggage for the return journey!

You can book equipment like changing mats, monitors and so on in advance if you are staying at one of the Thanos hotels **(www.thanothotels.com),** through Tiny Tots Away **(www.tinytots away.com)** or via a service in Limassol (for the Limassol area) called Cyprus With Babies, ℆ 25 710 661, **http://cypruswithbabies. moonfruit.com.**

Babysitters Most of the major hotels can book a babysitter through the reception. Expect to pay around €8.50 an hour plus the babysitter's taxi fare home.

Breastfeeding This is perfectly acceptable in public although you may get stared at – but then, you may in the UK as well. You don't tend to see Cypriot women feeding in public; in fact, a fair few bottle feed.

Blue Flag Beaches In 2008, 52 beaches in Cyprus were awarded the EU's coveted Blue Flag. This means that the beaches meet strict criteria for water quality, safety and services, cleanliness, the provision of litter recycling facilities, clearly displayed information, access to disabled people (a minimum of one Blue Flag beach in each municipality needs to have this), safe access and control of dogs and other animals. For a full list of Cyprus's beaches meeting the standards, visit **www.blueflag.org**.

Business Hours Shopping hours in Cyprus are 9am until

around 7pm in winter and until around 8.30pm in summer. Many shops close early on Wednesdays and in summer will take a siesta between 2pm and 5pm. Shops are open later on Fridays – until around 9pm – and are closed on Sundays. In the resorts, however, shops will be open as long as tourists are in the streets so you should always be able to buy essentials.

Car Hire See p. 30.

Chemists These are indicated by an illuminated green cross. Most pharmacists in the tourist areas speak English and will be able to advise on minor ailments. Most remedies you'd find at home are available over the counter. Remember to carry prescription medicines in your hand luggage and if you are likely to need a repeat, to bring the prescription with you.

Churches Even the smallest village church can contain valuable icons and as a result, many are kept locked. If you want to look inside, ask at the village taverna or coffee shop and the keeper of the key will be summoned!

Climate See p. 40.

Dentists Enquire through your hotel reception if you need an emergency dentist. Dental treatment is not free and you will need to claim via your travel insurance.

Doctors See p. 23.

Drinking Water Tap water is safe to drink in Cyprus. Water

pollution is negligible and every home has fresh running drinking water. Tap water in hotels, restaurants, public premises, etc., is also safe to drink. On some of the mountain walks, you'll find fresh water in springs (channelled through drinking fountains) – it's absolutely delicious.

Driving Rules See p. 29.

Electricity The electricity supply in Cyprus is 230 volts, a.c. 50 Hz. Sockets are usually 13 amp, square pin in most buildings, the same as in the UK, so you won't need an adaptor.

Embassies and High Commissions UK Cyprus High Commission, 93 Park Street, London, W1K 7ET, ℂ *0870 005 6711*, *www.cyprus.embassyhome page.com*; Ireland Embassy of the Republic of Cyprus, 71 Lower Leeson Street, Dublin 2 ℂ *01 676 3060*, *E: embassyofcyprus dub@eircom.net*; USA Embassy of the Republic of Cyprus, 2211 R. St. NW Washington, DC 20008, ℂ *202 462 5772*, *www.cyprus embassy.net*.
Cyprus British High Commission, Alexandrou Palli, P.O. Box 21978, CY 1587 Lefkosia, ℂ *22 861 100*, (daily) ℂ *90 916 666*.

Emergencies (English spoken): ambulance/fire service/police: ℂ *199, 112*. Narcotics emergency service: ℂ *1401*.

Holidays See p. 20.

Internet Access See p. 25.

Legal If you need urgent legal advice, ask the British High

Commission's consular section to recommend a local English-speaking lawyer (the services of whom will be at your own expense). If you are buying property, it's a whole different issue and very complicated but the main rule of thumb is NOT to use a lawyer recommended by an estate agent as backhanders often take place.

Mail See p. 37.

Maps The CTO provides a free set of maps which are quite adequate for most tourists. Get them from the airport when you arrive, or from your car rental company. Note that the spelling of place names often varies, and that many places have the same name! Google Earth (*www.google earth.com*) is actually a brilliant resource for Cyprus as the mapping is so clear and you can search for place names on that, too.

Marriage Cyprus is a popular place in which to tie the knot and a lot of British couples get married here. It can be the ideal place if, for example, it's your second marriage and you don't want the big church wedding you may have had first time round but you do want your children with you. Several tour operators have marriage experts who will set everything up but if you want to do it independently, you need to apply in person to the Marriage Officer in the municipality in which you wish to get married, and present your birth certificate, passport and

evidence that you are free to marry (i.e. divorce papers if you're divorced). You can then marry 15 days after the appointment, although this can be brought forwards. A wedding can be held at the registry office or by a minister of religion in a church or place of worship by prior arrangement. Some hotels have lovely settings in which you can have the ceremony, such as the chapel at the Columbia Beach Resort in Pissouri.

For more information on getting married, visit *www.ucm.org. cy/eng/civil_marriage.htm.*

Media Cyprus has two English language newspapers, the *Cyprus Mail* and the *Cyprus Weekly*. Both are a useful guide to what's on. They are also fairly political, with an understandable bias against anything to do with the Turkish occupied north, so do not expect a clear picture of the situation from the press.

You can buy English and other international newspapers from most large tourist shops, usually a day after they're published.

Cyprus has several English radio programmes, with daily news in English on CyBC (Cyprus Broadcasting Corporation) and many private music stations. BFBS Forces radio is on 89.7 FM.

CyBC TWO television broadcasts news in English at 6.45pm daily. Almost all hotels have satellite nowadays through which you can get Sky News and BBC World.

Money & Credit Cards See p. 18.

Newspapers & Magazines See p. 36.

Opening Hours See p. 34.

Parking You cannot park on a double yellow line and you can only stop on a single yellow to load or unload. There are car parks and parking meters in major towns but the reality is there is often free parking as well, if you check out the side streets. The rules are less stringent than in the UK.

Places of Worship Cyprus enjoys an exceedingly high level of freedom of worship. While the majority of Greek Cypriots are Greek-Orthodox Christians, other denominations are represented on the island, including Armenians, Maronites and Roman Catholics. The Turkish-Cypriot community is predominantly Muslim.

There are Anglican churches in Nicosia, Limassol, Paphos, Larnaca and Ayia Napa. Nicosia has a mosque and synagogue services are held in Larnaca. You must dress respectfully to enter a church.

Police Dial 📞 199 or 📞 112 for emergencies. There are police stations in all major towns. Crime is relatively low in Cyprus.

Post Offices You can send letters from post offices located throughout the island and at the airports, or using the yellow mailboxes on the street. Stamps may be purchased from all post offices, postal agencies, as well as from many hotels, news stands, kiosks, etc. Post offices offer other services, including courier service (data post), money orders, parcel post, etc. Post office opening hours are generally 7.30am–1.30pm and 3pm–6pm Mon–Fri, closed on Wednesday afternoons. Saturday opening is 8.30am–10.30am in major towns.

Safety Cyprus is generally a very safe place; towns do not have no-go areas after dark, as such. There is an ongoing threat of terrorist attacks, just as there is anywhere in the world today, but no more so than anywhere else. While there are occasional flare-ups between Turks in the north and Greek Cypriots in the south, these do not tend to affect tourists.

The Population of Cyprus

Cyprus has a total population is only 837, 300, of which 77.8% are Greek Cypriots, 10.5% Turkish Cypriots and 11.7% foreign residents, the majority of them English and German. These figures are swelled every summer by hundreds of thousands of visitors and by immigrant workers from all over Europe, particularly the former Eastern Bloc countries.

Average Daily Temperature and Rainfall in Paphos

	Temp (Centigrade)	Rainfall (days)
Jan	12	9
Feb	12	7
Mar	13	7
Apr	16	5
May	20	2
June	23	0
July	26	0
Aug	26	0
Sept	24	1
Oct	21	3
Nov	17	6
Dec	14	7

Average Daily Temperature and Rainfall in Larnaca

	Temp (Centigrade)	Rainfall (days)
Jan	12	8
Feb	12	6
Mar	14	6
Apr	17	5
May	22	2
June	26	0
July	27	0
Aug	28	0
Sept	26	0
Oct	22	4
Nov	17	5
Dec	14	6

The main threats to personal safety in Cyprus are bad driving (locals and tourists), inexperienced motorbike and quad bike drivers (tourists) and excess drunkenness (tourists, usually in concentrated areas of nightclubs).

Taxes Cyprus has four rates of VAT: 15%, 8%, 5% and 0%. VAT is automatically included in prices shown so should not be a concern. For information concerning VAT refunds, see p. 17.

Taxis See p. 31.

Telephones To dial Cyprus from abroad, call 00357 and then the eight-digit phone number.

To call abroad while in Cyprus, dial ℓ 00, followed by the country code and the telephone number (leaving out the initial 0).

International calls can be made from public telephones available at various central locations in all cities and villages, as well as at international airports, harbours and elsewhere. There are three

Tourist Guides

Tour guides in Cyprus attend a special tourist guide school and are all licensed by the Cyprus Tourism Organisation when they pass their exams. They complete a one-year course which includes topics such as archaeology, geology, Byzantine and mediaeval history, nature, arts and crafts, food and wine. Although it's expensive, if you're travelling as a group it may be worth hiring your own guide for a more in-depth look at the island - or perhaps a tour more geared to your family's interests.

You can contact a guide directly via the website **www.cytourist guides.com** where there is a helpful listing of guides in each of the main towns, with details of the languages they speak. The website also displays the fees charged by a guide which start at 75.99 euro for a half day, 119.57 euro for a full day with supplements for public holidays, Sundays or activities like trekking. Bear in mind that a good guide is likely to be fully booked in the summer, so plan ahead if you decide to go down this route. Tel. +357 22 765755 or email **cytouristguides@cytanet.com.cy**. You can also enquire in any tourist information office.

types of public telephones – coin phones, outdoor card phones and indoor card phones. Public payphones can be used for both national and international calls. Dialling instructions as well as rates are displayed in all payphones.

Calling within Cyprus simply requires dialling the eight-digit telephone number. Area codes Nicosia 22; Ayia Napa area 23; Larnaca 24; Limassol 25; Paphos 26.

Time Zone The time zone in Cyprus is GMT + 2. Clocks go forward one hour on the last Sunday of March and back to standard time on the last Sunday of October.

Tipping Although a 10% service charge is normally included in hotel and restaurant bills, it is common to round up bills for good service. Tip taxi drivers 5%–10%.

Toilets and Baby Changing

Toilets in Cyprus are pretty civilised but it does depend where you are! The plumbing system is not as sophisticated as it is at home so do remember not to put anything down the toilet, including loo roll.

Baby-changing facilities are not provided as a matter of course so you may have to improvise.

Tourist Information The CTO publishes useful free booklets in English on the following: **List of Events** – an annual what's on guide. **Nature Trails** – slightly confusing list of the marked nature trails – you'll need a more detailed map if you want to do any. **The Hidden Cyprus** – lots of information on off-the-beaten-track Cyprus. **The Cyprus Wine Story** – interesting for enthusiasts. **Flavours of Cyprus** – excellent guide to Cypriot food beyond the meze! **Cycling Routes** – for experts only, although there are a couple of short routes in there.

CTO tourist offices overseas. UK 17 Hanover Street, London W1S 1YP, ☏ 020 7569 8800, ☏ 020 7569 8808, *E: informationcto@ btconnect.com*. **USA** 13 East, 40th Street, New York, NY 10016, ☏ 212 683 5280, *www. cyprustourism.org*.

Weather and Climate Cyprus has a southern Mediterranean climate of long, dry, hot summers and mild winters between December and February. There are, however, still usually six hours of sunshine daily in December and January. There are daily weather forecasts on the radio on CyBC's Programme Two, 91.1 FM, after the news at 1.30pm and 8pm.

The summer months from May to October are best for beach lovers: day temperatures are warm (around 33° C) and nights are pleasant (though the beaches can still be nice into October, when it is usually about

5° C cooler). Inland, temperatures can get much hotter in the summer, rising as high as 40° C. Most of the annual rainfall occurs from December to March. The Troodos Mountains on the Greek side, rising to more than 1,970 m, are snow-covered from mid-January to mid-March. The mountains are particularly beautiful in the autumn.

Daily temperatures during the hottest months of July and August, range between 29° C on the central plain and 22° C on the Troodos Mountains. The average maximum temperatures for these two months range between 36° C and 27° C, in other words, very hot indeed. Humidity is low, although there are some muggy days. Nights can be stifling and if you have a baby, you may want to consider making sure your villa or accommodation is air conditioned. In January, the coolest month, the indicative daily temperature is 10° C on the central plain and 3° C on the higher parts of the Troodos Mountains, while the average minimum temperatures are 5° C and 0° C.

You can swim in the sea from Cyprus between June and November.

3 Paphos, Coral Bay & Pissouri

PAPHOS, CORAL BAY & PISSOURI

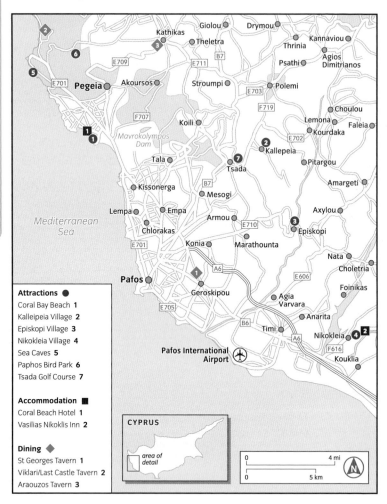

Attractions ●
Coral Bay Beach **1**
Kalleipeia Village **2**
Episkopi Village **3**
Nikokleia Village **4**
Sea Caves **5**
Paphos Bird Park **6**
Tsada Golf Course **7**

Accommodation ■
Coral Beach Hotel **1**
Vasilias Nikoklis Inn **2**

Dining ◆
St Georges Tavern **1**
Viklari/Last Castle Tavern **2**
Araouzos Tavern **3**

O nce a sleepy fishing village, Paphos is now a buzzing, international resort, perched in the south-west of the island where
scrub-covered hills and pine forest flatten out onto a broad coastal
plain. The climate here is more humid than in the east and although
much of the agricultural land has been covered by villa developments,
you'll still see banana plantations on the road north to Coral Bay.

Many people visit Paphos and barely stray from their hotel pool,
but behind the increasingly sprawling town, the developed area comes
to an abrupt end and gives way to olive and almond groves, steep hills
and sleepy, whitewashed villages. This is also the gateway to the wild,
rugged Akamas Peninsula, in a way, the last wilderness of Cyprus,

where you can still look for huge griffon vultures, trek craggy gorges and in season, see baby turtles hatching on Lara Beach (see p. 78).

Paphos itself has everything you could need for a family holiday, from the excellent Paphos Bird and Animal Park (see p. 55) to a medieval fortress, a bustling market, shopping, ten-pin bowling, Blue Flag beaches and every watersport imaginable, as well as some you probably hadn't imagined. But it's the contrast between the urban area and the countryside that makes a trip here so rewarding.

Paphos has extended tentacles of development to encompass the new resort area of Coral Bay, 15 km to the north. Coral Bay is worth considering in its own right for a family holiday, thanks to its quieter atmosphere, gorgeous beach and superb hotels – and, for adventurous types, the fact that Akamas is right on the doorstep.

To the east, the coast stretches away through a series of quiet villages to Pissouri, a hilltop settlement with another lovely beach at its foot, but best known for the nearby beach where Aphrodite, goddess of love, is said to have emerged from the foaming sea.

In between all these places are pretty villages, most of them off the beaten track. None of them offer anything specific for families – you have to stay in the big resorts for that – but the warm Cypriot welcome adults and children will find in these places is living proof that the famous hospitality is more than a myth.

ESSENTIALS

Getting There

By Air Paphos International Airport, 20 minutes from Kato Paphos, has fewer international flights than Larnaca but is served by **Cyprus Airways, easyJet** (see p. 26) and in summer, numerous charter airlines. The flight from the UK takes about four hours. Flying direct is much easier with children but for a much wider choice of airlines, you can fly into **Larnaca** (see p. 30) and easily rent a car.

By Car All the main car rental companies have offices at **Paphos Airport** (see p. 30),

although it's best to book in advance. Alternatively, do without a car for a few days and rent one in town, or through your hotel, when you need it.

The drive from the airport to the beach area on Poseidonos Avenue, where most of the hotels are located, takes a maximum 20 minutes in average traffic and the signposting is reasonably clear.

The drive to Paphos only takes about 1 hour 20 minutes. If you're doing a two-centre holiday and driving from Limassol, allow 40 minutes on the motorway or an hour or so on the prettier, quieter coast road.

VISITOR INFORMATION

The Cyprus Tourism Organisation (CTO) has two offices in Paphos, including one on the main hotel strip of Poseidonos Avenue. There's a booth at Paphos Airport, too, operating until 11pm. The CTO has a lot of excellent information and a complete set of island maps, which are good enough for navigating your way around. Its website is **www.visitcyprus.com**.

Orientation

The town itself is divided into two parts. The resort area is called Kato (lower) Paphos and stretches out along Poseidonos Avenue, which runs parallel to the beach from the harbour and fortress; it's along here that most of the smart hotels are located. Pano Paphos, the commercial part of town, is slightly inland and has little of interest apart from a couple of museums and some shopping.

The strip of coast from the harbour to the north is an archaeological park where you'll find the famous antiquities, the Tombs of the Kings and the Mosaics.

As recently as 10 years ago, there were a few kilometres of banana plantations between Paphos and the new resort of Coral Bay, 15 km to the north, but nowadays, the bananas have been replaced by luxury villas, as one of Cyprus's most glitzy

suburbs has sprung up. This is a great area to rent a villa – it's quieter than Paphos itself and has some good beaches. Coral Bay is now a self-contained mini-Paphos with a lovely beach but not much in the way of culture.

In the opposite direction, about 20 minutes along the A6 motorway, the village of Pissouri spills over a hilltop with amazing views. The village itself is delight-fully unspoilt and there are a couple of lovely hotels down on the beach, perfect for a quiet but luxurious family holiday.

Getting Around

By Car Hiring a car is by far the best way of getting around the Paphos area, although you can do it by bus if you have time and patience. While I'm the last per-son to recommend that you hire a giant, polluting SUV, you will need a four-wheel drive if you plan to visit the Akamas penin-sula. The dirt tracks can be negotiated by a smaller car. You'll also need a car to visit Polis and Latchi, Limassol and the Troodos, all easy day trips, unless you book on a coach tour.

It's also easy to hire mopeds, quad bikes and dune buggies, all of which are allowed on the road, and mountain bikes, but unless your children are big, burly teenagers, cycling round here is a bit risky when you take into account nervous holiday drivers and speed-loving locals.

By Foot If you're staying in one of the beach hotels, bear in mind that the coast path runs through all of them – all beaches in Cyprus are public – and the walk from the harbour down to the resort properties is very pleasant.

Child-friendly Events & Entertainment

Paphos Aphrodite Festival

📞 *26 822 218, www.pafc.com.cy.*

At a push, you may get a baby or toddler to doze in their buggy through this popular opera festival on a balmy August night! It's outside, set against the magical backdrop of the Paphos Medieval Castle, with the whole harbour area turned into a massive auditorium. Past performances include *La Traviata, Tosca* and *Madame Butterfly*.

Aug. **Admission** €32–72.

WHAT TO SEE & DO

Children's Top 10 Attractions

❶ **Scrambling** around the Tombs of the Kings (see p. 55).

❷ **Exploring** the history of olive oil at the fun, interactive museum, Oleastro (see p. 57).

❸ **Kayaking** into the mysterious Sea Caves at Agios Georgios (see p. 53).

❹ **Watching archaeologists** at work on the Paphos Mosaics (see p. 56).

❺ **Spotting** 65 types of parrot at the outstanding Paphos Bird and Animal Park (see p. 55).

❻ **Taking a thrill ride** on a high-speed boat from Paphos Harbour (see p. 61).

❼ **Swimming** under a waterfall at the Baths of Adonis (see p. 52).

❽ **Going wild** on the slides at the Aphrodite Water Park (see p. 60).

❾ **Riding a donkey** in the mountains and trying traditional Cypriot food at a working farm (see p. 59).

❿ **Bumping along** dirt trails on an exciting jeep safari (see p. 59).

Towns & Cities

Paphos ★★★

Once a tiny fishing port and now a huge, sprawling resort with an international airport, Paphos is extremely pleasant – but not terribly Cypriot. For Cypriot, you need to stalk the back streets of Pano Paphos (Upper Paphos), a busy but not wildly attractive urban centre with a market, a couple of museums and a lot of shops. Kato Paphos (Lower Paphos), the resort area, is hugely favoured by British tourists, who flock here between April and November and in many cases, buy property in the suburbs, one of which, **Peyia**, famously has more British than Cypriot residents.

Paphos is nonetheless a great place for a family holiday with

PAPHOS TOWN

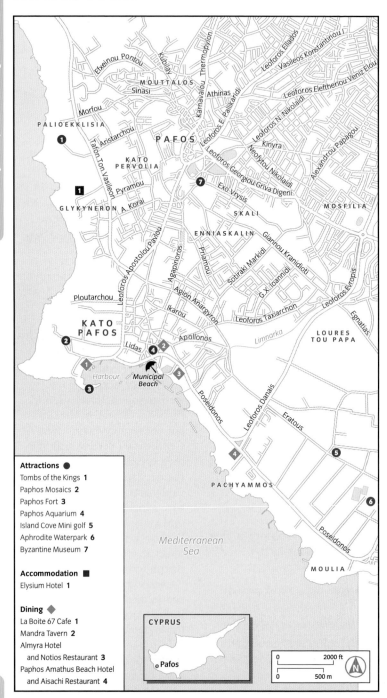

Attractions ●
Tombs of the Kings **1**
Paphos Mosaics **2**
Paphos Fort **3**
Paphos Aquarium **4**
Island Cove Mini golf **5**
Aphrodite Waterpark **6**
Byzantine Museum **7**

Accommodation ■
Elysium Hotel **1**

Dining ◆
La Boite 67 Cafe **1**
Mandra Tavern **2**
Almyra Hotel
  and Notios Restaurant **3**
Paphos Amathus Beach Hotel
  and Aisachi Restaurant **4**

CYPRUS

Pafos

0   2000 ft
0   500 m

its wide, palm-lined waterfront boulevard and friendly holiday atmosphere. There are some gentle, child-friendly cultural attractions, the **Mosaics** and the **Tombs of the Kings**, the popular **Bird and Animal Park**, clean, sandy beaches, a seriously good **waterpark**, decent enough shopping and a vast choice of places to eat and drink.

The focal point is the **harbour**, packed with yachts and pleasure boats and a smattering of brightly coloured fishing boats alongside replica Jolly Rogers and giant powerboats with teeth painted on the front. This is the place to come for morning coffee, Sunday lunch, an evening promenade, or just for a night out – the coolest places are **Boite**, which is part-pub and part-lounge, and the **Hobo Café**. There are plenty of nick-nack shops for children, and a solid medieval fort to scramble around. The whole sweep of the waterfront is lined with bars, some more basic pubs and others with smart cane chairs and tables and big, squashy chill-out cushions.

Paphos also has a disproportionate number of superb, five-star hotels for families looking for the full spa experience, exciting children's clubs and gourmet food. These places include the gorgeous **Almyra** and the wonderful **Paphos Amathus Beach Hotel**, with its vast pool that children adore. The resort's biggest lure to me, though, is its proximity to the untamed western tip of the island, **Akamas** (see p. 80), where I personally could spend days exploring, hiking, visiting remote beaches, wildlife-spotting and breathing in the mountain air (and have done so), all with my children.

Coral Bay ★

Coral Bay used to be, well, just a bay, with some pretty beaches and rippling plantations of glossy, green banana palms basking in the sun between the sea and the mountains. This was just 15 years ago. Now, the area is a sprawling tourist resort and although it's not exactly an eyesore, my burning question to the

Paphos Harbour

developers is 'What were you thinking?' There's way too much neon, tacky fast-food restaurants and shops full of tat – but that's only in the centre of this man-made place. The good news is that there are lots of gorgeous family villas round here, really lavish ones; you're near the amazing **Sea Caves** and the **Paphos Bird & Animal Park**; **Akamas** and its natural attractions are just along the coast; and Paphos is close by for shopping and better restaurants. The resort development itself is fine – it just makes you (or me, at least) long for a sleepy Cypriot village with a local taverna and some donkeys. Luckily, there are plenty of these within easy reach!

If you stay at Coral Bay, do venture up the coast to tiny **Agios Georgios**, which has to be one of the only beaches in the world where you can rent a sun lounger but you can't swim. It's only a place to stop for drinks on the way back from a day on Akamas – you can watch the sunset from the tavernas up on the hill overlooking the pretty harbour – and there isn't a lot for children, but for half-an-hour, this is a quiet and serene place. The monastery is beautiful, too.

Pissouri ★★

Pissouri is a real escape-from-it-all place – maybe somewhere to chill if you have a new baby and just want to relax, or young toddlers whose holiday needs are no more than a bit of sand and a splash pool. Few tourists travel through the village, as it's away from the road, perched right at the top of a mountain, spilling over the hillside, although a lot of visitors come to pay homage to the **Rock of Aphrodite**, further along the coast. This is still a working Cypriot community, with a lot of locals involved in the wine trade. Go out for dinner in the village centre and you'll hear more Greek than English spoken, for once,

Rock of Aphrodite at sunset

FUN FACT ▸ Eternal Youth ◂

A local myth states that anyone who bathes in the sea under a full moon at the Rock of Aphrodite will achieve eternal youth.

---

although canny property buyers are snapping up the gorgeous hillside villas here at a fraction of the price of those across the valley at the swish golf resort of **Aphrodite Hills**, so the expat community is growing fast.

Wednesday nights in summer are the time to be here in the village square, when there's live music and dancing, shared by all the tavernas that line the square. Provided you can get your children onto Cypriot time to stay up late, it's a great family occasion and they can run around quite safely while you finish your meal.

There are two distinct areas to Pissouri, the village and what used to be Pissouri Jetty, which served the village, but is now surrounded by the little resort of Pissouri Beach – no more than a handful of beach bars and tavernas, villas and two stylish hotels, the **Columbia Beach Resort** and the **Columbia Hotel**, both of which are completely family-friendly. The occasional yacht pitches up here for the day but apart from that, it's blissfully quiet.

The other string to Pissouri's bow is the new and very flashy **Aphrodite Hills Resort**, along the coast from the village and set up in the hills. Aphrodite Hills is a new departure for a Cypriot resort complex as it's not on the beach, and it aims to be completely self-contained, complete with tavernas, village square, golf, spas, bars and children's club. It's extremely stylish and very eco-friendly – but the price tag is high.

Scenic villages

Kallepeia ★

Only 13 km from busy Paphos is another world, where old men sit outside the *kafenion* (village café) gossiping, and donkeys bray in the afternoon sunshine. Kallepeia is a largish village of whitewashed houses with traditional terracotta roofs, sprawling over a hillside and surrounded by vineyards. The village has no attractions for children as such but is peaceful and pretty. Wander round and look out for stone houses with hidden, flower-filled courtyards, and the many structures made of beautiful marble, including the very impressive Monastery of the Holy Cross. The old church of Agios Georgios is worth poking your nose into, with gold icons and a lingering aroma of incense. There's also a small art gallery, showcasing the work of local and international artists. In the tavernas, look out for *palouze*, *resi*, *soutzouko* and *zivania* – variations on the local grape-based hooch.

Choulou ★

East of Tsada and south-east of Polis on the E702, Choulou is another spectacularly pretty village, beautifully restored with grants from the Cypriot agro-tourism scheme. Stay here and you'll be woken by donkeys braying and cockerels crowing (we were), miraculously hangover-free thanks to the fine organic wines served in the village taverna. There's not a lot to see in Choulou, which is its biggest charm, but I mention it because the couple of stone houses here for rental are ideal if you want a taste of village life.

Episkopi ★

Combine a stunning, if somewhat white-knuckle, drive through the hills with a visit to this dreamy village (not to be confused with the larger village of the same name just west of Limassol), which clings to the hillside underneath a craggy cliff some 11 km east of Paphos. To get there, follow the signs to Marathounta and stay on the twisty road past the village. Episkopi was famous for its resident saint, Ilarionas, who lived a simple life in a cave in the cliff, where he also died, in 371AD. The white church on top of the cliff was built in his name, supplementing the much older church in the village.

The best thing to do with children here is to take a walk along the river bed, which is dry for much of the year. See how many birds and lizards you can spot – and watch out for snakes (see p. 144)!

Nikokleia ★

Between Paphos and Pissouri, and just off one of the main roads leading up to Troodos, this lovely little village is probably somewhere you'd stay in the local inn (see p. 68) rather than devote a day trip to, but as a base from which to reach **Pissouri**, the **Rock of Aphrodite**, **Paphos** and **Troodos**, it's ideal.

> **INSIDER TIP ▶**
>
> The area is also famous for its bird, butterfly and reptile life, so young enthusiasts should come equipped with a good book; Collins publishes field guides to British and European butterflies and reptiles.

Beaches & Resorts

All the beaches in Cyprus have public access via a coastal path, almost always paved, that runs right through the grounds of the seafront hotels. The hotels in Paphos have developed their own little patches of beach, building breakwaters and dredging sand to deepen the often rather meagre strips. Each hotel beach has watersports concessions offering paragliding, water-skiing, banana boats and all the usual toys. These concessions are usually externally run, although the hotels put their own sunbeds on their respective strips of sand.

Within Paphos itself, you really are better off using your hotel's beach if you have a need to feel the sand between your toes – the reality here is that most people stick to the swimming pools. What is nice, though, is to take children for a walk along the coast path late afternoon, have a paddle at some of the undeveloped bits between the hotels, enjoy watching the sun set over the distant fortress and stop for a drink/milkshake at one of the beach bars.

Paphos Municipal Beach
Like most of the town beaches, this one is OK rather than stunningly beautiful, with coarse, yellow sand and umbrellas and sunbeds to rent. It flies the EU Blue Flag for meeting certain environmental criteria, but you can only get into the sea by

clambering over a low concrete wall and the seabed is rocky, with more rocks either side of the narrow sweep, so invest in jelly shoes and watch children really carefully. It's attractive enough, but far from ideal for a family.

Far more locals than tourists use the beach; if you are staying in a beach hotel, your children can use its lawns that slope down to the sand and are better for playing on. There are shops right opposite the beach selling drinks, ice cream and beach toys.

Located just before the Municipal Gardens, a 10-minute walk from the harbour.

Vrysoudia B
In case you're wondering, Vrysoudia A is near the winery on the main beach road stretching

Coral Bay beach

east from Paphos! Both are regularly awarded EU Blue Flag status. B is really only a narrow strip of sand in front of the Alexander the Great Hotel on Poseidonos Avenue but the seabed shelves gently and the water is beautifully clear.

Coral Beach ★ ★ ★

Easily the most beautiful beach in Paphos and perfect for families. A 15-minute drive north of the town, Coral Beach is a beautiful arc of golden sand with sandstone cliffs at either end. The gently shelving sea floor is perfect for small children to splash around. There are sunbeds and umbrellas to rent and pretty well anything you can dream up in the way of water toys from kayaks and pedalos (with slides) to banana boats, inner tubes, wake boarding and paragliding, all run by **Coral Bay Watersports**.

In addition, the beach has a decent snack bar serving salads and sandwiches – and even a massage pavilion. Parking is free and a wooden boardwalk leads down to the sand.

Needless to say, as one of the loveliest beaches in the west and with a Blue Flag into the bargain, Coral Beach gets very, very busy. It's worth going at sunset when the crowds have left – the light is breathtaking and we all know that most children will plunge into the sea however late in the day it is!

Pissouri Bay ★ ★

Pissouri Bay used to serve as the dock for fishing boats belonging to residents of the eponymous village, high up on the hillside. Nowadays, it's a quiet, relaxing resort with just a few tavernas, rental villas and two hotels. The beach itself is wide but not very deep and has EU Blue Flag status. At the western end, you can rent pedalos, kayaks and windsurfers and book banana boat rides, inner tubes and water skiing. A strong wind can kick up here and children will enjoy watching the kite surfers zipping across the waves at amazing speeds. Kite surfing isn't a sport for young children but rugged teenagers may want to have a go, in which case contact **Surf Cyprus** before you leave; the company is based in Worcestershire and Pissouri and runs a variety of courses.

There are some excellent restaurants in Pissouri, if you want to make a lunch stop out of it. **Captain's Bay** is right on the beach, next to the **Kastro** fish tavern, which has a stone terrace overlooking the water and **Limanaki**, where you have to book three days ahead (see p. 71).

Surf Cyprus, ☎ *99 755 536,* ***www. surfcyprus.com***.

Natural Wonders & Spectacular Views

Baths of Adonis ★
AGES 5 AND UP

Signposted from the Paphos–Coral Bay road, 1 km before Coral Bay.

This pretty waterfall is nice enough as a detour if you

happen to be driving along the Paphos–Coral Beach road, but is not worth hiring a car for. The water cascades about 3 m over a rock and tumbles into a cool, green pool in which you can bathe. Legend has it that Adonis, lover of Aphrodite, used to bathe here and some believe he even died here in Aphrodite's arms. Although there's not much to the site, it's better than the disappointing Baths of Aphrodite to the north of Akamas and children will love jumping into the cool water.

Admission *Approx €3.50.*

Sea Caves ☆ ☆ ALL AGES

Tours are operated by Zephyros Adventure Sports, Shop 7, Royal Complex, Tombs of the Kings Road, Kato Paphos, ☎ 26 930 037, www. enjoycyprus.com.

The Sea Caves are a few minutes' drive north of Coral Bay. On top of the cliffs here is the Beverly Hills of Paphos – huge, expensive and, it has to be said, very desirable villas with views to die for.

The cliffs themselves are white limestone, hollowed out by millennia of waves pounding at their base to create a series of dark caves and bizarrely shaped stacks and arches. The caves are about 30 m deep and have jolly names like Jonah, Purple Haze, Standing Room Only and The Big One, which belie their more grisly past as smugglers' hangouts. You can get inside on a **sea canoe safari** but only take children on a very calm day as there are some legendary currents here, including a spot called the Washing Machine which spins the kayaks around. It's suitable for all ages (there are double canoes so adults can paddle with a child in front) but whether you can go is subject to sea and weather conditions.

If all this is too much, spend a morning basking on the flat rocks facing the caves, where the sea is an almost Caribbean shade of turquoise and there's some great snorkelling for older children.

Admission *All tours €41.*

Sea Caves, west of Paphos

Petra tou Romiou (Aphrodite's Birthplace) ★ ★

ALL AGES

On the old B6 coast road (not the motorway) from Limassol to Paphos.

The best times to visit what is essentially a hunk of rock are sunrise, if you can get up early enough, or more likely, sunset, when its chalky, slab-sided west face turns a beautiful shade of pink and you can watch the sun sink over Paphos in the far distance. The spot where the goddess of love allegedly emerged from the foam is the subject of endless myths and legends. The name Petra tou Romiou means the 'rock of the Greek' and actually refers to the Byzantine hero Dighenis, who lobbed rocks at approaching pirates to protect his lady friend. The connection with Aphrodite possibly comes from certain weather conditions that cause the waves to form a column of water that dissolves into a pillar of foam, resembling an ethereal, rather ghostly goddess.

The scenery is undeniably beautiful, with great chunks of limestone separated from the cliffs and jutting out of the water, but it's not a great place for a day on the beach, first because it's stony, second because there are currents and a steep shelf and third, no lifeguard. Go late afternoon and let children have a supervised splash around in the shallows or a scramble over some of the lower rocks. Watch the other families and see all the dads clambering up the big rock – it must be a boy thing! Plenty of young lovers come here to watch the sunset and tie a ribbon (or more messily, a piece of tissue) to a wishing tree, hoping their dreams of love will come true.

Amenities *Free car park, tourist pavilion with snacks and drinks on sale. Disabled access limited.*

Aquaria & Animal Parks

Paphos Aquarium OVERRATED

1 Artemidos Street, Kato Paphos, ☎ 26 953 920, www.tsiolis.com.cy. Behind the shopping centre on Paphos waterfront, opposite the Municipal Beach and next to Theokapasti Church.

I had hoped to recommend the Paphos Aquarium (some other guidebooks do) for a rainy day – but it would have to be very rainy indeed to merit a visit to this grim place. Of course an aquarium in a holiday resort can't be expected to be on the same scale as a multi-million dollar attraction in the USA or London – but the specimens in this gloomy place looked so forlorn, I felt desperately sorry for them. There's a solitary crocodile in a fairly bleak cement enclosure and a rather bedraggled shark, as well as assorted 'Nemos' and other tropical fish. The tanks don't have enough greenery or rock features for hiding places that make up the natural habitat of the fish, surely a fundamental of running an aquarium? Children, though, are unlikely to notice the aquarium's shortcomings and the displays are well lit. It's also very cool and dark inside if you need to escape from the sun. There's a small gift shop (selling shells and dead coral – another black mark) and a cafeteria.

Open *Daily 9am–8pm summer; 9am–6pm winter.* **Admission** *Adults €6, children €3.50.* **Amenities** *Shop, cafeteria.*

Paphos Bird and Animal Park

★ ★   **ALL AGES**

St George, Peya, ☎ *26 813 852, www.pafosbirdpark.com.*

15 km from Paphos and 6 km from Coral Bay, well signposted from the St George suburb. The final stretch is up a dirt track. Buses include 10 and 15 from Paphos to Coral Bay and 10a from Coral Bay to the park. Free transfers operate from the hotels daily except Fri, at 9.45am and 12.30pm.

Paphos Bird and Animal Park is a great family day out and a change from the beach. It's compact but very well arranged, with plenty going on; the peacocks wandering around the car park are a good indicator of what's to come. Animals include snakes, iguanas, various species of deer and gazelle, giraffe and crocodiles. Birds, the park's real strength, are kept in decent enclosures and include hawks and eagles, ducks, geese, swans, game birds, ostrich, a staggering 64 types of parrot and nine types of cockatoo! New arrivals include snowy owls and meerkats.

The park has a captive breeding programme and a clinic and on Wednesday afternoons, you can watch the vets at work.

Meanwhile, there are daily talks and parrot and owl shows in the amphitheatre (parrots on roller skates, playing basketball and so on; luckily the owls get off more lightly). Small children will enjoy the petting zoo, with rabbits, guinea pigs, chickens, ponies and goats.

Open *Daily 9am–5pm Oct–Mar; 9am–sunset Apr–Sept.* **Admission** *Adults €9, children €5.* **Credit** *MC V.* **Amenities** *Souvenir shop, handicraft shop, restaurant, snack bar, traditional Cypriot house, playground, petting zoo, ice-cream kiosk, amphitheatre, disabled access, plenty of free parking.*

Historic Buildings & Monuments

Tombs of the Kings ★ ★
AGES 5 AND UP

On the Paphos–Coral Bay road, ☎ *26 306 295.*

Actual kings weren't buried in these vast, fourth-century AD tombs but rather, local dignitaries and nobles, following the Egyptian philosophy that the resting place for the dead should closely resemble a home for the living. Despite the lack of royalty, this UNESCO World Heritage Site is really impressive, spread out on a wide, rocky ledge overlooking the sea west of Kato Paphos, and the best thing from a child's point of view is that there seems to be no limit as to what you can climb on, or in!

The seven cavernous, underground tombs have been skilfully excavated and although there's no treasure in them, you can climb down inside and absorb the silence. Check out number three in particular, which is supported by graceful Doric columns. In some of the others, you have to scramble down a stone stairway; get children to look for the niches in the wall, where the bodies were kept.

Open *Daily 8am–5pm Nov–March; 8am–6pm Apr–May; 8am–7.30pm June–Aug.* **Admission** *Approx €1.71. No easy disabled access due to rocky paths and steps.*

Paphos Mosaics ★ ★ ★
AGES 5 AND UP

In Kato Paphos, near the harbour, ☏ *26 306 217.*

The stunning Paphos mosaics and the antiquities around them are all part of the Paphos Archaeological Park, which is still being excavated. Children with leanings towards Indiana Jones will enjoy watching the archaeologists at work. The whole site is part of Nea Pafos, which confusingly means New Paphos and actually refers to

ancient Paphos, dating back to the fourth century BC, when the city was encircled by walls. In those days, Paphos was the centre of cultural and political life in Cyprus, a golden age which lasted until the fourth century AD, when the city was destroyed by a massive earthquake. After this, it went into decline and Salamis in the east became the focus of the island.

The mosaics themselves are in four houses, of Dionysos, Theseus, Aion and Orpheus. If your children have studied Greek mythology at all, there are lots of things to look out for. The House of Dionysos is the most impressive, featuring intricately designed and coloured mosaics depicting the god of wine; look for the grape symbols. Other images tell the story of Pyramos and Thisbe, or the Four Seasons. Children will probably like the House of Theseus best, a second-century home with mosaics clearly telling the thrilling and grisly

Tombs of the Kings

Paphos Medieval Fortress

tale of Theseus and the Minotaur. Get Marcia Williams' brilliant and funny children's book, *Greek Myths*, before you go and read the chapter on Theseus (remembering to add all the voices, of course).

On the same site is the Paphos Odeion, not a cinema but an ancient amphitheatre, which was restored in 1970 and is used today for concerts and plays. It's a good place for a sit down in the heat and children can clamber on the stone tiers. There's one spot in the middle (you can see it as it's the most worn part of the ground) where the acoustics are perfect, should any family member with Thespian leanings be in the mood for a quick turn.

Open Daily 8am–5pm Nov–Mar; 8am–6pm Apr–May; 8am–7:30pm June–Aug. **Admission** €3.42.

Paphos Medieval Fortress

Paphos Harbour.

The fortress, a chunky-looking block guarding the harbour, was built in the 13th century to replace an earlier castle. It's a solid square with tiny windows and a central courtyard. There's not much to see but that doesn't usually stop children who enjoy stories of daring sea battles and raiding pirates. This particular fort was dismantled by the Venetians in 1570 so that the Ottomans, who had begun to attack the island, wouldn't be able to use it. Only the empty shell remains today but it's a good way to finish a stroll around the harbour.

Open Daily 8am–7.30pm June–Aug; 8am–6pm April–Oct; 8am–5pm Nov–Mar. **Admission** €1.71.

Top Museums

Oleastro Olive Park ★ ★ ★
FIND **GREEN** **ALL AGES**

10 km off the A6 motorway, past the village of Anogyra, ☎ *99 565 768,* **www.oleastro.com.cy**.

Situated inland from Pissouri, just beyond the sleepy, unspoilt village of Anogyra, the Olive Park is a great family outing and an insight into olive cultivation and production. Designed and run by Andreas and Lina Ellinas and their two children, this is how museums should be – interactive, fun and in harmony with their environment. In fact, the park has won environmental awards and Lina was in 2007 voted Cyprus's 'Woman Entrepreneur of the Year' for the project, which only opened in 2006.

Oleastro nestles on a hillside amidst an organic olive grove, its stone walls, wooden balconies and terracotta tiles reminiscent of an old Cypriot house. Visitors learn about 60,000 years of olive cultivation and oil extraction, from old-fashioned pressing to high-tech, eco-friendly techniques. The museum illustrates all the by-products of olive cultivation, including soap and beautiful wood from the ancient trees. You can visit the eco-mill, too, and learn how the waste from the pressing (skins and kernels) is crushed and recycled as compost and fuel as part of the organic process. Between mid-October and February, the mill is in action.

There's a playground, pony rides and an art corner for children, as well as an organic café serving recipes handed down in the owner's family. And, of course, a gift shop where you can stock up on fantastic going-home presents of wooden boxes containing bottles of oil with balsamic vinegar, mountain honey, bags of herbs and even carob honey.

Open Daily 10am–7pm. **Admission** Adults €2.56, children €1.71. **Amenities** Shop, restaurant, pony rides.

Paphos Byzantine Museum

5 Andrea Ioannou, 📞 26 931 393.

This little museum in Pano Paphos, just off the main square, is worth visiting if you like icons, although most parents would be hard-pushed to get children into this subject. One icon dates back to the ninth century and is said to be the oldest on the island.

Open 9am–3pm Mon–Fri; 9am–1pm Sat. **Admission** Adults €2, under-12s free.

Child-friendly Tours

Special Village Tour ★

📞 99 632 472, **www.paforentals. com**.

Sometimes, it's good to sit and enjoy the scenery rather than concentrate on the driving (and on some of the Cypriot mountain roads, you need to concentrate hard). The guided Special Village Tour run by **Pafotravel** gives passengers an insight into village life, pottering round some of the hill villages surrounding Paphos, some of which have points of interest for children. In **Geroskipou**, for example, you'll visit a place making Cyprus Delight (a confection similar to the Turkish version) and have a chance to taste it, and the local sugared almonds. In **Mesogi** village, children can watch old ladies weaving traditional bamboo baskets, while in **Polemi** the group visits a traditional house where the owners demonstrate weaving on a loom. There's a stop for lunch in the village taverna of **Akoursos**.

Open Daily in summer, 9am–3pm. Admission €17.09 excluding lunch. The same company operates tours to all the main attractions (Limassol, Troodos and so on) as well as 'Fun Bus' tours, using a vintage Cypriot bus.

Jeep Safaris ★ ★ ★

Ascot Jeep Safaris, ☎ 25 329 388, www.ascotrentacar.com.

It doesn't really matter where the jeeps go – in my experience, children love them anyway because they're rugged and hilariously bumpy. You'll see jeeps everywhere in the western end of the island, mainly bound for Akamas (see chapter 4) and the Troodos (see chapter 6). Be careful when you book one as some use minibuses, not jeeps, and going off-road in a minibus is not fun in any way. **Ascot Jeep Safari** is one of the better operators and uses Land Rovers. We had an absolutely brilliant guide who could identify every herb, bird, plant, butterfly and reptile at 50 paces and was a mine of information – and opinion. Ascot operates an Akamas tour out of Paphos, driving up the wild, rugged west coast and through the forest, mainly on dirt tracks, to Polis and Latchi in the north, heading back to Paphos via the mountains and the village of Stroumpi. There's also a Troodos tour (see chapter 6)

through pine forests and villages that calls at a winery, the beautiful Venetian Bridge, buried deep in the forest, Kykkos Monastery, Mount Olympus (the highest point on the island) and the Caledonian waterfall.

Open Akamas tour: Mon, Wed and Fri. Troodos tours: from Paphos Tues, Thurs and Sat. Admission Akamas tours: adults €59.85, children €34.20. Troodos tours: adults €63.27, children €34.20.

Donkey Safaris ★ ★

Argonaftis Tours, ☎ 25 586 333, www.argonaftis.com.

Cyprus has some 2,000 working donkeys and a fair few of them are employed in the tourist trade. These donkey safaris are unashamedly touristy but children love them and if you enter into the spirit, it's fun. The tour picks up in Paphos and there's a coach ride to Kelokedara, in the hills behind the town, where the fun starts. From here, it's a bumpy ride in a vintage bus to the Donkey Park, where the donkeys are kept. A few snacks are served – halloumi village cheese, olives, traditional oven-baked bread – washed down with wine and *zivania* (the local firewater) for adults and juice for children. Next, you ride through the countryside on the donkeys in a long string. It's pretty safe for children – the donkeys are very docile, used to it and essentially just plod along nose to tail. The ride traverses fields and olive groves with a snack stop to taste local fruit. Then, it's back to the animal park to say good-bye to the donkeys and tuck into a traditional meze, followed by riotous Cypriot entertainment.

This tour can attract several bus loads at once, so don't expect anything exclusive!

Admission Adults €69, children €38, including transfer, snacks, donkey trek, dinner or lunch with wine, and musical entertainment. Tours are offered daily in the summer; check the website for the winter pro-gramme, which tends to be lunch instead of dinner.

For Active Families

Aphrodite Water Park ★ ★ ★
ALL AGES

Off Poseidonos Avenue, Paphos, ☎ 26-913-638, www.aphrodite waterpark.com. Take bus 15 or bus 11 and your bus fare will be refunded at the entrance.

One of the best things about family holidays is that you get to go to waterparks and make a fool of yourself. This is a good one, well laid out and with plenty of consideration given to shade. All the small children's activities are together in the chil-dren's pool: a couple of slides, a wet bubble for bouncing on, splashing rainforest, shooting water clown, a mini-volcano and pirate ship slides. There's a big wave pool with DJs playing loud music; and a lazy river ride and a brilliant family rafting slide, one of the longest in Europe. Advice: don't cram two adults and two teenagers into your raft like we did – it nearly tipped because of the weight.

All the scary rides like Kamikaze, Free Fall and Black Hole start from the top of the hill (which is handy so you can pick the one with the shortest queue) and have height restric-tions, usually 120 cm.

Open 10.30am–5.30pm May–June; 10am–6pm July–Aug; 10am–5pm Sept–Oct. Admission Adults and over 12s €25.63, children (3–11) €13.67, under 3s free. You can also buy two-visit tickets and season passes. Amenities Showers, chang-ing rooms, ice-cream kiosks, fast-food restaurant; Cypriot restaurant, first-aid station, free parking. Disabled access.

Funbuggy Cyprus

76 Tombs of the Kings Road, Paphos, ☎ 26 912 491 or mobile ☎ 99 118 250 or ☎ 99 325 753, www.funbuggycyprus.com. On the out-skirts of Paphos, almost opposite the entrance for the Tombs of the Kings, next door to the Rocking Chair Pub; head out of Paphos town on the E701 (the coast road to Coral Bay).

Normally I wouldn't recommend anything that involved driving on beaches, or riding with rela-tively little protection on Cypriot roads. But if you've got teenagers, it will only be a mat-ter of time before you are per-suaded to let them have a go on the quad bikes or dune buggies which zip around all over Paphos and you will need to weigh up the pros and cons by yourself. Funbuggy Cyprus is British-owned and run and operates safaris in groups on and off-road to Akamas, Coral Bay, the Sea Caves, Agios Georgios and fur-ther afield into the Troodos for die-hard adventurers. Despite its eco-unfriendliness, buggy driving is undeniably exhilarating.

Phone for prices; there are several different tours.

Cosmic Bowling

1 Ifaistou, Paphos, 📞 *26 220 033.*

If you're stuck for ideas on a rainy day, this state-of-the-art bowling alley has 18 lanes and a cafeteria and is located in the middle of Paphos.

Open *Daily.* ***Admission*** *From €3.41.* ***Amenities*** *Restaurant, play area, Internet access.*

Island Cove Mini Golf

📞 *26 991 177.*

On bus routes 11 or 15 of if you're driving, just inland from the Riu Cypria Maris Hotel, which is on the beach in Kato Paphos.

A proper mini-golf course with greens and water features, suitable for all ages. Note that this is a putting course, not crazy golf, so there aren't any gimmicks as such, but the little greens are completely flat and children will enjoy knocking a ball around. There are 18 holes and the course is floodlit at night. You can repair to the café for ice creams if golf rage takes over!

Open *Daily 9.45am–6pm Nov–March; 9.45am–8 pm Apr; 9.45am–9pm May; 9.45am–10pm June, Sept and Oct; 9.45am–11pm July and Aug.* ***Admission*** *€3.* ***Amenities*** *Café.*

Balloon Flights

Ikaros Balloon Flights, 📞 *26 271 933.*

Take a balloon flight over the Paphos area at sunrise, a magical time to watch the patterns of the arid landscape beneath you and look at the dark shadows of rocks in the turquoise sea. A ground crew follows the balloon, so you're not just dumped in the middle of nowhere and left stranded!

Open *Times vary.* ***Price*** *€150 approx.*

Thrill Rides

Tiger Trips, Paphos Harbour. Office address: Shop no. 2, Block A, Byzantium Gardens, Tombs of the

RIB rides from Paphos harbour

Kings Road, Paphos, ℂ 99 665 753, www.tiger-trips.com.

While strolling around Paphos Harbour, you'll spot some menacing-looking RIBs (rigid inflatable boats) painted with fangs and butch-sounding slogans like 'Tornado' and 'Extreme' painted on their brightly coloured hulls. I can fairly well guarantee that any child over about 10 will make a beeline for them and next thing, you'll be hard in negotiation and wishing you'd taken a seasickness pill in preparation. These craft operate thrill rides along the coast south of Paphos and north towards Akamas. Yes, they do actually take off out of the water and yes, it is a white-knuckle ride.

The British-run Tiger Boats takes safety pretty seriously and runs two different tours. One is a straight zap along the coast with top speeds in excess of 100 kph and some serious bumping. More appealing (if you're over 30) is the 90-minute coastal tour, which takes in the rocky scenery north of Paphos and points of interest like the freighter that's wrecked on the rocks just beyond the harbour, and the bird sanctuary on Geronisos Island.

Admission *From €20.51 for the short ride and €37.60 for the tour. Parents must sign a waiver for under 15s.*

Mountain Biking

Bike rental from Zephyros Adventure Sports. Book ahead online or write to: Shop 7, Royal Complex, Tombs of the Kings Road, Kato Paphos, ℂ 26 930 037, www.enjoycyprus.com/ bikerental.

The best bike trails are really in the mountains and east of Paphos and are too tough for children. There's one pleasant trail, though, that goes along the coast and is suitable for children aged about 11 and above (the round trip is 24 km). You'll need mountain bikes as there are dirt as well as paved roads. There is a map of the route in the free booklet 'Cyprus Cycling Routes' from the Cyprus Tourism Organisation. Essentially, though, the trail goes from Paphos Harbour along the coast all the way to the Geroskipou Tourist Beach. If you've got younger children, you could bail out here, have a swim and head back. If you want to carry on, there is a dirt track that passes the airport and crosses the Esouza river bed. Follow the airport perimeter road and turn right before Timi into a eucalyptus grove where there's a picnic spot and a small beach. Head back the way you came.

Admission *Rentals from €8.54 per day, less if you rent for longer. Children's bikes available, as well as guided family cycle rides along the coast.*

Shopping

Like any holiday resort, Paphos has its share of tourist tat; you will never run out of beach balls or lurid, non-absorbent towels here. There are a few gems in amidst all the beachfront stores and shopping malls but you have to head away from the tourist areas for real quality.

All around the harbour there are shops selling lace from the village of Lefkara, as well as leather bags, pretty ethnic sandals, designer flip flops, belts and wallets. Leather is generally cheap here. Strangely, so are glasses: if you are in the market for a new pair, bring your prescription with you and order them when you arrive – you will save up to 50% on UK prices for designer frames. The same goes for sunglasses. There are decent opticians' shops all along the seafront of Kato Paphos. Several expensive-looking jewellers are based here, too, selling gold at reasonable prices.

An unexpectedly good buy is a goatskin rug. Goats are farmed here for their meat (not their skins) and the rugs are a small but useful contribution to the local economy, as well as being stylish looking. Look out for them in the shops that line the main seafront road west from the harbour.

INSIDER TIP >>

Watch out for pirate CDs and DVDs, which are everywhere. Buying these is illegal and besides, the quality is laughably awful.

Debenhams

Near the harbour at 62 Konstantinou Kanari, 8010 Paphos, 📞 *26 811 532.*

Debenhams department store is to Paphos as Harvey Nicks is to Knightsbridge. Locals love it, particularly for the designer labels, children's clothes and the deli. Needless to say, prices are cheaper than in the UK.

Open *9am–2pm.* **Credit** *MC V.*

Lemba Pottery Gallery

Eleftherias Street 18, Lemba Village, 8260 Paphos, 📞 *26 270 822.*

A very pleasant gallery in the village of Lemba, off the main road to Coral Bay. The pieces are all hand-thrown and there's a mixture of traditional and more

Fresh produce at Paphos Market

contemporary designs, many in a beautiful sea-blue. Children will enjoy watching the potters at work, getting nice and messy.

Open 9am–2pm and 5pm–7pm. **Credit** MC V.

Paphos Market

There is a covered market in Ano Paphos selling souvenirs as well as fruit and vegetables – huge piles of citrus fruit, watermelons, prickly pear and bananas. Look for leather, ceramics, silverware, copperware and lace from Lefkara.

Open 9am–2pm Mon–Sat. Arrive early for the best fruit. **Credit** Cash only.

The Beach Hut

31 Tombs of the Kings Road.

Surf shop selling Rip Curl, Roxy and Scorpion Bay surf gear – all super-hip labels. Also stocks FCUK and its own label gear.

Open 9am–2pm and 5pm–7pm. **Credit** MC V.

Cyprus Handicraft Service

64 Leoforos Apostolou Pavlou, Paphos, 📞 *26 306 243*

This service was set up to provide income for those displaced by the Turkish occupation. The Paphos branch of the shop sells folk art, wood carvings, lace, pottery, woven goods and copperware. It's good for souvenir shopping and is a worthy cause into the bargain.

Open 9am–2pm and 5pm–6pm. **Credit** MC V.

FAMILY-FRIENDLY ACCOMMODATION

Paphos

EXPENSIVE

Paphos Amathus Beach Hotel ★ ★ ★

Poseidon Avenue (on the beach, about five minutes' drive east of the harbour), 📞 *26 883 300,·www. paphosamathus.com.*

An elegant and friendly five-star hotel in a prime location on the beach – you can see the harbour in the distance from the grassy lawns that slope down to the sea shore and the walk along the coast is a very pleasant half-hour or so.

The hotel has undergone lots of refurbishment and as a result has a beautiful restaurant, inside and outside dining at various locations (including one with a wood-burning pizza oven) and a hip Asian-fusion outlet, Asiachi. The whole lobby is open plan, with stunning views straight through and down to the sea. Rooms are huge and there are decent sports facilities, a huge pool, children's club and a small-ish spa. There were plenty of families here when I visited and all the guests I spoke to were repeat visitors who come year after year for the friendly service.

Rooms 272. **Rates** From €341 per room per night, B&B. **Credit** MC V DC AE. **Amenities** Several restaurants, spa, children's club, babysitting, pool, beach, tennis, watersports, gym, playground.

The Almyra's pool, Paphos

Almyra ★ ★ ★ FIND

Poseidon Avenue (on the main beach road east from the harbour), 📞 *26 933 091, www.thanoshotels.com.*

This ultra-hip four-star hotel attracts beautiful people, many of them with babies. It's the perfect combination of stunning decor and sophistication with baby-friendliness – you can pre-order all your baby equipment and supplies online, for example. There's also a crèche for babies from six months – unusual for Cyprus.

The hotel embodies minimalist chic, with a black slate-tiled pool, sumptuous double sun-loungers and a fantastic Japanese restaurant, Notios, and really romantic dining right on the beach.

If you can stretch to a Kyma Suite, do. They can accommodate two adults, one child and a baby in a cot and open right onto the gardens and beach. You can put your children to bed and climb up to your private roof terrace, where dinner can be served under the stars. Fabulous.

Rooms *190.* **Rates** *From €208 per room per night, B&B.* **Credit** *MC V DC AE.* **Amenities** *Four restaurants, spa, two pools, beach, watersports, tennis, gym, crèche, Baby Go Lightly pre-order service.*

Elysium Beach Resort

Queen Verenikis Street, 📞 *26 844 444, www.elysium.com.cy.*

Another very chic five-star resort, located next to the Tombs of the Kings, so you get fabulous sunsets from here. Book a Royal Garden Villa and you get your own pool, or play in the imaginatively designed main pool, which is beautifully landscaped. There's an ESPA spa, the reason a lot of people come here, and a diving school. The hotel has several restaurants, including a sushi bar and a wonderful Mediterranean restaurant on the beach, where you can set children free on the

Elysium Beach Hotel

lawns if you want to linger over a meal.

Rooms 249. **Rates** From €246 per room per night, B&B. **Credit** MC V DC AE. **Amenities** Several bars and restaurants, spa, children's club, several pools, beach, watersports, scuba diving, gym.

MODERATE

Laura Beach Hotel

Chlorakas, 5 km north towards Coral Bay, ☏ *26 944 900,* **www.cyprotel hotels.com.**

Four-star, low-rise family hotel away from the bustle of downtown Paphos but within easy reach of Coral Bay and Paphos Harbour. There are huge gardens and a decent beach area, as well as children's club, children's pool, playground and indoor pool. The rate is all-inclusive of soft and alcoholic drinks and all meals – this hotel represents really good value.

Rooms 292. **Rates** From €68.40 per person on all-inclusive. **Credit** MC V

DC AE. **Amenities** Restaurant, bars, gardens, beach, pools, children's club, watersports, scuba diving, gym, regular entertainment for different age groups, playground.

Coral Bay

EXPENSIVE

Coral Beach Hotel ★ ★

Coral Bay, 12 km north of Paphos, ☏ *26 881 000, ·www.leptoscalypso. com.*

I love the layout and location of this hotel – it's in beautiful grounds with 500 m of beach and has its own small fishing harbour and yacht. The resort is out of town on the Akamas road, close to the excellent Coral Bay beach and the attractions of the far west of the island like the Bird Park, but still within easy reach of Paphos. I also like the fact that the Duplex rooms, on two levels, are specially designed for families and can sleep five, a fact larger families will appreciate.

Rooms 421. *Rates* From €324 per room per night, B&B. *Credit* MC V DC AE. *Amenities* Six restaurants, spa, children's club, babysitting, several pools, beach, watersports, scuba diving, gym, art studio, children's menus, boat cruises.

Pissouri

EXPENSIVE

Intercontinental Aphrodite Hills Resort ★ ★ ★

1 Aphrodite Avenue, Kouklia, ☎ *26 829 000,* ·*www.aphroditehills.com.*

Ultra-luxurious, self-contained resort, absolutely gorgeous if you don't mind the isolation in the countryside outside Pissouri. As well as the hotel, there are swish villas dotted around the golf course, and a village square area with restaurants and shops, including a pizzeria, taverna, Asian restaurant, pub, ouzerie and café.

The hotel itself is exquisite – really beautifully presented, with huge rooms spread around an enticing lagoon pool, decor you just want to take home and gracious service. There are several restaurants, from Italian to Mediterranean and Asian-fusion. There's an imaginative children's club from three to 12 years, and a beach club a short shuttle ride away. The spa is to die for and I seriously recommend at least one session in it. The hotel can arrange babysitting, children's menus, cots and high chairs.

Rooms 290. *Rates* From €242.73 per room per night, B&B. *Credit* MC V DC AE. *Amenities* Numerous restaurants, spa, children's club, babysitting, pool, beach with beach club, tennis, golf, shops, pub and taverna, watersports, gym.

Columbia Beach Resort ★ ★ ★

Pissouri Bay, ☎ *25 833 000, www. columbia-hotels.com.*

Not to be confused with its sister hotel next door – this is the more upscale of the two, in a very quiet, get-away-from-it-all location on the beach at Pissouri Bay between Paphos and Limassol. All the suites overlook one of the longest infinity pools I've ever seen, stretching the length of the resort, which slopes down to a pebbly beach. Suites are stunning – ours had a double height ceiling with fan, wonderful pool and sea views and beautiful decor with touches of island style – wooden beams and cool stone floors. There's a taverna by the beach, a very smart restaurant, magnificent spa with Molton Brown and Phytomer products. A lot of guests were here with their babies and I noticed the staff being especially helpful to them.

Rooms 94 suites. *Rates* From €287 per suite per night. *Credit* MC V DC AE. *Amenities* Two restaurants, spa, children's club, babysitting, 80-m pool, beach, watersports, scuba diving, gym, tennis, squash.

MODERATE

Columbia Beach Hotel

Pissouri Bay, ☎ *25 833 333, www. columbia-hotels.com.*

The little sister of the Columbia Beach Resort next door is also very family-friendly and with a fresh, contemporary design. The hotel has a beautiful little chapel, which is being used increasingly for christenings, and offers special christening packages.

Rooms 116. **Rates** From €276 per room per night, B&B, for a Bay Suite, accommodating two adults and two children. **Credit** MC V DC AE. **Amenities** Restaurants, pool, spa, children's club, children's pool, beach, watersports, gym, regular entertainment, chapel.

Kallepeia

INEXPENSIVE

Agrotiko

Perikli Demitriou 19, Kallepeia, ☎ 26 271 864, **www.agrotourism.com.cy**.

A complete contrast to the coast – two two-bedroom apartments with views to die for in a beautiful mountain village, still within 20 minutes or so and 13 km northeast of Paphos but also close to the Tsada golf course, the beach and 20 minutes from Polis.

The apartments share a shady garden with a stone oven and each has a fireplace, TV, air conditioning and modern kitchen. The owners have a travel agency in Paphos and will arrange excursions for their guests.

Rooms 4. **Rates** From €85 per apartment per night. **Credit** MC V if you book online; cash if you are paying the owner direct. **Amenities** Kitchen, garden, air conditioning.

Nikokleia

INEXPENSIVE

Vasilias Nikoklis Inn

Nokokleia, ☎ 26 432 211, **www. agrotourism.com.cy**.

In a village 17 km southeast of Paphos, this historic Cypriot inn was once used by travellers and their animals on the old trading routes – there are views of the Troodos and the coast and the inn sits in a (relatively) lush river valley.

The inn has a beautiful garden with a pool and lots of subtropical plants, surrounded by lemon and olive groves. This is a great area for birdwatching, too. There is a taverna attached to the property, which makes it handy for families. Rooms sleep a maximum of three and some have four poster beds.

Rooms 8. **Rates** From €58 per room per night. **Credit** MC V if you book online; cash if you are paying the owner direct. **Amenities** Garden, air conditioning, TV, fireplace, taverna attached to the hotel.

FAMILY-FRIENDLY DINING

Paphos

EXPENSIVE

Notios ★★

Almyra Hotel, Poseidonos Avenue, ☎ 26 888 700, **www.thanoshotels. com**.

East meets West at the gorgeous Almyra Hotel. Notios isn't exactly the place to take your children but if you're staying in the hotel, it's worth getting a babysitter for one night to sample the sushi or the smoked duck with noodles in this romantic, Mediterranean-Japanese fusion poolside restaurant. So many parents go to the Almyra that it's quite OK to have a sleeping baby in a buggy or car seat next to your table. The atmosphere is more casual during the day, although there isn't a children's menu (as the hotel offers numerous other outlets for children's dining). You can also try the 'Omakase' option, which means 'trust the chef', and take pot luck (vegetarian Omakase is available and you meet the chef beforehand to discuss your tastes) or for the ultimate in romance, book a Kyma suite, the best rooms in the hotel, put the children to bed and head upstairs to your private roof terrace, where Notios' delicious dishes will be served under the stars.

Open *Daily 12.30pm–3.30pm (for a snack menu), 7.30pm–10pm Apr–Oct.* **Main course** *From €18.* **Credit** *MC V DC AE.*

Asiachi ★★

Amathus Beach Hotel, Poseidonos Avenue, ☏ *26 883 300,* **www. amathus-hotels.com**.

An excellent Asian restaurant serving sushi, other Japanese and Thai dishes, in the Amathus Beach Hotel. Diners include locals as well as hotel guests. Because it's indoors (actually suspended above the hotel's spacious lobby) and relatively formal, Asiachi isn't suitable for small children but if you are staying here, the hotel will happily book you a babysitter. Teens may enjoy the restaurant, too. Dishes are mainly Japanese, with some Thai, and are designed for sharing.

Open *Daily 7.30pm–10.30pm.* **Main course** *From €15.* **Credit** *MC V DC AE.*

MODERATE

Seven St Georges ★★★ FIND
GREEN

Anthypolochagou Georgiou Savva, Yeroskepos, ☏ *99 655 824 or* ☏ *26963176,* **www.7stgeorges tavern.com**.

Surely the most fun and fascinating place on the island for a Cypriot meze! Everything here is home-made, or organic, or both. The herbs are grown in the garden and picked wild and the fabulous meze is made up almost exclusively of local produce, including samples of the 1,950 edible plants growing on Cyprus, from wild artichokes to mushrooms harvested from the Paphos forest. Seafood is delivered daily, meat and cheese are from local farms and George, the owner, shoots the game himself. George and Lara, his wife, even make their own wine. There's no menu as such; just sit and see what comes. Expect home-made bread, local olives, melt-in-the-mouth grilled halloumi cheese and a huge variety of meats, from chicken to spiced sausages and *kleftiko*, a local speciality, in which lamb is baked for a whole day in a sealed pit, making it blissfully tender. There are fantastic vegetarian dishes and such a huge choice that even the fussiest child will find something

The Last Castle Taverna, Akamas

they like. Allow the whole afternoon if you've come for lunch, or a long evening. Children are warmly welcomed and George will take great pleasure in explaining Cypriot lore to them; which herbs are edible, which snakes are poisonous. If there were ever a place to epitomise the slow food movement, and the art of reconnecting with what you are eating, this is it.

Open Daily except Mon. **Meze** Around €17.50 with wine (there's no menu). **Credit** MC V DC AE. **Amenities** Highchairs.

Deep Blue

12 Pafias Aphrodites (Tombs of the Kings area), 📞 26 818 015.

A pleasant fish taverna in a quiet location away from traffic noise, near the Tombs of the Kings, with wooden tables and chairs and a cheerful blue decor. The fish meze starts with the usual salads and dips and moves onto fresh seafood – calamari, mussels, crabs and octopus – before a main course (as if you can eat any more) of succulent swordfish kebabs, or whatever the catch of the day is. As if that's not enough, more fish comes, with perfectly fried chips. Children won't be able to eat a whole meze but there are things like fish cakes and pasta on the menu, too.

Open Daily, lunch and dinner. **Meze** €19.65. **Credit** MC V. **Amenities** Indoor and outdoor seating, high chairs.

Mandra Tavern

Dionysou 4, Kato Paphos, 📞 26 934 129.

Mandra has been around for decades, since the time Kato Paphos was little but grazing land. Popular with locals and visitors and welcoming to children, it serves Cypriot classics like *kleftiko* and *stifado* and stuffed vine leaves are a house speciality. Vegetarian dishes are less exciting, though.

Open Daily 6pm–. **Main course** Meze from €17. **Credit** MC V. **Amenities** High chairs.

La Boite 67

Apostolou Pavlou, on the harbour,
📞 *26 234 800 116.*

More of a pub and ice-cream parlour than a restaurant but the nicest place to sit around the harbour and watch the world go by. The pub itself has been here for 20 years. There are big barrels for tables on one side of the pavement and squashy chairs and sun umbrellas overlooking the water. Gets noisy on weekend evenings, when there's live music and a young crowd, but ideal for an afternoon ice-cream break.

Open *Daily mid-morning till late.*
Credit *MC V.*

Akamas

MODERATE

Viklari/Last Castle

On the edge of Akamas; drive past Agios Georgios towards Akamas and follow signs to Avakas Gorge. Viklari is on top of the hill up a steep, unmade road, 📞 *26 991 088.*

A big, jolly taverna with stunning views over the sea to the west and Akamas to the north, constructed on the foundations of an old castle. You sit at stone tables under the shade of vines, or on a wooden deck, raised above the restaurant with stupendous views towards the gorge. A lot of walkers come here for a beer after hiking the gorge but it's also popular with expatriates, families (keep a careful eye on climbing toddlers, as it really is on top of a cliff) and parched holidaymakers who have spent the day exploring Akamas, where there are no facilities. The menu is a simple barbecue, freshly prepared, with chicken and pork, plenty of salads, bread, olives and baked potatoes. Combine Viklari with Akamas or walking the gorge (see p. 81), or just come for a drink at sunset.

Open *Daily lunchtime only Apr–Oct.*
Barbecue *About €9.* **Credit** *Cash only.* **Amenities** *High chairs.*

Kathikas

MODERATE

Araouzos

Georgiou Kleanthous 17, Kathikas village (on the E709 from Coral Bay), 📞 *26 632 076.*

A traditional stone house in a pretty village in the heart of the wine-growing area. The food, typical Cypriot meze, is slow-cooked and fresh and there's an excellent vegetarian menu. Sunday roast is served (there are a lot of expats round here). Saturday is another good day to visit as special home-made bread is baked in the village ovens and is served in the restaurant.

Open *Daily 12.30pm–11.00pm.*
Meze *€13.68.* **Credit** *MC V.*
Amenities *High chairs.*

Pissouri

MODERATE

Limanaki

Pissouri Bay, on the waterfront, 📞 *25 221 288.*

Once a carob store and then an unassuming taverna, Limanaki is now one of the hottest restaurants in Cyprus, combining Lebanese and Cypriot cuisine to create a fabulous range of wraps, salads and stuffed pittas at lunchtime and meze with different dips and flavours in the evenings, as well as a spectacular prawn curry. Locals say you need to book three days ahead for dinner. There's plenty on the menu children can eat and older ones who don't want to linger on the table can go and play on the beach right outside.

Open Daily except Mon, lunch and dinner. **Main course** From €11. **Credit** MC V. **Amenities** High chairs, right by the beach.

Pissouri Square Taverna

In the centre of Pissouri village, 📞 25 221 579.

One of three restaurants in a row in Pissouri Square, where there is a buzzing atmosphere on a warm night, especially on Wednesdays, when the three restaurants share live music and dancing. Everything is grilled over charcoal or oven-baked and there are a few more traditional dishes than you'll find on the coast, like slow-baked rabbit.

There's no children's menu as such but Aristos, the owner, is very friendly and there were plenty of children running around the square when we ate here, and lots of meze items on the menu for them to pick at.

Open Daily. **Meze** Around €25 including wine. **Credit** MC V. **Amenities** High chairs, live music Wed nights.

Bunch of Grapes

9 Ioannou Erotokritou Street, 📞 25 221 275.

With its gorgeous, flower-filled courtyard with candlelit tables and chairs, this is one of Pissouri's best-known restaurants and it's getting popular – you have to book ahead. The menu is eclectic, from traditional English Sunday lunch to mountain trout, *stifado* (beef or goat stew) or duck liver with bacon and walnuts in garlic butter. Despite the slightly higher prices than the other village tavernas, the restaurant is very welcoming to children.

Open Daily lunch and dinner. **Main course** From €11.88. **Credit** MC V. **Amenities** Children's menu, high chairs.

4 Polis, Latchi & the West

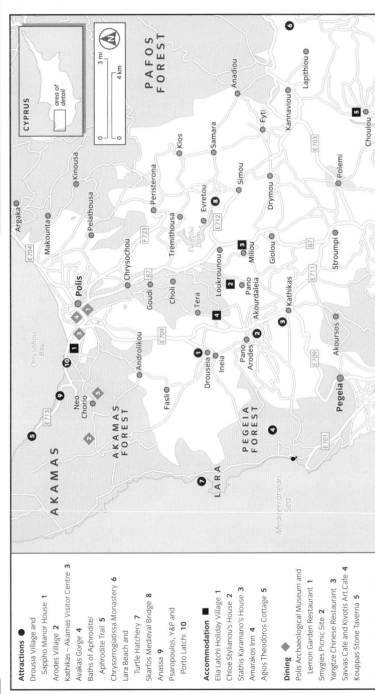

CYPRUS

area of
detail

PAFOS
FOREST

Lapithiou

Anadiou

Fyti

Kannaviou

Choulou

Kinousa

Samara

Polemi

Kios

Argaka

Makounta

Pelathousa

Peristerona

Simou

Drymou

Stroumpi

Tremithousa

Evretou

Evretou
Dam

Giolou

E703

B7

Chrysochou

E704

Choli

Loukrounou

Pano
Akourdaleia

Kathikas

Akoursos

Polis

Goudi

B7

Tera

Miliou

Chrysochou
Bay

Androlikou

E709

Pano
Arodes

Drouseia

Ineia

Pegeia

Neo
Chorio

Fasli

E713

AKAMAS
FOREST

PEGEIA
FOREST

AKAMAS

LARA

E701

E709

E711

E712

E723

Mediterranean
Sea

This sleepy corner of Cyprus is for adventurers and escapists. You won't find any nightlife or shopping malls here – not even a glimmer. What you will find is dazzling wildflowers, abundant herbs, birds and butterflies, mountain streams, craggy cliffs and tiny offshore islands.

This is the place to come if you want to introduce your children to village life, where they'll encounter goats, donkeys and chickens, or if you're looking for family-friendly tavernas right on the beach serving fish caught that morning. Grapes and olives grow on the steep hill terraces, sloping up to the Paphos forest where there are picnic sites and marked walking trails, many of them manageable for young children.

Polis is the only town, slowly expanding towards its tiny neighbour, Latchi, as more tourists discover the charm of this peaceful area and pockets of holiday villas spring up. But the mountain villages are coming back to life, thanks to 'agrotourism', an initiative to fund and promote rural tourism, and even if you're looking for a beach holiday, do spend a couple of nights in a traditional stone house in the hills, just for the experience.

The pointy north-west tip of this corner of the island is the Akamas Peninsula, a protected area with no development, criss-crossed with bumpy dirt tracks and walking trails and fringed with gorgeous sandy beaches. There are no facilities here so you'll need water, a picnic, your own shade and a four-wheel drive, but you'll see a side of Cyprus a million miles from the big resorts of the south.

ESSENTIALS

Getting There

By Air Paphos International Airport is the nearest entry point by air, about an hour away by road. Paphos is served by **Cyprus Airways**, **easyJet** (p. 26) and in summer, numerous charter airlines. The flight from the UK takes about four hours.

By Road Pick up a rental car at Paphos Airport, an hour's drive from Polis on the B7, a decent enough mountain road that passes through some beautiful scenery. With luck, you won't get stuck behind a lorry or tractor, which slows things right down.

There are buses, but they are slow and a hassle if you have small children, as these vehicles potter along from one village to the next and have timetables designed for villagers, not visitors, which is reasonable enough.

VISITOR INFORMATION

The CTO website, **www.visit cyprus.com**, has fairly comprehensive information on the area but I strongly suggest you visit the Akamas Visitor Centre in Kathikas village for more information on touring Akamas.

Cyprus car bingo

Make car bingo for your children to encourage them to look at the countryside! See who can be the first to cross off the squares in their bingo card containing the following:

A goat
A donkey
A vineyard
Olive trees
A prickly pear
A fig tree
A fruit stall
A brown sign (to a tourist attraction)
An old Cypriot bus

You can vary the bingo according to the time of year, of course – citrus fruit in winter, pomegranates in October.

There's a CTO office in Polis at Vasileos Stasioikou (📞 26 322 468).

Orientation

Paphos is by far the biggest town in the area and somewhere you'll probably visit, to see the harbour, the mosaics and the Tombs of the Kings (see chapter 3). It's an easy day trip from the resorts further north.

In the far north-west, tiny, sleepy Polis, on the wide sweep of Chrysochou Bay, is the biggest centre of population, sandwiched between the protected Akamas Peninsula (where there is no development) and the Paphos Forest, a mountainous area of pines bordering olive groves and vineyards.

Polis has a sleepy resort feel about it but most come to this part of Cyprus to experience village life, or to stay in a remote villa with its own pool, rather than indulging in shopping and nightlife.

Getting Around

A car is pretty essential here; local buses are slow and don't always run to convenient schedules for sightseeing. You can be green and hire a bike, but the whole north-west region is mountainous so you'd have to be a family of real enthusiasts and probably stick to the coastal areas. Other than cars, there are quad bikes, mopeds and 4x4s for hire. An off-road vehicle is a good idea if you want to explore Akamas; a normal rental car won't cope well with the rocky trails.

Child-Friendly Events & Entertainment

Orthodox Easter

This is a magical time to be staying in a small village as it gives a real insight into rural life and its rhythms and is fun for children, too. Good Friday and Easter Saturday are solemn occasions but at midnight on Saturday, bonfires are lit and effigies of Judas burned. Days of feasting follow, with whole lambs and giant *souvla* (kebabs) being cooked and coloured eggs and special Easter buns, *flaounes*, consumed, alongside singing, dancing and general partying.

Check the dates of Orthodox Easter as it's different from 'western' Easter and always falls in April or May.

Summer Nights in Polis

There's a regular programme of cultural events throughout the summer, including Cypriot dancing in the village square and a jazz festival in September.

Throughout summer, ☏ 26 321 321, **www.polis-municipality-cyprus. com.**

WHAT TO SEE & DO

Children's Top 10 Attractions

❶ **Holding** a baby turtle in your hand at Lara Beach. See p. 78.

❷ **Riding** in a donkey safari at Lysos. See p. 83.

❸ **Coasting** 20 km downhill on a mountain bike. See p. 84.

❹ **Looking for** (but don't touch) wildflowers in the Akamas forest. See p. 80.

❺ **Cooking** your own *souvlakia* over a barbecue at a woodland picnic site. See p. 85.

❻ **Posing** for pictures in the Avakas Gorge, 'propping up' the sides. See p. 81.

❼ **Counting** how many different kinds of lizard and butterfly you can spot. See p. 81.

❽ **Learning** to identify edible plants and herbs (but not through trial and error!). See p. 79.

❾ **Taking** a boat trip and jumping off the boat for a swim. See p. 83.

❿ **Plunging** underwater in the Blue Lagoon on a Bubblemaker diving course. See p. 85.

Beaches & Resorts

Polis

Polis is the biggest resort in the north-west, and by the standards of the rest of Cyprus, it's no more than a sleepy village. This is the place to come if you like a really laid-back holiday, quirky cafés, toes-in-the-sand tavernas, a bit of walking and probably, no nightlife to speak of.

Polis is also slightly 'alternative' – in cafés, you'll see ads for Pilates and yoga, reiki and aromatherapy. There's a small British expat community here and quite a few Germans. Because it's so quiet, the area appeals to families and older people.

Polis is not actually on the beach. To get to the water, you have to drive down a country lane to the campsite through an area of lime trees and palms. Pass through the campsite, which is a tatty affair in a eucalyptus grove (definitely not somewhere to consider for a family holiday), and you arrive at a rather good beach, greyish sand but gently sloping and curving around a pretty bay. There are toilets, lifeguards, a café and a small playground.

Latchi

Latchi is the little sister of Polis, even smaller and even sleepier. It's not much more than a string of fish tavernas along the beach, a half-finished marina with some watersports, another, rather grey beach and a series of developments of apartments and small hotels.

Nonetheless, there's a certain dozy charm and the people in the tavernas have the look about them of having discovered something good. This is certainly the place to come for a fantastic fish meze, fresh that day, right by the water.

Latchi is also the location of the swish Anassa resort, the only officially rated five-star hotel in this region, and as such is attracting a growing number of well-heeled families.

Lara Beach ★★★

Lara Beach is one of the most beautiful beaches in the whole of Cyprus, delightfully inaccessible unless you're prepared to hire a four-wheel drive and bump your way across Akamas. It's an absolute must for families in turtle-hatching season (July to September) for the wonderful educational opportunity of seeing the turtle hatchery. I held a baby turtle in the palm of my hand and it was quite amazing, a perfect miniature.

There are steps going down to the beach, which is long, unspoilt and sandy, with no facilities except a small café with erratic opening hours and no shade. Take a picnic, lots of water and a UV tent if you have small children. The beach is rarely crowded and at either end,

Latchi Harbour

you'll see people skinny dipping. The turtle hatchery is manned by volunteers who live here all season, guarding the nests, which are marked by metal cages (see p. 86 for more information on turtles).

Drousia ★

Drousia is one of the prettiest of the mountain villages, a tiny place with a population of fewer than 400. Many of the stone houses have been beautifully renovated and the village is popular among holidaymakers looking for peace and quiet. The name, Drousia, means 'cool and fresh', after the breeze that blows off the sea, over Akamas. Stop to admire the stupendous views, across the Bay of Chrysochou to the north, the Troodos Mountains to the east and the rugged limestone formations of Akamas to the west.

There's not a lot going on here – old men sitting outside the café, sheep and goats in the fields around the village – but it's a pretty place to stop and stroll if you're passing through.

Arodes

Nearly 600 m above sea level, the hamlet of Arodes, which has a population of about 70, is the place to go if you want a glimpse of the dramatic Avakas Gorge (see p. 81), but don't want to do the hike in from the more accessible end, for example, if you have a very young baby or toddlers not confident enough for the scrambling bits. From the rim of the gorge, you'll see a lot of walkers here clambering out of the gorge head. These are the hardy ones who have trekked up from the bottom and are doing the 14-km round trip back to Lara beach, where the gorge begins. We managed a short walk here years ago when my daughter was in a baby backpack and the views of the rock formations were amazing.

Laona Project Villages GREEN

The Laona Project is a small non-governmental organisation that has used its grants to renovate 26 traditional buildings in authentic Cypriot style in five villages close to the border of the Akamas area. The renovations were finished in 1994 but the Foundation continues its work in sustainable development on the island.

An Akamas visitor centre has been established in Kathikas (open 11am–4pm daily), a good place to visit before setting off into the wild; you'll find trail maps, information, field guides and local produce and handicrafts for sale here.

These villages really are as remote and quiet as you could imagine but have great charm, and are a wonderful place to stay if you want to introduce your children to rural life. In Pano Akourdalia, for example, there's a herb garden where you can identify island herbs and in Kato Akourdalia, if you can get hold of the key, you can poke around the tiny Rural Life Museum. Ask at the Amarakos Inn where the key might be found! In Milio, a very green village nestled amidst citrus orchards,

Famous Cypriots

Several famous popular musicians have connections to Cyprus. Singer George Michael was born to Cypriot parents in London, and the father of musician Yusef Islam (formerly known as Cat Stevens) was from Cyprus. Australian singer Peter Andre, husband of Katie Price, aka Jordan, has close family on the island.

you can buy local honey and see village ladies weaving on traditional looms.

All of these villages have accommodation suitable for families (see p. 87).

Kato Pyrgos ★

A visit to this peaceful beach village in the far north is a white-knuckle ride via a UN-patrolled dirt track over a steep mountain, but worth it if you seek the slightly dubious thrill of being right up against the Green Line, the UN buffer zone that separates the Republic of Cyprus from the Turkish-occupied north. The scenery here is amazing – you really are as far from the big resorts of the south coast as you could possibly imagine – and the tiny fishing village has clean beaches and cheap fish tavernas. It's extremely popular with Cypriots in summer, escaping the fleshpots of the south, so if you want a taste of where the locals go on holiday, here's your chance.

Other Natural Wonders & Spectacular Views

Akamas ★★★ ALL AGES

The wild, untamed Akamas peninsula is the last real wilderness of Cyprus. If you're an outdoorsy family, it's possible to spend ages here, exploring the remote sandy beaches, hiking the mountain trails and pottering around the rocky coast by boat. At the very least, do it as a day trip.

We drove the relatively short distance from the Smigies picnic site (see p. 85) at Neo Chorio through the forest to the coast, following the trail down past Lara Beach (see p. 78), stopping to hike the Avakas Gorge (see p. 81) and emerging, extremely hot and dusty, at Agios Georgios. That took a day, and that was at speed. You need plenty of time and lots of stops to appreciate Akamas. Ideally, you'd walk the whole way, for the sake of this fragile environment, but with younger children that's not really practical, as you could take several days! Older children may enjoy some of the tougher walks, though.

The tarred road runs out at the village of Neo Chorio (the whole of which appears to be in a state of permanent siesta) in the north and at Agios Georgios in the south. In between the two, it's dirt track, with rocks, potholes and scary narrow bits with a drop to one side.

Most of Akamas is fairly exposed, the winds having twisted the trees into stunted shapes, the rocks pounded smooth by the sea. Juniper, pines and rock-rose cling to the boulders, with summer snowflakes and pink orchids sprouting from the sand. Occasionally, the wind brings a waft of rosemary or thyme. Lizards bake in the sun, insects hum and birds wheel overhead. Occasionally, you might spot a rare griffon vulture, the island's largest bird, with a wing span of 3 m.

Away from the trail, you can soak up the sounds and scents for ages, but the roads do get busy in summer with unappreciative people thundering past in their four-wheel drives and not even stopping to look.

The northern tip, Cape Arnaoutis, is greener, shaded by juniper and broom, the grassy meadows dotted with cyclamen and gladioli. There's a lovely walk here, the Aphrodite Trail (see p. 85), which is suitable for families.

Avakas Gorge ★ ★ ★ FIND
AGES 5 AND UP

1 km north of Agios Georgios; look out for the sign on the right as you head north. The tar road becomes a dirt track leading down to the car park.

To my mind, this is a highlight of the whole of the west of Cyprus. The gorge is almost a secret; you can't see it from the road and the only way in is by foot. If you have a buggy or a baby in a backpack, you won't be

The Avakas Gorge

able to go too far as there's a fair bit of scrambling from the western side, but you can go to the gorge head from the other end and admire the view.

Either way, wear shoes with good grip as the rocks are slippery and there will be a fair amount of hauling children over some of them. If it's just rained hard, don't attempt the walk, as you might not be able to get very far because of the water.

The walk into the gorge is pretty in itself, and children will love spotting lizards (of which there are many), birds and plants, which are helpfully labelled. Look out for olives, juniper and oleander, and close to the ground, pretty anemones in rich colours.

Before you know where you are, the trail narrows and descends into a steep chasm, with boulders blocking the route and towering cliffs of bleached limestone almost meeting above you. The path snakes around the boulders and in some cases, over the top.

After rainfall, there should be pools to paddle in but when I walked the gorge at the end of a long, hot summer, the water was pretty stagnant. The air was pretty rancid, too, as an unfortunate sheep had toppled off the towering cliffs and met its end in the path, causing an unholy stench. But this is nature!

Dead sheep aside, children will love the clambering, and the photo-opportunities to record the walk with your infant 'holding up' a giant boulder that's wedged between the sides of the chasm (it was dislodged from the top by an earthquake in the 1980s). The whole walk takes about 40 minutes in and out, but you can turn back at any time and repair to the Last Castle taverna at the end for ice-cold beers.

One word of warning: anybody with a bird phobia should avoid this walk as there were huge flocks of screeching birds wheeling overhead, diving and pooping on us.

It is possible to carry on and clamber up the path to the escarpment ridge close to Ano Arodes, but the forest trail back round to Lara means a round-trip walk of 14 km, too much for most children on a hot day.

Baths of Aphrodite `OVERRATED`

Making the journey all the way beyond Latchi especially for the slightly laughable Baths of Aphrodite is not worth it; I won-der when I see the coaches in the car park if their passengers are feeling slightly ripped off. Yes, the scenery around here is undeniably beautiful and there is some lovely walking, but the 'baths' themselves... well, it's no more than a mossy rock pool in a half-cave. The sense of anticipation as we scrambled up a well-marked path was quite exciting (you can take a buggy up here if you're still interested in going), but the pool itself is a non-event, even if you close your eyes to the crowds and try to imagine the goddess frolicking here in the dappled shade with her lover, Adonis. There are a few souvenir stalls in the car park but the only real reason to come here is for the start of the Aphrodite Trail walk (p. 85).

Top Museums

Chrysorrogiatissa Monastery

⭐ AGES 5 AND UP

About 40 km northeast of Paphos, signposted from Pano Panagia, 📞 *26 722 457.*

This is one of the most beautiful of the Troodos monasteries, set high in the mountains and dedicated to Our Lady of the Golden Pomegranate.

The monastery was founded in 1152 by a monk, Ignatios, who found an icon of the Virgin Mary off the coast of Paphos and had a calling to build a monastery on this site. The building that stands today dates to 1770 and houses a rich collection of icons and religious artefacts.

The monks are also famous for their excellent wine, which is sold here.

Of interest to children? Not obviously, but you can make it come alive with a little effort. Look for the ostrich eggs and incense burners in the small museum, and the ancient monks' habits. Take a stroll through the peaceful cloisters; you may see the monks quietly going about their business in near silence, a life pretty hard for most of today's children to comprehend! After the visit, stop at the entrance to admire the stupendous views and see what points of interest you can spot.

Open *Daily 9.30am–12.30pm and 1.30pm–6.30pm May–Aug; 10am–12.30pm and 1.30pm–4pm, Sept–Apr.* **Admission** *Free.*

Polis Archaeological Museum of Marion-Arsinoe
AGES 5 AND UP

📞 *26 321 321,* **www.polis-municipality-cyprus.com.**

This compact little museum in the centre of Polis displays artefacts from around the area dating back to Neolithic times. Exhibits are mainly pots and amphorae but it's interesting to learn about the history of Polis, once called Marion and actually referred to in an Egyptian temple dating back to 4498 BC. Marion was a thriving commercial centre, an exporter of gold and copper and an importer of pots from Athens, some of which you can see. The museum is not especially geared to children but if you're interested in local history, a visit doesn't take

long and can be traded off for an ice cream at one of the surrounding tavernas afterwards.

Open *8am–2pm Mon, Wed and Fri; 8am–6pm Thur; 9am–5pm Sat.* **Admission** *€1.28.*

Child-friendly Tours

Donkey Trekking ★ ALL AGES
📞 *99 086 721.*

There's a donkey trekking operation at Lysos, 12 km inland on the F733, ideal for an hour or two of family fun, walking in a sedate line through the olive groves and past vineyards, with children on a lead rain. It's a good way to appreciate the countryside, which is too often only seen from a car.

Admission *€17.09 per hour, or €59.82 for a family of four.*

Boat Trips ★★
Various operators including Polipafo, 📞 *26 323 422,* **www.polipafo.com.**

Several companies offer day trips by boat from Latchi, a relaxing and extremely scenic voyage to the tip of Cape Arnaoutis. Boats usually leave around 9.30am, stopping at the tiny Agios Georgios islet in Chrysochou Bay for swimming in the crystal clear water of the 'Blue Lagoon'. There's a barbecue lunch on board and various further swimming stops throughout the day, returning at about 5.30pm. These trips are very laid back and more than a little cheesy, what with the free-flowing plonk and bouzouki from 'Captain Zorba', but they're fun for all the family and it's always good to see a place from the water.

Open *Daily, departing from Latchi harbour. Book in advance.* **Admission** *From around €25.64 for adults, €13.67 for children.*

Self-Drive Boats

Latchi Watersports Centre, ☎ 26 322 095, www.latchiwatersportscentre. com. Based in Latchi harbour.

Hire a motorboat by the hour, half-day or whole day and make your own way along the coast and even as far around Cape Arnaoutis to the western beaches of Akamas. Alarmingly, you only need a full UK driving license; tuition is given on driving the boat. All boats come with life-jackets, masks and snorkels. Pack your own picnic and drinks and head off into the blue yonder!

Admission *Contact Latchi Watersports for prices.*

For Active Families

Wheelie Cyprus ★ ★ ★ GREEN
AGES 14 AND UP

☎ 99 350 898, www.wheeliecyprus. com.

If you have teenagers over 14, hire well-maintained mountain bikes or join a guided tour with two expat Brits, Helen and Alistair, living in Polis. The bikes can be delivered to your accommodation (in Polis) or they can arrange the whole holiday.

One of the best services for a family bike ride is the one-way routes from Drousia to Latchi. You'll be taken to Drousia, a

village 600 m above the beautiful Akamas peninsula, and left to your own devices for an easy, 20-km ride, downhill almost all the way, past olive groves, villages and vineyards. There's a handy taverna for a lunch stop, although if you're going in summer it's best to start really early and make it a breakfast stop instead!

Participants must be 14 or over and minimum 153 cm tall.

Go-Karting
There's a go-karting circuit just outside Polis, about 1 km from town on the road to Argaka.

Open *Daily 10am–10pm.* **Admission** *From €10.25*

Tsada Golf Club AGES 12 AND UP
☎ 26 642 774, www.cyprusgolf.com.

The first proper golf course in Cyprus opened at Tsada, north east of Paphos, in 1994. It's a pretty course, winding through hilly scenery with stunning views, and visitors can play with a handicap (men 28, ladies 36) or after 12pm at the discretion of the starter. So while small children won't be allowed to hack their way round the course, golfing families in which everybody is of reasonable standard will be welcome. Book in advance, though. There's also a restaurant, bar and pool, with a country club feel. You'll see a lot of expats here, especially on Sundays for the carvery lunch.

Admission *From €42 a round.*

Scuba Diving ★ AGES 8 AND UP

Latchi Watersports, ✆ *26 322 095,*
www.latchiwatersportscentre.com.
Latchi Harbour.

Children as young as eight can
do a **PADI Bubblemaker** course,
where they learn to use scuba
equipment in shallow water and
come away with a certificate and
a badge. If your child is confident in the sea and happy in a
mask and snorkel, northern
Akamas is a wonderful place for
a first underwater experience;
the Blue Lagoon, off the islet of
Agios Georgios, is shallow, calm
and crystal clear.

Special child-sized equipment
is used and instructors are all
highly qualified. Once a child
reaches 10, they can do a
Discover Scuba Diving day, also
at the Blue Lagoon, descending
to 6 m. If they decide they like
it, the tuition counts towards the
first PADI open water certifica-
tion, which takes another two
and a half days to complete and
means you can dive pretty well
anywhere in the world!

Hiking Trails

Akamas and the Paphos forest
are well marked with signposted
hiking trails and the CTO produces a guide to all the official
trails, as well as maps.

Aphrodite Trail ★

Walking the Aphrodite Trail is the
only real reason to include the
Baths of Aphrodite in your holiday plans. This circular walk from
the car park at the Baths is 7.5
km, with some fairly steep gradi-
ents and rocky paths, so it's quite
a hike for little ones, but manage-

able enough for most older children. Things to look out for after
the Baths of Aphrodite are the
ruins of Pyrgos tis Rigainas, once
part of a medieval monastery, and
also the site of a wonderful old
oak tree, reckoned to be over 100
years old.

Further along, you can see the
whole of Cape Arnaoutis, the
pointy bit at the very far north-
west of Cyprus. It's often pleasantly breezy up here but you'll
still need to take a supply of
water and load up with sunblock
before you set off.

Smigies Trail ★

This trail has the advantage of
starting at the gorgeous Smigies
picnic site just off the road west
from Neo Chorio, deep in the
pine forest with no sound apart
from the whisper of the wind in
the pine trees. There are big barbecue pits, clean toilets and
plenty of wooden chairs and
tables for picnics. This spot is
popular with locals in summer,
trying to escape the heat of the
coast. There's also a decent play
area with see-saws, swings, baby
swings and a slide, all built out
of wood in keeping with the
forested surroundings. Some of
the smarter hotels do picnics and
fancy barbecues here, but you
can have your own, too, if you
bring barbecue coals or wood
and all the gear.

All the trails are well signposted. The short walk from
Smigies is 2.5 km, and with children will take no more than an
hour, meandering through the
forest with lovely views of
Akamas and Lara Bay.

Turtles in Cyprus

You might see two species of turtle – Green Turtle (*Chelonia mydas*) and Loggerhead Turtle (*Caretta caretta*) – in the warm waters around Cyprus. Both are endangered; in the past, they were captured to make turtle soup, but a more recent threat is the encroachment of tourism projects on their nesting sites. Green turtles especially are on the verge of extinction in the Mediterranean.

Although turtles live in the sea, they still breathe air and lay their eggs on remote beaches, from the beginning of June to the middle of August.

During the breeding season, each female lays three to five clutches of eggs, each one of about 100 eggs, in a hole she digs herself. Seven weeks later, the baby turtles, or hatchlings, dig their way out and head straight for the sea. They find the sea by following the moonlight reflected off the water, but sadly, will be attracted to any other light source, like a taverna, or a torch, which is why it's so important that the turtle beaches are dark. Another danger is foxes, which will eat some 80% of the eggs, given half a chance.

The Lara Turtle Conservation Project aims to protect the beach, protect the nests, and keep an eye on the turtle population. All the nests are collected and moved to a special fenced-off part of the beach, where they're reburied in cages to protect them from the foxes.

Thanks to the project, over 6,000 hatchlings are now released every year, more than three times the number that would make it if the nests were left open to foxes. And if a female turtle survives, she will return to this very same beach in 15 to 30 years to lay her own eggs.

Agiasma Trail

This is a much shorter walk, only 2 km, starting 1 km from Kathikas village on the road to Pegeia. Pick up a map at the Akamas Visitor Centre in Kathikas before heading off. The path follows the ridge of a deep gorge before descending into the valley among citrus trees, wild herbs and dramatic rock formations.

Evretou Dam and Skarfos Medieval Bridge ★★ FIND

This is a lovely excursion with a picnic, and a little trip back in time to the Middle Ages, when the only way from Polis to Paphos was by donkey or on foot across the mountains – a journey of several days.

Head for the villages of either Sarama or Simou and follow the signs to Skarfos Medieval Bridge. Park the car and walk – the roads are pretty deserted here. The ancient bridge is curiously positioned in a flower-strewn meadow, next to the crumbling remains of a stone watermill that was once used for grinding flour. The stream the bridge was built for no longer flows under it, and the bridge looks a bit forlorn as a result.

The scenery is beautiful, though. Follow the stream towards the abandoned Turkish village of Evretou and you'll see the Evretou reservoir, created by the third-largest dam on the island and a popular spot for walking, birdwatching and fishing, glinting metallic blue in the sunshine. You can walk right round, a distance of 20 km, but as that's a bit ambitious for children – just wander as far as you like before stopping for a picnic and then heading home.

FAMILY-FRIENDLY ACCOMMODATION

Polis & Latchi

EXPENSIVE

Anassa ★★★

On the Baths of Aphrodite Road, between Polis and Latchi, ☎ *26 888 000,* **www.thanoshotels.com**.

By far the most luxurious hotel in the north-west and wonderfully geared to families in every way. The whole hotel is built around a 'village square' in the style of an old Byzantine village, in lush gardens sloping down to a spotless sandy beach. There are four gorgeous pools, and the suites also have their own plunge pools. Families might prefer the studios in the main building, which are essentially big doubles accommodating two extra beds or cots, all stone floors, gauzy curtains and cream rattan furniture.

For children, there's the Smiling Dolphin club, catering for four to 12 year olds from April to October and in the Christmas holidays. Some of the activities carry a fee. There are also children's menus in two of the four restaurants and lessons in tennis, scuba diving (on site) and waterskiing for older children. Baby-sitting can be arranged for a fee.

The hotel has a stunning thalassotherapy spa using organic products, tennis, squash, loads of watersports and its own yacht, which you can charter for the day for cruises around the Akamas peninsula.

There are also occasional yoga-themed weeks run by **Yogoloji**, offering separate sessions for parents and children. Little ones, or **Teeny Yoginis**, have their own classes to attend where they can learn postures like 'The Cat' or 'The Lion'.

Anassa is very popular with well-heeled families and like its sister in Paphos, Almyra, goes out of its way to help. A **Baby Go Lightly** service has been introduced, whereby you can pre-order absolutely anything, from nappies to baby food. You can, in fact, book a two-centre holiday with Almyra, which gives a good contrast of being in a buzzy resort and staying somewhere more tranquil and in the midst of nature.

Rooms 183. ***Rates*** *From €420 per room per night, B&B.* ***Credit*** *MC V DC AE.* ***Amenities*** *Four restaurants, spa, children's club, babysitting, four pools, tennis, squash, watersports, scuba diving, yoga, regular entertainment.*

MODERATE

Elia Latchi Holiday Village

200 m from the harbour at Latchi, on the waterfront, 26 321 011, www. eliavillage.com.

A big holiday village on the sandy/pebbly beach at Latchi. Very popular with families as there's a children's club (four to 12), children's pools, playground, adventure theme pool, and all sorts of activities like football, mini-golf and volleyball. Sometimes, special events are laid on, like village donkeys being brought in for beach rides!

For adults, there's also a gym. The resort is all-inclusive and has two restaurants, with regular theme nights and bouzouki dancing.

Accommodation is in a mixture of twins, studios and apartments, all with kitchenette, which is handy if you're travelling with a baby. Expect an international atmosphere – Brits, Germans and some Cypriots. It's a busy, lively place and a lot of visitors won't go out and explore much, preferring to sunbathe and enjoy the all-inclusive food and drinks, but Latchi port is a stone's throw away, as are the delights of Akamas and the mountain villages.

Rooms 142. **Rates** Expect to pay under £2,000 for a family of four for a week, all inclusive with flights with a tour operator such as Libra Holidays, 0871 226 0446, www.libraholidays. co.uk. **Credit** MC V. **Amenities** Football, volleyball, several pools including one indoor, playground, several bars, two restaurants, gym, watersports, beach, regular entertainment.

Self-Catering in Villages

MODERATE

Chloe Stylianou's House

Pano Akourdalia, 26 952 268, www.agrotourism.com.cy. In the village, next to the Museum of Flora and Fauna

This traditional stone house has cool, flagstone floors and high, wood-beamed ceilings. There are two double bedrooms, living/dining room, bathroom, kitchen and vine-covered terrace, also with pomegranate and olive trees.

Rooms Two bedrooms. **Rates** €103 per night for the house. **Credit** MC V if you book online. **Amenities** Parking, TV, fireplace, nature trails nearby.

INEXPENSIVE

Loukas Karamano's House

Miliou. Driving from Paphos, bear left at the village square, away from the coffee shop and the church, and follow the road straight and then sharply to the right. The houses are on the left, 26 321 443.

Three renovated limestone houses stand around a shared pool and a pretty courtyard in the tiny village of Miliou. Arch House is probably best for families, as it's on the ground floor and has two bedrooms. Air conditioning, TV and a cot are available. The village, with a population of 60, has no supermarket (the nearest shops are 4 km away) but there's a small coffee shop where old men sit in the shade, discussing politics, local issues and life in general.

Rooms Two bedrooms. **Rates** Around €77 per night. **Credit** MC V.

Amarakos Inn ★ FIND GREEN

Kato Akourdalia, ☎ *26* **www.agro**
tourism.com.cy.

A gorgeous, 150-year-old stone
house converted into an inn
through funding from the Laona
Project. There are seven rooms,
four opening onto the terrace
and pool and three upstairs with
views of the hills and vineyards
beyond. Two of the first floor
rooms have interconnecting
doors. All rooms are big enough
for a third bed and are beautifully furnished, with stone
floors, ceiling fans and wooden
beams. Breakfast is served on the
terrace and owner Mrs Angela
will cook in the evenings, too,
although there's no set menu.

Rooms *7.* **Rates** *Around €72 per
night, B&B, per room (two people).*
Credit *MC V.* **Amenities** *Swimming
pool, 10 acres of olive and citrus
groves, TV, small restaurant, walking
nearby.*

Sappho Manor House

*Apodimon Drousioton 3, at the cen-
tre of Drousia village,* ☎ *26 332 650,*
www.agrotourism.com.cy.

This restored manor house was in
its heyday the focus of the social
scene in this quiet village. The
house was done up in 2002 and
now has seven studios sleeping
between two and four, with room
in each for an extra cot. Each one
has a kitchenette and bathroom
and all seven have shared access
to a pretty pool area.

The village taverna is a short
walk away – a mere 30 m, in
fact. There are two small supermarkets. Don't be surprised to

Sappho manor House

see sheep and goats wandering
around – the villagers breed
them. You'll need a car to stay
here; the nearest beach is 10 km
away. The views and sense of
silence, though, are spellbinding.

Rooms *Seven units.* **Rates** *From
€48 per night, accommodation only.*
Credit *MC V if you book online.*
Amenities *TV and air conditioning on
request.*

Agios Theodoros Cottage ★

*Opposite the Agios Theodoros
chapel in Choulou village centre,*
☎ *25 750 761,* **www.agrotourism.
com.cy**.

This beautifully restored cottage is
ideal for larger family groups, as it
sleeps eight, and is probably best
for shoulder seasons, as there's no
pool. Instead, you'll be in the
heart of a lovely village of traditional stone houses, with donkeys
braying and cockerels crowing at
dawn to add to the rustic feel!

The house is spacious, with
wood-burning stoves or fireplaces in every room, TV, washing machine and a decent-sized

kitchen, as well as a courtyard with shade from a sycamore tree. The local taverna does a fine line in meze with organic wines.

Choulou is a good base if you have a golfer in the family, as the Tsada Golf Club is only 10 minutes or so away.

Rooms *Four double rooms.* **Rates** *From €171 per night, accommodation only, for the whole house.* **Credit** *MC V if you book online.* **Amenities** *TV, linen, towels, heaters, logs for the fire €8.50 per basket.*

FAMILY-FRIENDLY DINING

Polis & Latchi

Anassa Beach Barbecue ★

Anassa Hotel, Latchi, 📞 *26 888 000,* **www.thanoshotels.com.**

A wonderful opportunity for a top-notch beach barbecue if you don't mind keeping your children up late. Expect lots of Cypriot specialities and delicious grilled *souvlaki* and fish, accompanied by a guitarist and bouzouki player. The barbecue is perfect for children as they can run around on the sand and paddle as the sun sets, while you sip an expensive cocktail.

Anassa does have other, more formal restaurants, Amphora and Pelagos, with children's menus, but if you're not resident at the hotel, you have to book in advance.

Open *Sun and Mon nights in summer. Advance reservations essential.* **Main course** *Adults €76.92, children*

€33.33 for the whole menu. **Credit** *MC V DC AE.*

Yangtze Chinese Restaurant

On the Polis–Latchi Road, 📞 *26 323 047.*

You can't miss this exotically ornate temple structure on the road from Polis to Latchi. Favoured by visitors and locals who have had their fill of Cypriot meze, the restaurant is Chinese-owned and run and has an extensive menu including an all-you-can-eat buffet on Sundays from 12pm to 4pm.

Open *Daily in summer. Phone to check times in winter – typically, Thurs, Fri and Sat for dinner only, from 6pm.* **Buffet** *€13.67.* **Credit** *MC V.*

Lemon Garden

Makarios Avenue, just before the village square on the way into Polis, 📞 *26 321 443,* **www.lemongarden. com.cy.**

A family-run taverna owned by the Karamano family, who also rent stone houses in Miliou village. George catches the fish. Nikki does the cooking. Lucas and his son, Alverto, are the hosts. All the vegetables are bought fresh from the market and all the dishes are from family recipes, washed down with home-made village wine. There's a terrace and garden.

Open *Daily.* **Main course** *From around €9.* **Credit** *MC V.*

Psaropoulos

On the waterfront in Latchi, 📞 *26 321 089.*

Lemon Garden

This is the kind of place to spend a whole afternoon working your way through a fish meze and a crisp local white wine; children can go and play on the beach when they've had enough (older children only as the play area is a little along from the restaurant). It's quite a big restaurant, popular with families, although it feels more romantic in the evening when you can hear the waves lapping on the shore. The fish meze, the speciality, includes seven types of fish.

Open *Daily 11am–11.30pm.* **Meze** *€14.52.* **Credit** *MC V.* **Amenities** *High chairs, beach and playground in front of the restaurant.*

Y&P Taverna ★

Latchi (on the beach, next to the old harbour master's house), ☎ *26 321 411.*

Y&P is something of a local institution, offering a vast array of fresh fish. You can choose your own from a chiller cabinet, which children may or may not enjoy! There's a vegetarian and meat menu as well as the fish. The setting feels slightly cavernous but the food is great.

Open *Daily 8.30am–11pm.* **Main course** *From €10.21.* **Credit** *MC V.* **Amenities** *High chairs.*

Porto Latchi

☎ *26 529 530,* *www.portolatchi.com.*

Just what you want from a seaside taverna: a shaded deck with blue and white checked tablecloths, overlooking the beach. Inside, there's an airy feel thanks to the high ceiling of traditional stone arches. The building was originally a carob store and has been carefully renovated in local style.

There's an eclectic menu of fish, traditional Cypriot dishes, pasta, a couple of incongruous Chinese ideas and children's dishes, although these are of the chicken nugget variety – better to let them pick at the fish meze, a plate of hummous and a big bowl of chips!

Open *Daily until around 11pm.* **Meze** *From €14.52.* **Credit** *MC V.*

INEXPENSIVE

Savvas Café ★

In the main village square of Polis, ☎ *26 321 081.*

A good place to stop for morning coffee, or a yummy breakfast of pancakes with toppings or the Cypriot version of a fry-up – eggs with halloumi cheese. You can check your email, or if you've got a laptop, use the free WiFi.

Savvas is very much the gathering place for expats in Paphos, and in summer, gets busy in the evenings, too, thanks to its giant screen showing live sports, should you need a football-mad child as an excuse to have a night off your Cypriot experience!

Open Daily 7.30am until late. **Snacks** Cappuccino €2.22, eggs with halloumi €4.27. **Credit** MC V. **Amenities** High chairs, TV, free WiFi.

Kivotis Art Café ★★

A fantastically quirky place to chill out with a newspaper, linger over lunch or enjoy a game of chess. There are stone tables dotted round a pretty, shady garden, filled with curious *objets* that make up a permanent sculpture exhibition. Children can play on the swings or mess around with the owner's toddlers, who roam freely around the garden. Indoors, there's a little library with board games, books and films, which are shown in the afternoons at siesta time.

Open Daily, all day. **Snacks** Cappuccino €2.05,; waffles €3.41. **Credit** MC V.

Villages

INEXPENSIVE

Kouppas Stone Taverna ★
FIND

Neo Chorio, 📞 26 322 526.

A particularly good taverna in this sleepiest of the Akamas villages, where you'll find all the usual Cypriot specialities and more, including rabbit and occasionally, snails. Everything is prepared with island herbs and fresh vegetables, while meat dishes are simmered for hours until the meat falls off the bone. The 'big' meze includes vast amounts of steak, so is for the brave only; even the 'small' meze is a feast for most. Children are best off picking at what adults are served, as there's so much!

Open Daily, lunch and dinner. **Main course** From around €10.

Mansoura Tavern

Outside Mansoura village, near Kato Pyrgos, 📞 26 522 493. On the rocks above the water's edge before you get to Kato Pyrgos; drive north from Polis on the coast road and detour round the Turkish enclave of Kokkina.

A tiny fish taverna in the middle of nowhere, guaranteed to make you feel far from the madding crowds! The Turkish occupied zone is only a few kilometres from here. Come to Mansoura for the best, freshest fish, simply but deliciously prepared, and an uninterrupted view of the sea. Like anywhere in Cyprus, children are welcome.

Open Phone first to check, especially in low season. **Main course** Prices vary according to the catch of the day.

5 Limassol

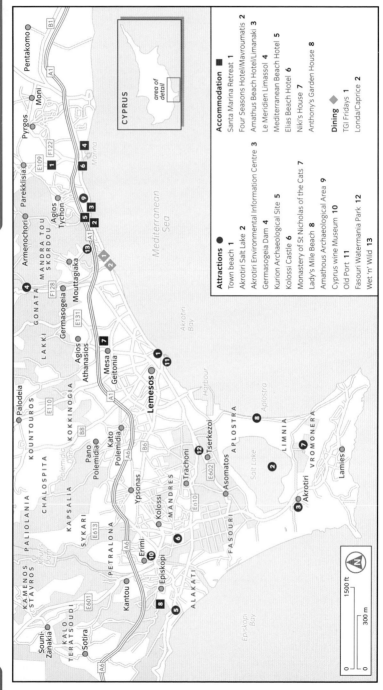

Accommodation ■
Santa Marina Retreat 1
Four Seasons Hotel/Mavroumatis 2
Amathus Beach Hotel/Limanaki 3
Le Meridien Limassol 4
Mediterranean Beach Hotel 5
Elias Beach Hotel 6
Niki's House 7
Anthony's Garden House 8

Dining ◆
TGI Fridays 1
Londa/Caprice 2

Attractions ●
Town beach 1
Akrotiri Salt Lake 2
Akrotiri Environmental Information Centre 3
Germasogeia Dam 4
Kurion Archaeological Site 5
Kolossi Castle 6
Monastery of St Nicholas of the Cats 7
Lady's Mile Beach 8
Amathus Archaeological Area 9
Cyprus wine Museum 10
Old Port 11
Fasouri Watermania Park 12
Wet 'n' Wild 13

Limassol, or Lemesos in Greek, was built between two ancient sites, Amathous to the east and Kourion to the west, so was originally known as Neapolis, or 'new town' in Greek during Byzantine times. It's the biggest port of the Republic of Cyprus, and the most populous town, at over 170,000 residents. Limassol is also the epicentre of Cyprus's wine industry.

While Paphos is laid-back, Limassol today is big, bustling and buzzing. It has many of the island's best and fanciest resort hotels and some amazing spas, and is the place to come for more eclectic nightlife than that of Ayia Napa (by which I mean Limassol tends towards girlie bars and neon-lit 'theme' bars alongside English pubs showing reruns of *Only Fools and Horses*, so we're still not exactly talking St Tropez). Your teenagers will thank you for it, though, and some of the new beach lounges and sunset chill-out bars are a step in the right direction.

This is also a good place to aim for in a low-season holiday. It's got lots to do for families, good shopping, a pleasant waterfront and some excellent restaurants. Limassol is also at the centre of the coast, so you can take day trips to Paphos, the Troodos, Larnaca and Nicosia without subjecting children to too much time in the car.

Like much of Cyprus, a mere 20 minutes inland is another world of sleepy villages, friendly tavernas, vineyards and country walks. It's this contrast that really makes this island so enchanting.

ESSENTIALS

Getting There

By Air Limassol is mid-way between Larnaca and Paphos, the two international airports of Cyprus, so easily accessible. Larnaca is served by more flights, including British Airways, Cyprus Airways and most European airlines. Larnaca is about 40 minutes' drive away, while Paphos is about 45 minutes in the opposite direction.

By Boat Limassol is a busy commercial port and the gateway to the island for cruise ships, which often call here. Cruises also depart from Limassol on mini-breaks to Israel and Egypt. These voyages are operated by Salamis Cruise Lines and Louis Cruise Lines (see p. 112) and offer a chance for children to visit the Pyramids and the Sphinx just outside Cairo.

By Car Limassol is an easy drive from the airport at Larnaca, where you can pick up a car. The journey takes about 40 minutes and it's straight along the motorway. If you fly into Paphos, it's about 45 minutes' drive along the motorway from there. Most of the hotels are on the same road, which runs about 15 km all the way from the old port to the end of the Amathus area.

VISITOR INFORMATION

Orientation

Limassol is a surprisingly big, sprawling town, although the tourist areas are very much concentrated into one part. The western side is bordered by the Akrotiri peninsula, where the British Sovereign Base is located. The town and the big, commercial port spread along the vast sweep of Akrotiri Bay and towards the eastern end, the hotels stretch out along a long, busy strip into an area called Amathous. The further from the centre, the more upmarket the hotels, broadly speaking.

Behind the town is a range of low hills covered with olive groves and vineyards, rising up to the foothills of the Troodos Mountains.

Getting Around

Limassol is easy to navigate and can be done without a car. Buses run along the strip to the centre of town, for the old castle and museums. There are plenty of taxis, too.

Child-Friendly Events & Entertainment

Limassol Children's Festival

℡ *25 887 227,* **www.limassol** *festival.com.*

This is a fantastic two-day festival in Limassol's municipal gardens, celebrating everything to

do with childhood. There's a packed programme of art, drama and concerts, all performed by local schools as well as visiting schools from abroad. Children will be amused by puppets, clowns, trampolines, art workshops, painting and singing.
Sept.

Limassol Wine Festival

www.limassolmunicipal.com. **cy/wine**.

A huge, 10-day celebration of the end of the wine harvest, taking place in Limassol's Municipal Gardens. Most of the action is in the evenings but children will enjoy watching the dancing, soaking up the general festivities, and in particular, having a go at grape treading.
Last week of Aug.

Cyprus Rally

℡ *22 313 233,* **www.cyprusrally.** **org.cy**.

The Cyprus Rally is a major event on the international rally circuit. While children won't normally be able to watch the race itself, which takes place in the Troodos Mountains, all the cars are lined up on the first evening in the Municipal Gardens alongside displays from each team – every would-be rally driver's dream.
One weekend in Oct.

Music and Dance at Kourion

All summer long there is a wonderful programme of music, dance and orchestral concerts at

LIMASSOL CENTRE

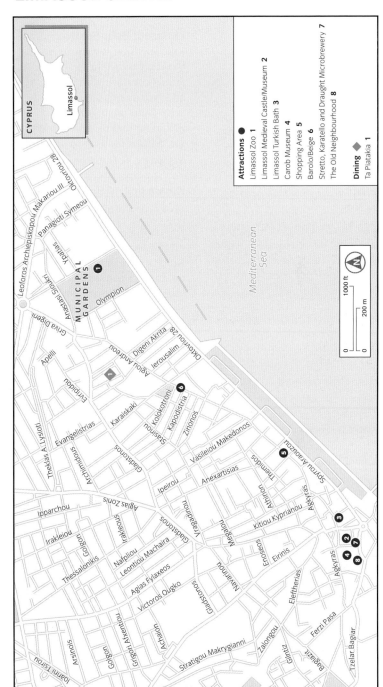

Attractions ●
Limassol Zoo **1**
Limassol Medieval Castle/Museum **2**
Limassol Turkish Bath **3**
Carob Museum **4**
Shopping Area **5**
Barolo/Beige **6**
Stretto, Karatello and Draught Microbrewery **7**
The Old Neighbourhood **8**

Dining ◆
Ta Piatakia **1**

CYPRUS
Limassol

Mediterranean
Sea

0   1000 ft
0   200 m

the Kourion (Curium) Amphitheatre. These concerts are a magical occasion and worthwhile for the whole family, although do remember to take a cushion as the stone benches around the amphitheatre can get very uncomfortable!

Throughout summer; check the local press or with the tourist board for details.

Limassol Carnival

www.limassolmunicipal.com.cy/ carnival.

The 10-day Limassol Carnival is an excuse for the locals to parade the main streets decked out in all manner of fancy dress. Carnival takes place during the two weeks before Lent and is a great time to visit the city. Children will love the parades and the generally festive atmosphere, and a lot of the hotels and bars lay on big parties during the celebrations.

Over the two weeks before Lent.

Kataklysmos

The Festival of the Flood, or Kataklysmos, is an annual event which takes a slightly different form in each of the coastal towns. In Limassol, there's a procession to the sea in which people sprinkle water on each other, perhaps to commemorate the birth of Aphrodite, the goddess of love, or to remember the great flood as depicted in the Old Testament. The festival is actually over Pentecost, and is a happy occasion, with singing, dancing, funfairs, food stalls and lots of water-themed events.

Pentecost (50 days after Orthodox Greek Easter).

Limassol Beer Festival

Like anything in Cyprus, this beer festival on the beach is a family occasion with entertainers and face painters as well as all sorts of different beers to try, including that of the main sponsor, KEO.

July, on the municipal beach.

Kypria International Festival

www.kypriafestival.com.

Kypria International Festival is a month-long cultural festival where a host of events focused on music, theatre and dance are staged throughout Cyprus, particularly Larnaca, Nicosia and Limassol. It's probably more of an adult event but if you are here, take advantage of some of the superb performances.

Sept and Oct.

Pastelli Festival

A local event in the village of Anogyra to celebrate the end of the carob harvest. Try all manner of food and sweets made from carob!

Third Sat of Sept.

Mallia Village Fair

Local specialities, drinks, arts and crafts at a lively village fair.

Aug; check with the tourist board for dates.

Vouni Village Festival

Another local celebration with dancing, feasting and drinking.

Mid-Aug.

WHAT TO SEE & DO

Children's Top 10 Attractions

❶ **Cooling off** on a hot day at Watermania. See p. 113.

❷ **Grooming, feeding and riding** a donkey at the Vouni Donkey Sanctuary. See p. 102.

❸ **Riding a bike** all the way along Limassol waterfront.

❹ **Counting** the flamingos at the Akrotiri Salt Lake. See p. 100.

❺ **Climbing to the top** of Kolossi Castle and seeing where the residents poured boiling oil on their enemies' heads. See p. 105.

❻ **Getting up close** and personal with an ostrich at Wild Valley Resort. See p. 102.

❼ **Seeing** where prisoners were kept in Limassol Medieval Castle. See p. 107.

❽ **Swimming from the boat** on a day cruise along the coast. See p. 112.

❾ **Playing beach volleyball** on Limassol town beach. See below.

❿ **Exploring** the Troodos Mountains in an off-road jeep. See p. 110.

Beaches & Resorts

Limassol Town Beach
Beaches are not the strongest selling point of Cyprus but Limassol's main beach is pleasant enough and has a great buzz, as urban beaches often do, with a cycle lane, playground and beach volleyball.

A long seafront promenade stretches from the Old Port to the start of the Blue Flag Akti Beach, a greyish sandy strip protected by breakwaters and offering a variety of watersports, with shops and cafés along the seafront with plenty of beach showers and umbrellas to rent.

Even if you're here in winter, take time to stroll along the beach and soak up the atmosphere. It's lovely on a hot summer's day, too, after sunset when the heat of the day lessens and Cypriots nip down for a quick swim after work. If you've got very small children, this can be the best time of all for a dip.

From the end of this beach, the waterfront is dominated by luxury hotels instead of apartment blocks, but because all beaches in Cyprus have public access, you can use any of them. If you are staying in accommodation away from the seafront, the town beach is perfectly good for children, although it does get busy.

Governor's Beach
30 km east of Limassol on the old Larnaca road; bus service.

Governor's Beach is a decent strip of dark sand flanked by towering, white cliffs, about half-an-hour east of Limassol. Because it requires some effort to get here, it may be slightly less crowded than the town beaches but will still get busy at weekends. There's a nice restaurant, Panayotis, up on the

Governor's Beach, west of Limassol

cliff, with bougainvillea around the terrace and blue-and-white tablecloths. If you stop here for lunch, children of responsible age and good swimming ability can play on the sand at the bottom of the cliff, and splash around in the shallows while you relax with a chilled white and a plate of fish.

The power station to the west does mar the view somewhat but you soon get used to it.

Lady's Mile Beach

On the east side of the Akrotiri peninsula; no public transport.

A 7 km stretch of sand, which is pleasant enough, but you need to bring shade for children as there isn't any. Go midweek, as the beach is packed at weekends. The seabed shelves gently so this is a good spot for families and there are a couple of tavernas for lunch. Think about visiting this beach in combination with Kourion and/or Kolossi Castle, as both are nearby.

Kurion Beach

Off the B6, just below the Kourion archaeological site.

Part of the British Sovereign Base Area on the Akrotiri peninsula, this part pebbly, part sandy beach is worth a stop after visiting the Kourion archaeological site, but not really worth the journey specially. Only the western end is safe for swimming. There are three tavernas but no shade, so take your own umbrella.

Natural Wonders & Spectacular Views

Akrotiri Salt Lake ★

The Akrotiri Salt Lake is surrounded by marshland on the Akrotiri Peninsula, sandwiched between the British Sovereign Base residential area and a more mysterious piece of RAF property at the southern tip of the peninsula, where there's a large airfield and no public access. You can, however, get to the salt lake, which is only worth visiting in winter. In summer, it's a dust bowl.

This is, though, a strangely forgotten area of Limassol for most visitors. Since the new motorway to Paphos opened in the 1990s, tourists have no real reason to pass through this part of town but it's worth a detour to see the beautiful flamingos, which come here to feed on the algae.

The **Akrotiri Environmental Information Centre** overlooking the Salt Lake is a centre for exhibitions, displays, video and presentations and educational programmes about the unique natural elements of the peninsula. From the first floor, you can look out over the lake and see the flamingos, and there are also occasional nature trails and visits to Akrotiri village to see local basket makers at work.

Most British visitors quite like a nose around the Sovereign Base, too. You can only drive through it but what you can see from the road is like a slice of 1970s Britain, with neat ranks of houses and an emerald-green cricket pitch, maintained by recycling waste water.

Open Akrotiri Environmental Information Centre: daily, 8.30am–3pm. Call in advance for information on walks and visits to the basket makers, ☎ 25 826 562.

Germasogeia Dam

The best hiking trails in this region are in the Troodos Mountains (see p. 142) but if you don't want to make a whole day of it, head the shorter distance to the Germasogeia Dam, a short drive inland in the direction of Foinikaria.

The reservoirs behind the dams of Cyprus are always an extraordinary sight, as the countryside is so barren at first glimpse. These tranquil, man-made lakes glimmer deep blue in

Richard the Lionheart

Richard the Lionheart landed at Limassol in 1191 en route to his third crusade, accompanied by his French fiancée, Berengaria of Navarra, when their ship was wrecked in a storm. Richard's stay turned out to be longer than planned as he ended up in battle against the island's ruler, Isaac Comnemos, and after defeating him, married Berengaria at Limassol Castle, crowning her Queen of England.

Richard had conquered Cyprus but was short of funding for his crusades, so sold the island to the Knights Templar in 1192 to raise money for an army. However the conditions of the sale made the Templars unable to rule, as they did not have the necessary funds to pay Richard any more after they had put down four-tenths of the price he asked. To raise the rest of the money, they taxed the Cypriot people, who rebelled and were cruelly crushed by the Templars.

The Templars eventually gave Cyprus back to Richard, who promptly sold it to Guy de Lusignan, a Norman knight, whose family ruled the island for nearly 300 years, until the Venetians annexed it for themselves in 1489.

The Akrotiri Salt Lake

The salt lake is actually below sea level, 2.7 m at its lowest point (which, combined with the fact that it is only 1 m deep, is what makes it so saline). Geologists believe it was formed after an offshore islet was gradually joined to the mainland, cutting off the water on the other side.

In many areas, the lake is only 30 cm deep, making it perfect for wading birds which stand in the water and feed on the algae. As well as the greater flamingos, you will spot cranes, other migratory birds and birds of prey.

the sunshine, with pines and deciduous woodland around their sides. Cypriots come here for fishing (for which you need a permit) and birdwatching.

The easy walking trail at Germasogeia is only 1.3 km and takes about half-an-hour, circling a small peninsula extending out into the reservoir. It's a lovely stroll with small children, and the views are stunning. For something more challenging, there's a circular woodland walk (3.7 km) from Foinikaria starting at Moutiss tis Kyparissias, or a two-hour hike from here to the dam (3.9 km). Before you do either of these, pick up a free hiking map from a CTO office.

Aquaria & Animal Parks

Wild Valley Resort ★

5 Akadimos Street, Kato Polemidia, 📞 *25 711 110; the farm itself is 4 km from Pissouri, signposted from the motorway.*

This is Cyprus's second ostrich farm (the first is near Nicosia), opened in 1999 as a breeding and ostrich-rearing centre and expanded to include a visitor

centre and shop. It's an interesting enough visit but be careful how you present it to your children: the fact that there is a list of menus for ostrich meat on the website should be a clue. This is not a zoo but a working farm – although in theory, it shouldn't be any more traumatising than a farm stay back home.

There is a visitor centre where you can meet ostriches first hand, tour the farm in a 4x4, taste the meat and buy products made from all parts of the bird – meat, skin, oil, eggs and feathers. The recipes are an interesting twist of Cypriot tradition combined with this unusual, high-protein, very lean meat – vine leaves stuffed with ostrich mince, or ostrich steak with Commanderia sauce.

There's a playground, too. So you can certainly justify a couple of hours here and you never know, you might come away with a decent handbag!
Open Daily. Admission Free.

Cyprus Donkey Sanctuary, Vouni ★★

Follow the E601 towards Troodos and turn off at the sign to Vouni,

☏ *25 944 151, E: donkeycy@ cytanet.com.cy.*

Formerly run by a British couple and recently taken over by the British charity, The Donkey Sanctuary, this donkey haven is a great treat for children and a happy ending for some 130 donkeys. The donkeys are either retired or rescued and now live in spacious stables and paddocks. Several of them are suitable to ride or to lead around on a lead rein. There's also a shop and a café. You can end the day by adopting or sponsoring a donkey!

While in Vouni, take time to explore the village, the architecture of which has Venetian influences. Look out for the two *havouzas*, communal water fountains, that were once the focal point of the village, where women would bring their washing and collect water for their homes.

There's one by a 300-year-old plane tree at the village centre.

Open *Daily 10am–4pm.* **Admission** *Free.* **Amenities** *Café, picnic area, souvenir shop.*

Limassol Zoo OVERRATED

In the Municipal Garden, off Octovriou 28, the boulevard running along the seafront, ☏ *25 588 345.*

Limassol Zoo is tiny – only one and a half acres – and pretty outdated, with small concrete pens and little foliage for the animals, many of which have been rescued from circuses. A larger site is at present being identified to create a modern facility with habitats more appropriate to their residents.

Should you want to visit, the current zoo has 300 animals, including big cats, bears, monkeys, mouflon and various species of bird. There's a small

Ostriches in Cyprus

According to legend, ostriches roamed freely around Cyprus during the time Richard the Lionheart was on the island (1191 AD) on his way back from the crusades.

Ostrich products are apparently in such high demand that the world supply will never be enough. The ostrich is indeed a useful creature; as well as its meat, you can make things from the skin, eat the eggs, and use the feathers.

Ostrich meat is low-fat, low-calorie, low-cholesterol and high in protein, making it much sought after by health-conscious Europeans.

Ostriches can live up to 70 years and can reproduce up to their 30th year. Their height reaches 2 m and their weight averages around 120 kg. Ostriches can run at speeds of 65 km per hour and if frightened, can deliver a vicious kick.

Visit the beautiful mosaics at Kourion

petting zoo for children and a play area, as well as a café.

The animal population varies as bigger creatures are being re-housed in more modern facilities in other countries.

Animal rights campaigners are vehemently opposed to the Limassol zoo, saying the enclosures are unacceptable and do not meet EU standards for animal welfare. Two brown bears were actually rescued from the zoo by the World Society for the Protection of Animals and Animal Responsibility Cyprus, and re-homed in a Hungarian sanctuary.

If you go, don't expect to come away with a warm, happy feeling; the Paphos Bird Park is a better day out.

Open *9am–7pm summer; 9am–4pm winter.* **Admission** *Adults €1.36, children €0.68.* **Amenities** *Café, playground.*

Historic Buildings & Monuments

Kourion ★ ★ ★ AGES 7 AND UP

19 km west of Limassol; take the old road in the direction of Paphos and it's well signposted.

Kourion is without doubt the most impressive archaeological site on the island and has been really well presented so that children will get something out of the visit, too.

Kourion was a city-kingdom, originally settled in Neolithic times because of its strategic position, high on the clifftop with views of the sea and surrounding countryside.

The structures you can see today are from the second century BC and later. Although the site is still being excavated, you can wander round the collection of villas with their beautiful mosaics and visit the spectacular amphitheatre. The original was probably smaller and was destroyed by an earthquake in the third century but its replacement is awe-inspiring and is used regularly for plays, ballets and music festivals. If you get a chance to see an outdoor concert here, take it.

The site is very spread out, so bring water on a hot day. After the amphitheatre, there are three houses to visit. The House of Eustolios is the most impressive, dating to the fifth century AD, with intricate mosaics and some fine examples of Roman baths and underfloor heating. Get children to see how many birds and fish they can spot in the mosaics.

The House of Achilles and the House of the Gladiators also have rich mosaics – spot the two gladiators, whose names were Hellenikos and Margaritis, fighting and try to imagine the real thing, which would have taken place in the amphitheatre in front of 2,000 spectators.

Another interesting element for children is the 'Earthquake House', a short climb down the hill. This more modest building was built in the second century and demolished by an earthquake in 365 AD. Archaeologists have left it much the way it was found as a reflection of life at the time. Children may enjoy trying to work out which rooms were used for what purposes – you can still see the animals' drinking trough, cracked into two pieces, right next to where the family lived.

There are two other sites nearby if you're in the mood for more, although neither has a huge amount of detail. The Sanctuary of Apollo Ylatis, which dates from the eighth century BC through the Hellenistic period to the Roman period, is 3 km from Kourion and covered by the same, very modest entrance fee. This ancient site was originally used for tree worship (Ylatis means 'of the woods' and Apollo was the god of the forest) – so you can imagine early tree-huggers here, 2,800 years ago. The graceful columns you can see today, rising incongruously from unkempt shrubbery and rubble, are from the Roman era and are the remains of yet another beautiful structure that was destroyed by the great earthquake of 365 AD. After this, the sanctuary was abandoned.

A short drive or 500 m walk away are the just-discernible remains of a vast stadium that would have seated 6,000, also dating to the second century AD.

Open 8am–5pm Nov–Mar; 8am–6pm Apr–May, Sept–Oct; 8am–7.30pm June–Aug. **Admission** €1.71. **Amenities** Refreshments at the main site of Kourion; nothing at the Sanctuary of Apollo or the Stadium.

Kolossi Castle ★

11 km east of Limassol; free parking on site.

There's not a huge amount to see at Kolossi Castle but it's worth a visit nonetheless if you're having a cultural day. And with a bit of imagination... I remember as a child being particularly fascinated

Entrance to Kolossi Castle

by the idea of pouring boiling oil over unwanted visitors and sure enough, as you cross the drawbridge into Kolossi, you can see the 'welcome' hole in the wall above, through which the intruders would have quickly got the message. Actually, this is the kind of castle children enjoy as it's uncomplicated and there is nothing inside. You can climb up the narrow, spiral stairs to the rooftop, imagine firing missiles at approaching enemies, look at the view, run around a bit and then demand an ice cream.

For those with more cultural inclinations, the castle, which is more of a fortified tower than a 'real' castle, is one of the last reminders of the occupation of the island by the Knights Hospitaller.

In 1210, the land on which Kolossi stands was given to the Knights by the Lusignan king, Hugh I, and in 1218 they moved to Cyprus from Acre in Israel after being defeated in the final crusade. Nearly a century later, in 1310, the knights relocated again, to Rhodes, but Kolossi was now rich and they kept it going for its wine production. It's from here that the **Commanderia** wine originates (Kolossi was known as a commandery) and you'll see it for sale all over the island.

It is believed that the original structure was destroyed in around 1425 and the current fortification built over the ruins by Grand Commander Louis de Magnac, in the mid-15th century. You can see his coat of arms on the castle's eastern wall. The ground floor was probably used for storage, while the kitchen would have been on the first floor and the Commander's accommodation on the second floor. The castle also produced sugar cane and the ruins to the east are of an old cane refinery.

Open Daily 8am–5pm Nov–Mar; 8am–6pm Apr–May, Sept–Oct; 8am–7.30pm June–Aug. **Admission** €1.71.

Limassol Medieval Castle ★

Only a fragment of 'old' Limassol remains but it will change your entire perspective on this busy town. It's hard to believe that thousands of visitors come to Limassol and never eat supper under the stars in the tavernas around the medieval castle. But they do, and they miss a great opportunity.

Just inland from the Old Port, the chunky castle sits in pretty gardens behind railings, with atmosphere added by the presence of an ancient olive press in the grassy surrounds. There are tavernas all around the site and when it's floodlit at dusk, this is a gorgeous spot in which to spend the evening.

The fort you see today was built by the **Ottomans** in 1590 but there has been a castle here for much longer than this. The most famous incarnation of the structure was the one in which Richard the Lionheart married **Berengaria of Navarra** in 1191

and crowned her Queen of England. This is long gone, the fortress having been rebuilt several times and destroyed by waves of invaders or those pesky earthquakes. There are some walls in the ground floor halls that are believed to be original; but what's definitely known is that the castle used to be much bigger.

Children will probably be interested to know that the basement of this castle contains cells and was used as a prison until as recently as 1950.

The castle incorporates the Medieval Museum (see p. 109) and the entrance fee covers both.

After visiting the castle and museum, wander around the old town for a while. There's a slightly hippie, new-age feel about the souvenir shops, which are marginally less tacky than those on the seafront. There are also some pretty amazing Cypriot hardware stores, the kind where it looks as though the owner lives in the shop and sells anything you could possibly ask for – completely incongruous amidst the trendy art galleries and outdoor cocktail lounges.

Open 9am–5pm Tue–Sat; 10am–1pm Sun; closed Mon. **Admission** €3.42.

Limassol Turkish Bath ★

Loutron 3, Limassol centre.

Tucked away in a side street between the castle and the mosque is a fantastic little hamam, or Turkish bath. This isn't a family attraction, or indeed a tourist attraction at all (although you could take

Women in Cyprus

The reality for women in Cyprus is that in the workplace they enjoy nothing like the freedom or equal rights of women in Britain, despite what the EU laws stipulate. Sexism is rife, particularly among older Cypriot men, even if it is not maliciously intended. Women in a Cypriot company will almost always have to answer to a man and however educated or senior their position, they may be expected to perform secretarial duties and make the coffee.

There are jobs for women, naturally, including British women (many of whom are employed in the hospitality business and in real estate), but advancement to senior level is difficult.

Having said this, there are more and more female role models for young Cypriot women, including politician Kate Clerides, daughter of former Cyprus President Glafcos Clerides. There are many active women's groups who campaign for peace between the north and the south, among them Women Walk Home, Women's Civil Initiative for Peace, Actions in the Mediterranean and Hands Across the Divide.

Whether they intend to work or not, women in Cyprus marry young. There is usually intense family pressure to find a husband and produce grandchildren. An engagement is cause for great celebration and a broken engagement is regarded by the family as a shameful tragedy. A very small percentage of the population still practices arranged marriages.

Most couples marry in the Greek Orthodox church, usually on a Sunday, followed by a lavish ceremony involving the entire local community, the bride in a frothy white dress, singing, dancing and bouzouki music. In urban communities, the invitation to the wedding is often in the form of an advertisement in the paper, ensuring a large turnout.

Many Cypriot girls still come with a dowry, usually in the form of property, although the reality is that both sides of the family will contribute towards the couple's first home.

teenagers) but if you're strolling around the old town, sneak a quick look at it. The hamam is the oldest building in Limassol, dating back to Byzantine times, and you can still see the original shapes of the windows and an Arabic inscription above the door. If you do want to go in, you can get a sauna, massage and scrub down for around €10, in a mixed session.

Holy Monastery of St Nicholas of the Cats

On the edge of the salt lake, between Akrotiri Village and Lady's Mile Beach.

Of course, with name like this, the monastery is bound to attract the attention of children and it does indeed have cats. If you're driving across Akrotiri, stop and pay a visit, especially in the winter months, when thousands of pink flamingos colonise the salt lake that occupies a large swathe of the peninsula.

The monastery was founded in 327 AD by Kalokeros, the first Byzantine governor of the island, in a lonely spot by the lake. The site was overrun with snakes and a shipment of cats was brought in to keep the numbers down. Needless to say, the cats thrived and can still be found in great numbers around the 13th-century church and the old monastery building, which has been through various stages of renovation and repair. It's a quiet place today, tended by just four nuns.

Amathous Archaeological Area

On the main coast road west out of Limassol, before the Atlantica Bay Hotel.

Given its importance as a city-kingdom of ancient Cyprus, Amathous is curiously nondescript nowadays, only part-excavated, plundered of its treasure and surrounded by modern hotels. About 10 km east of Limassol in the middle of the Amathous tourist area, it's somewhere you could drive by and hardly notice.

Nobody really knows how big the city was as there's a lot of development on top of the old site. You do, however, hear stories of locals starting to build houses and uncovering ancient remains, only to have their plot commandeered by the government.

According to mythology, Amathous was founded by King Kinyras and was where Theseus left the pregnant Ariadne to be cared for after his battle with the Minotaur. The first evidence of human settlement can be dated at around 1100 BC, and Amathous was without doubt a flourishing city, but over the centuries, Persians, Ptolemies, Romans and Byzantines chipped away at it, assisted by regular earthquakes, until it was finally destroyed and abandoned in the seventh century AD.

What's been excavated so far includes the Agora, an early Christian basilica, a sanctuary to Aphrodite, and the ancient harbour, which, rather excitingly, is now below sea level. There isn't a lot for children apart from clambering around the ruins but a quick trip here can be combined with a beach visit immediately afterwards.

Open Daily 8am–5pm Nov–Mar; 8am–6pm Apr–May, Sept–Oct; 8am–7.30pm June–Aug. Admission €1.71.

Top Museums

Limassol Medieval Museum

Inside the Medieval Castle, inland from the Old Port, ☏ 25 330 419.

A visit to the museum ties up the experience of the Medieval Castle. It doesn't take long to look round. Look out for gold jewellery, religious artefacts, pottery from Byzantine times, old weapons and suits of armour. You can climb up to the roof of the castle and look out over the rooftops of the town centre.

Open 9am–5pm Tues–Sat; 10am–1pm Sun; closed Mon. Admission Included in the entrance to the castle.

Carob Museum

Vasilissis Street, behind the Medieval Castle.

Carobs grow all over Cyprus and this free museum exhibits the equipment that used to be used in their processing. Carobs were used for making chocolate substitute, sweets and medicines. A visit here only takes a couple of minutes and there's a good restaurant in the Carob Mill for lunch or dinner.

Cyprus Wine Museum

Pafos Street, Erimi Village.

Limassol is at the heart of the island's wine-producing industry and this small museum takes you through the years of wine production via photos, audio-visual displays and objects including ancient vessels and grape presses. The entrance fee includes a glass of wine. There is not much for

children here but if you're passing, pay a visit.

Open Daily 9am–5pm. Admission €4.28.

Child-friendly Tours

Day Trips

Because Limassol is at the centre of the island, it's easy to get pretty well anywhere for a day. With children, sensible lengths of tour include the Troodos Mountains (p. 127), the wine-growing areas, Paphos (p. 45) and Akamas (p. 80), Nicosia (if it's not too hot) and Larnaca (p. 151). Ayia Napa is a bit too far unless you're especially keen to visit, although coaches do run there in summer.

Troodos 4x4 Excursions

Ascot Tours, ☎ 25 329 388, www.ascotrentacar.com.

Children love these as the jeeps suddenly veer off the road onto bumpy dirt tracks through the forest. There's only a little bit of off-road on the Troodos day but

Cyprus Wine Museum

enough to make it exciting, as well as plenty of stops.

From Limassol, these tours call at a winery, the Venetian Bridge (see p. 140), Kykkos Monastery (see p. 139), Mount Olympus (see p. 136) and the Caledonian Waterfall. There are plenty of chances for children to run around and burn off steam, and lunch is in a taverna in the Troodos, with child-friendly menus (when I did this tour there was an excellent buffet).

Admission *Approx. adults €60, children €35.*

Akamas Jeep Safari

Ascot Tours, 📞 *25 329 388,* **www. ascotrentacar.com**

Travel from Limassol via Aphrodite's Rock in a 4x4 to the Akamas Peninsula (see p. 80). This trip includes the Avakas Gorge, Lara Bay, the Baths of Aphrodite and the resorts of Polis and Latchi, with plenty of bone-shaking bumping across the Akamas peninsula.

Admission *Approx. adults €60, children €35.*

Visiting the North

Louis Tours, every Tuesday, 📞 *25 746 320; passports required,* **www.louis travel.com**.

Check out the north of the island without any of the worries of crossing borders in a rental car, getting lost, changing currency and so on. It's a long day but intriguing if, like me, you know and love the south but are keen for a look at the north. The tour crosses the Green Line in Nicosia and travels up into the Pentadaktylos Mountains to Bellapais, where there's a stunning, ruined Gothic abbey. There's time to visit Kyrenia and wander round the harbour and medieval fortress. There isn't a huge amount for children, specifically, but older kids can be encouraged to spot the differences between Muslim and Orthodox Greek lifestyles; a trip into the north is, after all, a journey into Turkish culture. Life here is a lot less frenetic and the infrastructure a lot less developed.

Boat Trips

Regency Travel, 📞 *25 320 905,* **www. regency-travel.com**.

The coastline around Limassol isn't rich with features but boats nonetheless operate from the Old Port in either direction – heading west as far as Pissouri Bay and east to Governor's Beach. Lunch is included in the price and there's a chance for swimming or in some cases, snorkelling or octopus fishing.

You can't just pitch up and book these boat trips as there's an element of security at the port. Instead, book in advance and a coach will collect you at your hotel.

> **INSIDER TIP** »
>
> There's a K Cineplex at 8 Ariadnis Street, Mouttayiaka in the Germasogia district of Limassol for rainy (or very hot) days, with six screen and films showing in English, Greek and sometimes other European languages. Box office: 📞 25 315 047.

Egypt for the Day

Regency Travel, ☎ 25 320 905, Tues and Fri, www.regency-travel.com.

This is a really ambitious day and it's not cheap, but then again, if you've never seen the Pyramids... The tour picks up at hotels in Limassol and drives to Paphos Airport. It's a 55-minute flight to Cairo, from where you join a coach and guide and visit the Sphinx and the Pyramids and time permitting, the Egyptian Museum in the city centre. After lunch at a five-star hotel (yes, it's still only lunchtime) the tour continues to a papyrus factory and the famous Khan el Khalili bazaar for a bit of lightning-speed shopping, before a cruise on the Nile. The flight back to Cyprus departs at 21.15.

Admission *Around €359; children under 12 €325. Get an Egyptian visa on entry.*

Mini Cruises

Louis Cruise Lines, www.louis cruises.com; Salamis Tours, ☎ 25 860 000, www.salamis-tours.com.

Two companies operate short-break cruises from Cyprus to Egypt, Syria, Lebanon, Israel, and Greece. If you're on a long holiday, take one as a mini- break from your vacation! They're not very expensive, the ships are reasonably comfortable and there is no shortage of sightseeing in each destination for the whole family.

You can go to Egypt and see the Pyramids (be warned, it's a long bus journey from where the boats berth at Alexandria to Cairo); to Israel and visit Jerusalem; to Lebanon to see Beirut (depending on the security situation there) or on a longer voyage to the Greek islands.

The ships of Louis cruises are pretty old, but they do have entertainment lounges, bars, duty-free shops and even a swimming pool on deck.

The other company offering cruises is called Salamis, and provides a similar experience.

Admission *Expect to pay about €300–385 per person for a two-day cruise, including all food and*

Watermania: the biggest water park in Cyprus

entertainment on board the ship. There are discounts for children.

For Active Families

Fasouri Watermania Water Park ★ ★ ALL AGES

Shuttle bus operates from all bus stops between Le Meridien and the Holiday Inn along the waterfront in Limassol, at 9.30, 10, 10.30 and 11, with four return trips in the afternoon. Buses also run from Paphos and Larnaca, ☎ 25 714 235.

Watermania is a fantastic waterpark and the best answer to a stiflingly hot summer's day – although it gets very busy, with shuttle buses bringing people from all over the island. Still, it's the biggest waterpark on Cyprus, has the biggest wave pool in Europe and has been voted one of the top three in the world in the last annual World Travel Awards.

The whole park has a Polynesian theme and there's plenty of shade under a series of tropical-looking pergolas. You'll find the usual white-knuckle rides – kamikaze slides, black holes, an evil thing called Black Cannon, and the curious Pro Bowl, where you're shot out of a slide into a giant bowl, propelled around the sides by your own momentum before plopping into the water at the bottom.

There's loads for smaller children – lazy river rides, family slides, a children's pool, for example – and the whole family will want to try the It's A Knockout-style Activity Pool, where you use ropes and

walkways to make your way across a series of giant, floating orange slices.

Restaurants in the park include a fast-food outlet, buffet with salads, a juice bar and a creperie. There's also beach volleyball, a football pitch, lockers, changing rooms and lawns to run around on.

Open 10am–6pm May–Sept; 10am–5pm Oct. Admission Adults €25.64, children €13.67.

INSIDER TIP ▶

If you're in Cyprus for a long holiday, get a season ticket for Watermania and save money. The season ticket also gives you discounts in various restaurants in Limassol and at the Aphrodite Hills golf course.

Wet 'n' Wild

Limassol–Nicosia Highway at Mouttagiaka Juction, ☎ 25 318 000, E: wetnwild@spidernet.com.cy.

Smaller than Watermania but more convenient if you're staying on the Amathous strip and don't want to cross town. It's cheaper, too. You'll find rafts, inner tubes, flumes, slides and a children's pool. The entrance fee includes a buffet lunch.

Open 10am–6pm Apr–Oct. Admission Adults €15.38, children €11.96.

Space Bowling Centre

1 Hercules St, Germasogia, ☎ 25 310 000.

Ideal for a wet or hot day, or a change of scene from the beach, the Space Bowling Centre has 16 lanes, air conditioning and all the usual trappings of a bowling alley, including loud music and fast food.

Open Daily 10am–2am.

Evening Walk

You can stroll 10 km all the way from Limassol Old Port to the Amathous tourist area, sticking to the beach pretty well all the way and avoiding the road. This is a long way for children but you can always turn back – and there are countless stops for drinks, swimming and resting. Early evening is the nicest time, just around sunset.

All beaches in Cyprus are public so while it may look as though you're traipsing through the grounds of a hotel, you are not trespassing. It's a good chance to have a look at other hotels, too!

Driving Round the Villages

The Cyprus Sustainable Tourism Initiative has produced a very helpful booklet called 'Discover the Real Cyprus', with details of a self-drive tour from Limassol through some of the prettiest villages in the area. Turn this into a family day out with a walk and lunch in a village taverna.

Heading west from Limassol, turn off at the exit for Avdimou. Either take a detour to the beach, where there are some pleasant tavernas for morning coffee, or head through the village towards Anogyra, a pretty village which was once the centre of the island's carob trade. Here, you can visit the ruined (although partly restored)

Monastery of Timios Stavros, dating back to the 14th century. The other curiosity in the village is a large, upright monolith with a hole in the centre. Mothers from the surrounding area have a superstition around this monolith; if you pass a sick baby through the hole, the baby will be healed.

> **INSIDER TIP ›**
> Look out in the village shops for *pastelli*, the local delicacy of carob toffee. You can also buy *teratsomelo*, carob syrup, to drizzle on yoghurt or, unusually, as a marinade for meat.

Other diversions in Anogyra include the Nicolaides Winery and the Oleastro Olive Park (see p. 57).

The tour carries on through the heart of the wine-growing country, through Pachna and Mallia, another pretty village, to Vasa, where (if your children aren't too restless) you can visit the Vasa winery, which has a mixture of high-tech equipment and very old, traditional artefacts (℡ 25 945 999 to make an appointment).

Carry on through Arsos and Agios Nikolaos to Omodhos (see p. 134), the epicentre of the island's wine business. The main street is lined with cafés and shops and it's a good place to stop for lunch (see p. 150).

Leaving Omodhos, head for Mandria and follow the signs to Vouni, with gorgeous views in every direction. Just past Mandria is the Castellanos Herb Farm, with a shop attached (see p. 116).

Cypriot Coffee

Cypriots tend to assume that foreigners want to drink Nescafé, or instant coffee, which is pretty insipid. Instead, go local and drink the same as the Cypriots. You'll see old men sitting in cafés all day long, playing backgammon, drinking coffee and gossiping.

Most of the coffee drunk in Cyprus comes from Brazil. It's ground up and put into a special coffee pot called an *mbrikia*. Sugar and cold water are added and the coffee is heated until it boils and begins to froth on the top. At this stage, it's poured into small cups and served very strong, always black and always with a glass of water.

If you order a Cypriot coffee, be sure to specify to the waiter how much sugar you want in it. Normally, you can ask for unsweetened, medium sweet or very sweet.

When you get to the bottom of the cup, leave a little behind or you will end up with a mouthful of coffee grounds.

In Pera Pedi, the winery produces orange and coffee liqueurs as well as table wines; book a visit on ☎ *99 681 431*.

By now, your children probably want some entertainment, so call in at the donkey sanctuary in Vouni for an hour or so of donkey rides and letting off steam in the playground.

You can follow the road back to the coast from here and if there's time, take a detour to the Akrotiri Peninsula (see p. 100) to see the salt lake (where there are flamingos in winter) and the Monastery of St Nicholas of the Cats before driving back to Limassol.

Santa Marina Retreat ★★
FIND AGES 5 AND UP

Towards Pareklisia, 5 km from Limassol, ☎ *25 99 545 454,* **www.santamarinaretreat.com,** *E:reservations@santamarina retreat.com.*

The Santa Marina Retreat is a new and very exciting activity centre for all the family, in the grounds of what was once the Elias Hotel's country club. The site is built on an old copper mine, which you can visit as part of a museum display, and includes a horse stud farm with over 250 horses. Children can try riding, archery, shooting, an assault course, climbing, football, mountain biking and quad biking around a special nature trail. Instruction is provided for all the activities and there's a restaurant on site with evening entertainment. The retreat is expanding all the time; a handmade wooden castle for toddlers has just been added. Book ahead as they handle some large corporate groups and it's important to make sure you can get in.

Admission *Adults €5.50, children under 12 free. Activities are charged* *individually, for example, the one-hour buggy trail on a quad bike is €20.50 each (only adults can drive).* **Credit** *MC V DC AE.*

Shopping

Limassol is probably the biggest shopping centre on the island, although the shops are fairly spread out and there isn't a great deal that's special to buy here. You'll see many of the same shops as in the UK; Dorothy Perkins, M&S, Next, Debenhams, Benetton, Zara and so on, as well as designer stores like Karen Millen and Fendi.

What's different are the prices. Although Cyprus has become more expensive since adopting the euro, it's still less, particularly the children's clothes, then in the UK. Designer glasses are also amazingly cheap, so bring your prescription if you need a new pair.

The main shopping areas in Limassol are on Anexartiatis and Agiou Andreou (St Andrew) Streets and Makarious III Avenue, which encircles the centre of town.

Bear Factory

34 K. Partasidi, Shop 5, 📞 *25 341 040.*

A must for children who love teddy bears! Children can custom design their own bear in five simple stages and create a lasting souvenir of their holiday.
Open *9am–7pm.* **Credit** *MC V.*

Mitsu Mitsu FIND ★

St Andrews Street, 📞 *25 359 291.*

A fantastic find in St Andrews Street – brilliant if you're planning a wedding in Cyprus or just want some floaty, sequinny evening-wear, spangled tops and pretty trousers. Good for teens, too.
Open *9am–7pm.* **Credit** *MC V.*

Tonia Theodorou Jewellery

Ayiou Andreou, Agora Anexartisias, No. 30, 📞 *25 355 244.*

Beautiful handmade jewellery from local designer Tonia Theodorou, who trained in Florence and now specialises in quirky, unusual designs, some contemporary, some classical, including clever rings that change from gold and amethyst to gold and diamond, by turning the middle stone, or bracelets with precious stones that can be converted into rings. Ideal for gifts and teenage girls will enjoy it, too.
Open *9am–7pm.* **Credit** *MC V.*

Vouni Art Gallery

📞 *99 775 426.*

This small art gallery is at the lower end of the village and is signposted from the main road. There is a permanent exhibition of paintings by local artists. It's not big enough to merit making the journey specially but if you're here to visit the Donkey Sanctuary, take the time to drop in.
Open *Every afternoon from 2pm.* **Credit** *MC V.*

Castellanos Shop and Herb Farm

Mandria, 📞 *25 433 961.*

This organic herb farm is a great place to stop if you're looking for gifts to take home. It's just past the church in the village and sells essential oils, herbal teas and products made from herbs grown on the farm.

To get there, follow the Castellanos Herb Farm signs from the main road past the village of Mandria.

Open 9am–2pm Tues, Thurs, Fri. **Credit** MC V.

FAMILY-FRIENDLY ACCOMMODATION

Limassol

EXPENSIVE

Londa ★★★

72 George A Street, Potamos Yermasoyias, Yermasoyia; just east of the centre of Limassol on the beach, ☎ *25 865 555, www.londacyprus. com.*

Super-chic gathering place for the town's beautiful people but this being Cyprus, a fair few guests had babies in tow when I stayed. The Londa is best for families with small babies or style-conscious teens, not so much for children in between, as it doesn't really have children's facilities.

What you get here is a cavernous lobby, all white and neutral tones with clever use of glass so if feels as though the whole space is open to the sea, and a variety of minimalist but sumptuous rooms. There's a gorgeous pool area with the kind of outdoor furnishings you see in *Vogue* magazine, a small beach and jetty with watersports and an outdoor bar/dining area.

Inside, the bright and airy Caprice at Londa restaurant (see p. 122) is one of Limassol's most stylish. The bar is gorgeous, with an open fireplace in winter and lots of squashy chairs for lounging in and looking cool. The hotel also has a spa with over 50 treatments, using products from Payot and Darphin.

Fruity decor at the Londa

Rooms 68. **Rates** From €109 per room per night, B&B, increasing in summer to more than €160. **Credit** MC V DC AE. **Amenities** Restaurant, spa, children's club, babysitting, pool, beach with watersports.

Le Meridien Limassol ★★★

Old Limassol–Nicosia Road (at the far end of the coast road leading east from Limassol centre), ☎ 25 862 000, www.starwoodhotels.com.

Le Meridien is the last hotel at the end of the Amathous strip, some 15 km from the town centre, but easily connected to everything by bus. This is an absolutely perfect hotel for families in every way as it has vast amounts of space, including an entire children's village, the Penguin Club.

The pool is enormous, like a beautiful lagoon, set in acres of grassy gardens leading down to a sand beach with watersports.

Rooms come in lots of different categories, only one of which, the Royal Spa Wing, is adults only. There are other categories of suite that give families more space, or family rooms. If you really want to splurge, the Presidential Suites on the roof are truly palatial, with a private pool and its own grotto!

The Penguin Village has a mini football pitch, bouncy castle, swimming pool, mini amphitheatre, climbing frames, and crèche facility for one month to three year olds (fee for the crèche) and teens will love Leisureland, which has tennis, basketball, volleyball, football, mini golf, pool tables, table tennis, archery, badminton, table football, air hockey, bicycles for adults and children as well as a bowling alley and a disco.

The hotel also has what I rate as the island's finest thalassotherapy spa. You must make time for this, even though it's adults only. Treatments are by Thalgo and Elemis and there are seven pools of varying salinity.

Le Meridien has several restaurants, including seafood, Italian and Asian. Le Nautile is posh Mediterranean and best for a night when you have a babysitter, while Le Vieux Village (summer only) is a great family taverna. There's also Mickey's, a children's restaurant.

Rooms 329. **Rates** From €92 per room per night, B&B in winter to anything around €290 in summer. **Credit** MC V DC AE. **Amenities** Nine restaurants, spa, children's club, teen centre, babysitting, several pools, beach, all watersports, scuba diving, gym, regular entertainment.

Four Seasons ★★★

Ag. Tychonas, on the main coast road heading east from Limassol, ☎ 25 858 000, www.fourseasons.com.cy.

This beautiful and very stylish hotel manages to combine family-friendliness with gorgeous and luxurious surroundings. Landscaped gardens slope down to a spotless Blue Flag Beach and the hotel has its own diving school. The hotel has indoor and outdoor pools (indoor is important if you're coming in winter with children) and a huge range of watersports. There are three levels of children's club, from kindergarten to a teen activity programme, and a video games room. You'll also be lured by a stunning Shiseido spa and six restaurants, from gourmet Greek (Mavroumatis – see p. 123) to Chinese, Italian and seafood, as well as lavish theme nights with entertainment round the pool.

Children love the Café Tropical, the main restaurant, the outside of which is built on bridges and islands over a koi carp lagoon. Just watch out for the mosquitoes on hot nights!

Rooms 304. *Rates* From €103 per room per night, B&B, in winter, rising to much higher in summer. . *Credit* MC V DC AE *Amenities* Six restaurants, spa, children's clubs, babysitting, several pools, beach, diving school, gym, numerous bars, tennis.

Amathus Beach ★★★

In the Amathus area on the main coast road, 9 km from the city centre (25 832 000, *www.amathus-hotels.com/limassol*.

Another fantastic top-class beach hotel, aimed at the family market (among others). If you book direct, children up to 14 stay free when sharing with their parents. There are excellent children's activities and clubs as well as a playground, paddling pool with a big shade umbrella, babysitting and a games arcade.

The Amathus Beach has four pools, one of which is indoors, and acres of grassy gardens sloping down to the beach and watersports centre. There's a big spa, the Amathusia, with various

treatments including Clarins and Decleor, and a gym.

Dining is in four restaurants, one of which, the Limanaki Fish Taverna (see p. 124) has won awards. There's a children's menu at the Kalypso Garden Restaurant and separate dinner for under fours in the evenings.

Rooms 239. *Rates* From €98 per room per night, B&B in winter, rising to over €200 in summer. *Credit* MC V DC AE. *Amenities* Four restaurants, spa, children's club, babysitting, four pools, tennis, watersports, scuba diving, regular entertainment.

MODERATE

Mediterranean Beach

In the Amathus area on the main coast road, about 9 km from the city centre, (25 311 777, *www.med beach.com*.

The Mediterranean Beach is a really good four-star hotel, with pretty well all the facilities of a five-star. It's located on the main strip of hotels, on the beach side, and has landscaped pools (one indoors) and its own Blue Flag beach. Accommodation is bright and airy, furnished in Mediterranean colours, and there are three restaurants. There's a spa, gym, Pilates studio, and a children's clubs in the grounds with play equipment on the grass. This is a good choice if you don't want to stretch to one of the flashier five-star hotels; essentially, the facilities are pretty similar.

Rooms 291, 54 of which are interconnecting. *Rates* €42–88 per person, B&B. *Credit* MC V DC AE. *Amenities* Three restaurants, spa,

Cypriot Food through the Seasons

For an economy that was once entirely rural, the Cypriot year is still very much based around the seasons and special dishes for every month and every occasion. You can have fun discovering these as a family, although some are only available at the time of certain festivals.

On New Year's Day, which is known as St Basil's day in Cyprus, each family bakes a special cake known as *Vasilopitta*, not dissimilar from our idea of a Christmas pudding. The person who finds a coin in a slice of cake is supposed to have good luck for the rest of the year.

January isn't normally a time you would associate with fruit harvest but this is when the citrus fruit is picked and you will see lorries piled high with oranges, tangerines, lemons and grapefruit on their way to the ports. Quite a lot of the fruit is exported but often the best way is to buy it straight from the back of a stallholder's van in the local market.

Carnival in Cyprus comes two weeks before the beginning of Lent and is a time of partying and festivity, especially in Limassol. Seasonal specialities at this time of year include a special pastry filled with cheese, called *bourekia*, and sticky sweets made with honey known *asdaktyla* and *kandaifi.*

Carnival is a pretty decadent time, with parties, street parades and general merriment but on the first day of Lent, things quieten down a bit and families traditionally pack a picnic and head for the countryside where they eat more simple fare of vegetables, bread, salad and village wine.

Lent is a more sombre period and a lot of people still take it very seriously, eating no meat or fish or dairy products. Instead, Cypriots live off

---

children's club, babysitting, two pools, tennis, watersports, scuba diving, Pilates, regular entertainment.

Elias Beach Hotel

In the Amathous area, on the beach, 11 km east of Limassol, ☎ *25 636 000, www.kanikahotels.com.*

Located 5 km from the city centre on the beach, this Cypriot-owned four-star hotel has recently had a big facelift, with a new indoor/ outdoor children's club, attractive free-form pools and some fun features, like Kids' Suites – special family rooms with a

sliding partition separating a children-only area with bunk beds, Disney bed covers, TV, games and PlayStation.

There's a main restaurant, a beach restaurant where theme nights are held, spacious grounds featuring all sorts of activities, and a beach with watersports.

Rooms *168.* ***Rates*** *From €90 per room per night, B&B.****Credit*** *MC V DC AE.* ***Amenities*** *Outdoor and indoor swimming pools, children's club, dive centre, tennis, health club with massage, two restaurants, several bars, beach with watersports.*

the land, eating vegetables, fruit and pulses, using ingredients including pumpkin, cracked wheat, spinach and greens that grow wild.

At Easter, rather than stuffing themselves with chocolate, Cypriots make a special soup of eggs and lemon in chicken stock, as well as savoury Easter cakes. Lunch on the Orthodox Easter Sunday is a time when the meat fast is broken and families gather in their gardens to roast huge *souvlaki* on their barbecues.

Summer, when most visitors are likely to be on the island, is a fantastic time for soft fruit and you should have no problem getting your children to eat cherries, apricots, plums, and juicy peaches and melons which you will see piled high by the roadside.

September is more about drinking and eating as this is the traditional time for the wine harvest and a lot of people flock to Limassol for the enormous Wine Festival. Shortly after this comes harvest time when you'll see a lot of dishes featuring almonds, carobs and olives. Try to get your children to try pastelli and carob honey on their toast instead of Nutella!

At Christmas, Cypriots don't eat turkey but instead slaughter a pig and even families living in urban areas will make and smoke their own special sausages, called *loukanika*. Cypriot Christmas cake will look more familiar, as it's very similar to ours, but if you are spending Christmas on the island also look out for *kourambiedes* – biscuits like shortbread sprinkled with icing sugar and spicy buns which are draped with honey syrup.

Limassol Suburbs

INEXPENSIVE

Niki's House

Rodou 18, Mesa Geitonia, Lemesos, 📞 *25 888 000, **www.agrotourism. com.cy**.*

It's possible to stay in a small village yet be only minutes from downtown Limassol if you fancy getting away from it all but still having all the attractions of a big town at hand. One of a couple of agrotourism projects in the suburbs, this is a 120-year-old stone farmhouse with just five rooms, in the village/suburb of Agios Athanasios. The village is only 3 km north-east of the city and has views right across the rooftops towards the sea.

The house itself is a listed building, refurbished in 2006 and situated in the middle of the village. There's a paved yard and grassy area in the centre, and a fireplace.

Rooms *Four studios and one apartment with fireplace.* **Rates** *From €48 per studio per night, self-catering.* **Credit** *MC V if you book online.* **Amenities** *Bank, taxi service and pharmacy in the village, a bus stop is five minutes' walk away.*

Anthony's Garden House ★

30 Makariou St, Episkopi, ☎ *25 932 502, www.agrotourism.com.cy.*

A pretty, two-storey house in the village of Episkopi, about 15 km from downtown Limassol. The house used to be a stable for camels but now has eight rooms on the ground floor and a studio upstairs with views towards the sea. There's a gorgeous court-yard filled with flowering trees and lots of original features, including wood-beamed ceilings and stone arches. Kourion Beach is only 3 km away and there are shops and tavernas in the village.

Rooms *Eight plus studio.* **Rates** *From €52 per room per night, B&B.* **Credit** *MC V if you book online.* **Closed** *Dec–Feb.* **Amenities** *The studio has a kitchen and can take a family of five.*

Villages

Vouni Lodge

27 Makariou Street, Vouni, ☎ *22 323 385, www.agrotourism.com.cy.*

A 200-year-old stone building in the middle of a beautiful village surrounded by vineyards. The house has a decent sized garden and courtyard for children to run around in and there are tav-ernas and the Vouni Donkey Sanctuary nearby. You can even see the sea on a clear day. There are three apartments, each sleep-ing up to four, so the Lodge is ideal for families.

Apartments *Three one-bedroom apartments with bathroom and*

kitchen. **Rates** *From €65 per night. Breakfast at the nearby taverna €5.* **Credit** *MC V if you book online.*

FAMILY-FRIENDLY DINING

Limassol Town

Caprice at Londa

72 George A Street, Yermasogia, ☎ *25 865 555, www.londahotel.com.*

This exclusive restaurant, related to the chichi Caprice in London, is super-smart, one of the most swish on the island, with mini-malist design and a whole wall of glass overlooking the sea. The menu has Italian influences, with plenty of fancy pasta and risotto dishes, as well as some delicious salads and pleasingly simple, sub-tle main courses of meat and fish. We had the fish of the day – a big sea bass – with lemon and olive oil and it was delicious.

There weren't any children here (we ate late and the Londa tends to attract parents with young babies) but I'd recom-mend it as a place to come for a special dinner on a night when you've hired a babysitter.

Open *Dinner only. Advance reserva-tions essential.* **Main course** *€15–49.* **Credit** *MC V DC AE.*

Barolo

248 Ayiou Andreou, Limassol, ☎ *25 760 767.*

Small and unpretentious, this restaurant serves classy and adventurous Cypriot dishes,

Hip restaurant Stretto

although there is pasta on the menu which children will enjoy. Try the *foie gras* in Grappa, or quail, or baked mozzarella in pumpkin seeds for a change from the usual meze. This is a great place for lovers of game, too, but less good for vegetarians unless you don't mind eating pasta.

Open *7pm–11pm Mon–Sat.* *Main course* *From around €12.82.* *Credit* *MC V DC AE.*

Beige

238 St Andrew's Street, ☎ *25 818 860.*

One of the island's most happening restaurants, east-west fusion in a funky setting of reds, earth tones and stone walls. The menu includes sushi and steak. This is better with teenagers than young children as it's busy and attracts a youngish, trendy crowd.

Open *6pm–12am Mon–Sat.* *Main course* *From €17.* *Credit* *MC V DC AE.*

Mavroumatis AGES AND UP

Four Seasons Hotel, ☎ *25 858 000,* *www.fourseasons.com.cy.*

There's a modern Greek theme here, using local stone, stainless steel and olive-gold linen.

Signature dishes include slow-cooked lamb shank and grilled feta cheese, mixed bean ragoût and minted radish, lamb jus scented with wild thyme. Children over five only are allowed in. While it's as friendly as anywhere else, the restaurant is more formal than many and is probably a special-occasion place rather than everyday supper.

Open *7.30pm–10.30pm. Advance reservations essential.* *Dinner* *From around €45.* *Credit* *MC V DC AE.*

MODERATE

Stretto ★

Lanatis Carob Mill, Vasilissis (behind the castle in Limassol old town), ☎ *25 820 465,* *www.carobmill-restaurants.com.*

In the same location as the Draught Microbrewery and Karatelo. Stretto is young and funky, part-café and part-restaurant, with light Mediterranean dishes, sandwiches, wraps and grills, so there's no shortage of things for children to pick at, especially the hot chocolate brownies!

Open Daily 11am–2am. **Main course** €9.50–19. **Credit** MC V DC AE.

Karatelo ★

Lanatis Carob Mill, Vasilissis (behind the castle), 25 820 46, **www.carob mill-restaurants.com**.

This busy restaurant is fun for children as you can make up your own meze; simply tick the boxes on the menu, which has a wide range of hot and cold meze starters. Specials include rabbit and moussaka, meat or vegetarian. There's live Cypriot music here in the evenings.

Open 7pm–11pm, dinner only. **Main course** From €9.50. **Credit** MC V DC AE.

Draught Microbrewery

Lanatis Carob Mill, Vasilissis (behind the castle in the old town), 25 820 470, **www.carobmill-restaurants. com**.

As the name suggests, a microbrewery, the only one in Cyprus. You can have a full meal or snacks in the bar – the food is unchallenging Tex-Mex, burgers and little infusions of Greek (salads, chops, pork marinated in beer, ostrich fillet). With children, it's a good lunch stop for a filling burger after visiting the castle.

Open 11am–2am, lunch, dinner and snacks. **Main course** €10–30. **Credit** MC V DC AE.

Limanaki ★

On the beach at the Amathus Hotel, 25 832 000, **www.amathus-hotels. com**.

An award-winning upmarket fish taverna right on the beach and one of the nicest hotel restaurants. The hotel is very family-friendly and children are welcome; as it's outdoors, there is plenty of space. Although the restaurant has been created by the hotel, it feels authentic and the quality is fantastic. Either have the meze or see what you think of the day's catch. Some dishes have a classy twist, like the stuffed kalamari.

Open Daily 8pm–11pm summer only. **Main course** From €17.50. **Credit** MC V DC AE.

The Old Neighbourhood

Angyras 14, 25 376 082.

Authentic fish taverna, friendly and packed in the evenings, with live music. There's nothing unusual about the menu but it's fresh, fresh, fresh, simply prepared and delicious – try kalamari stuffed with feta cheese, tomato and oregano.

Open Daily from 6pm. **Main course** From €17.50. **Credit** MC V DC AE.

Ta Piatakia ★★

Nicodemou Mylona 7, 25 745 017.

This quirky little restaurant is the kind of place hoteliers will suggest if you ask them for ideas for a night out, even though it's taking revenue away from them. There's nothing like it – the room is festooned with plates, on the walls, hanging from the ceiling, (the name means 'little plates') and the food is exciting and highly imaginative.

Chef/owner Roddy serves small dishes using Cypriot cuisine with a twist – bacon-wrapped feta, baked cherry tomatoes in a sweet and sour herb dressing and feta with duck. Although the restaurant is small, children who don't need to run around during dinner will be at home with the ambience and general buzz and there are enough things on the menu to please most fussy eaters to some extent at least.

Open 7pm–11.30pm Mon–Sat. **Small dishes** €1–12. **Credit** MC V DC.

TGI Fridays

333 28th October Street, ☎ 25 583 355.

I wouldn't normally recommend a fast-food restaurant, but if you are travelling with teenagers and you want to give them a bit of freedom in a safe environment, TGIF is a good place to let them out for the evening. It's right on the seafront on the main drag and is always busy, with tourists and locals. The menu is standard TGIF fare and everything most children love, from pizza to burgers, nuggets and fish fingers on the menu. There isn't anything Cypriot about the main menu – it's Tex-Mex/modern American with huge cocktails

(for adults) and shakes and smoothies for children.

Open Daily until late. **Main course** From around €10. **Credit** MC V.

Governor's Beach

MODERATE

Panayotis

Governor's Beach, ☎ 99 633 258.

A long-established fish taverna on the cliffs overlooking Governor's Beach, a stretch of sand framed by towering white cliffs. The restaurant, with blue and white chequered table cloths, specialises in fish meze and is a popular place for Sunday lunch. Older children will love it as they can be freed to play on the beach below while parents sit and relax on the shady terrace. There are high chairs for younger children, as well as items like burgers and omelette on the menu.

Open Daily, lunch and dinner. **Fish meze** €18. **Credit** MC V.

Avdimou

MODERATE

Melanda Beach Taverna

Avdimou, on Melanda Beach, ☎ 99 422 233.

Another good lunch stop, this pretty taverna is in an idyllic setting on the narrowish strip of Melanda Beach, just down the road from Avdimou village. It offers basic taverna fare under some shady trees and has fresh fish daily. Children can play on the beach, which is safe and gently shelving, if a bit narrow and lacking in shade.

Open *9am–5pm Mar, Apr, Nov lunch only; 9am–10pm May–Oct except Mon evenings. Book ahead.* **Meze** *Around €18.* **Credit** *MC V.*

Pachna

Nick's Fish Tavern

Last building on the cliff as you leave Pachna on the road to Limassol, ☎ *25 942 082.*

Also known as Aphrodite's Restaurant but if you get lost, ask for Nick the Fish. Nick claims to be the only fisherman in the Troodos and runs the taverna with his wife. The views are stupendous, across the mountains to neighbouring villages. As well as the fish for which Nick is known, the halloumi in the restaurant comes from his sister's goat herd.

Open *Dinner only; phone first.* **Main course** *From around €10. No credit cards.*

Vouni

I Orea Ellas ★ FIND

Ellados 3, Vouni village, ☎ *25 944 328.*

A real treat in this gorgeous village that has everything from

donkeys to herb shops. The owner, Mrs Phaedra, cooks authentic, regional Greek food with a Cypriot twist and makes restina wine on the premises. Combine this family-friendly place with a visit to the Donkey Sanctuary for a lovely, relaxing day out.

Open *12pm–3pm, 7.30pm–11pm Tues–Sun.* **Main course** *From €9.40.* **Credit** *MC V.*

Vasa

Ariadne

On the Vasa old road, at the top of the hill where the road joins the main road leading into the village, ☎ *25 944 064.*

Another authentic, family-friendly Cypriot taverna serving superb meze and wines grown in the village. Specialities include meatballs or courgette flowers stuffed with cheese – deliciously light.

Open *Daily 8am–11pm.* **Meze** *From €11.96. No credit cards.*

6 The Troodos Mountains

THE TROODOS MOUNTAINS

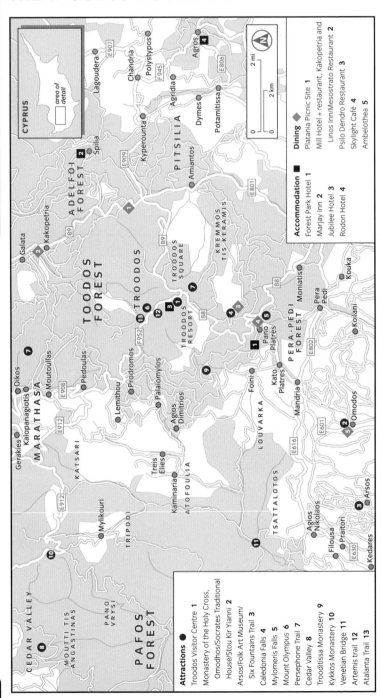

CYPRUS

area of detail

2 mi

2 km

Attractions ●
Troodos Visitor Centre **1**
Monastery of the Holy Cross,
Omodhos/Socrates Traditional
House/Stou Kir Yianni **2**
Arsos/Folk Art Museum/
Six Fountains Trail **3**
Caledonia Falls **4**
Mylomeris Falls **5**
Mount Olympus **6**
Persephone Trail **7**
Cedar Valley **8**
Trooditissa Monastery **9**
Kykkos Monastery **10**
Venetian Bridge **11**
Artemis trail **12**
Atalanta Trail **13**

Accommodation ■
Forest Park Hotel **1**
Marjay Inn **2**
Jubilee Hotel **3**
Rodon Hotel **4**

Dining ◆
Platania Picnic Site **1**
Mill Hotel + restaurant, Kakopetria and
Linos Inn/Mesostrato Restaurant **2**
Psilo Dendro Restaurant **3**
Skylight Café **4**
Ambelothea **5**

The Troodos Mountains form a long, forested spine along the centre of the island. To visitors, they are a constant source of amazement. This is a different world from the hustle and bustle of the coast, where the only sound is the wind whistling in the trees or the splash of waterfall. There's very little development here: the mountains are scattered with villages but there isn't any mass tourism. What you will find is beautiful walking trails, enormous monasteries crammed full of the most amazing treasures, vineyards clinging to steep slopes, and, in winter, skiing on the slopes of Mount Olympus, 1,951 m above sea level.

ESSENTIALS

Getting There

By Air If you're staying in the Troodos Mountains or visiting for a day, you really need a car to get around. The mountain resorts are equidistant from Paphos International Airport and Larnaca International Airport. The journey from the airport takes 1–1½ hours, depending on your destination.

By Car Roads through the mountains are in reasonable condition, although signposting can be a little erratic. Make sure you have a decent map before you set off. All of the **walking trails** are well signposted and there's usually somewhere to leave your car at the end of the trail.

> **INSIDER TIP**
>
> The Troodos falls into several different municipalities of Cyprus so doesn't have its own area code. Villages in the west have the dialling code 26 for Paphos, while those in the south and centre are in Limassol district, so begin with 25. Some places to the east fall into the Nicosia area, so start with 22.

VISITOR INFORMATION

Orientation

The Troodos can be quite confusing, as the region is mountainous, spread out and has no real centre of population. It's easiest if you imagine it with Mount Olympus (the highest point) at the centre, with Troodos Resort on its slopes and slightly lower down from here, the two Platres villages, Pano Platres and Kato Platres.

To the north-west is the Marathasa Valley and west of this, Kykkos Monastery and Cedar Valley. Due north is Solea Valley and the village of Kakopetria, while to the east is the Pitsilia area. Finally, on the southern slopes, you'll find the famous wine-growing villages, Omodhos, Arsos and Mandria.

Getting Around

Bus services to the Troodos region are sketchy at best. There are long-distance buses from Larnaca and Nicosia but only one in each direction per day.

Once you're in the mountains, the only other form of public transport is taxi, which can be expensive for longer journeys.

Getting around the Troodos depends entirely on how active you are! Most people choose to drive or take coach tours. You won't need a four-wheel drive unless you're planning to combine a visit here with the Akamas Peninsula in the west. There are off-road tracks but there isn't really any need to use them and besides, if you do have a hankering to be off-road, it's better to get someone else to take you on an excursion so you can appreciate the scenery.

The E4 European Long-Distance Path, part of an international network of walking and cycling trails, goes straight across the Troodos Mountains. It is possible to hike the trail and spend the night in different villages but this is extremely ambitious for a family, as it means long walks each day and carrying your own pack.

The mountains also have marked-out cycling trails and cycle lanes on the main roads, but these are pretty steep and unless your family consists of burly teenagers you're unlikely to see much of these. You'll see plenty of lycra-clad teams of cyclists, though; Cyprus has an active cycling community.

The nicest and greenest way for families to get around is to plan several walks on the marked trails. You will need a car to get to the start of each one, although if you're staying here and only want to do one or two walks, there are plenty of private hire taxis.

Child-friendly Events & Entertainment

The Troodos region has a lot of summer festivals and exhibitions, which tend to be moveable feasts. Contact the tourist board for details when you arrive in Cyprus.

The village of Agros has an annual **Festival of the Wild Rose** in May, with dancing and music, and exhibits of the products of the roses which are grown commercially around the village.

In August, the villages of the Marathasa area have a **folk art and crafts fair**, with various demonstrations of traditional arts and crafts, as well as food stalls. On the last weekend of August, the villages of Kalopanayiotis, Gerakies and Kambos have a **sweet exhibition**, where local people make sweets and candies using very old recipes and the bakeries present their products.

Nut and sweet stalls in Troodos Square

In the middle of September, the villages of Kyperounta and Kato Mylos show off their **sausages and meat products** (there are several small-scale meat-curing establishments here) and at the end of September, Omodhos and the surrounding villages throw a big **wine festival**.

All of these events are suitable for the whole family; there aren't any events in Cyprus that exclude children and there will always be something to amuse them.

Also look out for **saints' days**, when each village celebrates the commemorative day of its patron saint with religious ceremonies, parties, processions and festivals.

INSIDER TIP ⟫

In Cyprus, the 15th August is the day of the Assumption of the Virgin Mary and big ceremonies are held at all the monasteries – Kykkos, Agros, Chrysorrogiatissa, Kiti and Leopetri. It's worth the trip to join the celebrations.

WHAT TO SEE & DO

Children's Top 10 Attractions

❶ **Taking a dip** in a mountain stream at Caledonia Falls. See p. 137.

❷ **Finding out** how Cypriot sweets are made in Agros village, and sampling all the different ones. See p. 146.

❸ **Hiking** the mountain trails around the Troodos. See p. 142.

❹ **Catching a glimpse** of the rare mouflon (a type of wild sheep) on the steep sides of Cedar Valley. See p. 138.

❺ **Toasting marshmallows** over a camp fire in one of the mountain picnic sites. See p. 137.

❻ **Throwing a snowball** in the Troodos Mountains in the morning and then swimming in the sea in the afternoon.

❼ **Picking fruit** from the trees – cherries, peaches and oranges – but remember to ask permission first!

❽ **Discovering** how Cypriot families used to live at Socrates' Traditional House in Omodhos. See p. 141.

❾ **Getting savvy** about birds, animals and reptiles at the Troodos Visitor Centre. See p. 133.

❿ **Learning** about the life of a monk at Kykkos Monastery. See p. 139.

Mountain Resorts

Kato Platres and Pano Platres

Although it only has a population of 280, Platres, divided into upper and lower parts, is a reasonably smart mountain resort. This used to be where rich Cypriots would come to get away from the summer heat of the coast. It even has a slightly colonial feel about it and you can almost imagine taking Tiffin in the afternoon on a shady terrace.

Time Off

Cypriots do not share the same love of the beach and the outdoors as the holidaymakers to whom they play host. Many will be happy to live in an apartment in town rather than a suburban house with a garden. Anything more than a 10-minute commute is jokingly referred to as a long distance, so urban living is popular. Gardening is definitely not on; rather than cultivate flowers, a city-dwelling Cypriot will probably buy a plot in the countryside for growing olives, pomegranates, oranges and lemons to squeeze over the *souvlaki*.

Typical Cypriots' interests, generally speaking, include the village café/pub, backgammon and chess for men, particularly of the older generation and family life, shopping and home-making among women. Football is a passion, with many staunch supporters of British teams on the island. Families will go on outings at the weekend, either to the beach, or to Akamas Peninsula if they live in the west, or to the Troodos Mountains, usually for a big picnic.

There isn't that much to see here but Platres has does have a few shops, several tavernas and a few hotels, some of which have swimming pools, a blessing when you are travelling with children. It's really used mainly as a lunch stop by tour companies offering day trips into the mountains.

Platres is, however, a great base for a few days from which to do some walks, taste the local wines, which are surprisingly good, sample trout from the mountain streams and pay visits to some of the spectacular monasteries. There isn't a huge amount for children but in summer, getting away from the intense heat of the coast can be a relief and give the whole family more energy.

Troodos Square

Troodos Square, the name for the middle of the straggling Troodos village, is a bit of a one-horse town, and there isn't any reason to come here other than for a quick look at the views and give children a chance to stretch their legs in the playground at the centre. In summer, the breeze up here is welcome but in winter it can be cold and wet, with cloud covering the top of the mountain.

The main reason to be here is to join one of the many hiking trails radiating out from the mountain top. There are places to pick up supplies for a picnic in the main street. You'll also find a little cluster of market stalls by the car park selling the most delicious varieties of nuts, from great heaps of macadamia nuts to nougat, honey nut clusters and different flavoured peanuts.

Watch out for the confusing road signs around the Troodos, which may offer several different ways of getting to the same place!

Troodos Visitor Centre

By the car park, just off Troodos Square.

This small visitor centre has a token admission fee for which you get to see basic displays of the animals, birds and insects endemic to the region, as well as audio-visual presentations, all of which helps children understand the flora and fauna they'll encounter on walks. There's also a very short hiking trail around the centre where you can have a look at some of the plants that grow here. If you're planning on doing some hiking, this is the place to pick up trail leaflets. The most popular trails are well signposted and there's an individual leaflet for each one, pointing out areas of interest along the way.

Marathasa area

There's no one focal point of this area but you will find several pretty villages along this route through the Marathasa river valley. A good day out by car is to drive up to Troodos for a look at the view, explore some of the villages like Prodromos and Pedoulas, then follow the E908 from Troodos and the E911/912 to Kykkos Monastery (see p. 139), carrying on to Cedar Valley (see p. 136) further west if you have time.

Prodromos is a sleepy little place, known for its cool, oxygen-rich, unpolluted air and supposedly one of the healthiest places on the island, almost a vertical mile above sea level.

Further along, Pedoulas has a UNESCO-listed church dating from 1474 and several decent tavernas for lunch or coffee. The less touristy village of Moutoullas is from where much of the mineral water sold on the island originates.

Solea area and Kakopetria

Kakopetria is the main village in the Solea valley, clambering up the hills either side of the Karyiotis River. There's a real mountain village feel about the place, with wood smoke on the breeze, tiny, cobbled streets too narrow for a car, chickens scratching around and tumbledown stone houses interspersed with smart places obviously spruced up with agrotourism grants.

Some of the houses are empty, having been abandoned by Turkish Cypriots fleeing to the north after the island was divided in 1974.

FUN FACT **Wicked Rock**

Kakopetria means 'wicked rock' although the origin of the name isn't known. A local myth, however, says that a young couple were killed by a rock that fell on them during an earthquake, the tragedy giving rise to the name.

There are a couple of surprisingly good family hotels here, the Linos Inn and The Mill, both worth a stop for the night if you are touring.

Pitsylia area and Agros ★

Less visited than Platres or Troodos, but actually, I think, more interesting, Agros is a lovely village clinging to the eastern slopes of the Troodos and gaining a reputation for its cottage industries. There's also a hotel with a pool here, The Rodon (see p. 149), so it's a good base from which to explore the area with children.

The village is surrounded by fields of roses and a local entrepreneur has set up a business producing rosewater, rose tea, rose-infused wine, candles and organic cosmetics.

The village is also famous for its sweets and you'll see shops selling traditional *soutzouko* (grated almonds dipped in grape juice with flour) and *palouze* (jelly sweet made from grape juice and flour), as well as mountain honey, village halloumi and traditional smoked and wine-cured delicatessen meats. You're unlikely to leave empty handed!

Omodhos ★★

Omodhos is the epicentre of the island's wine production and consequently attracts a lot of visitors. It's really a small town

Souvenirs in Omodhos

rather than a village and is absolutely gorgeous, with beautiful views across the countryside and the lovely old cobbled centre with lots of shops selling lace, mountain honey, wine and other traditional products, as well as items for the young shopper, like stuffed donkeys and cheap jewellery. Although the village is inundated with coach tours during the day, the tavernas are friendly and there are some decent enough souvenir shops. Needless to say, several of the wineries offer tastings and it's well worth stocking up here – buying direct from the vineyard means better prices.

FUN FACT ≫ **Warm Welcome** ≪

In Greek Cyprus, the word for stranger (*xenos*) also means guest, providing linguistic evidence of Cyprus' warm hospitality.

How Cyprus Got Its Name

Cyprus was famous in antiquity for its copper resources and the copper gave the island its name, Kypros, thought to be a pre-Greek word for the metal (the Anglicised version comes from the Latin, *cuprum*). Copper was mined in the Bronze Age on the north slope of the Troodos Mountains – from certain vantage points, you can still see the old quarries that have been exploited over the millennia.

The whole of the village centre is pedestrianised and the main street is lined with tavernas and shops. At the end of the street is the Monastery of the Holy Cross, a rather beautiful Byzantine structure around which the village is built, dating back to 1150 but extensively repaired in the 19th century.

Arsos ★
Not far from Omodhos on the slopes of Laona mountain with views as far as Paphos, Arsos is a wealthy and attractive village at the heart of the wine country. In summer, the countryside around the village is swathed in emerald green as the vines ripen. Everybody in the village is involved in winemaking, even on the smallest scale, and you'll see big earthenware jars everywhere in which the red wine is kept.

Arsos suffered a lot in the 1960s as younger generations migrated to the coast and cities and its population has shrunk, but there is a strong community spirit today, with the Arsos Development Association, absolutely committed to agro-tourism and the preservation of the village's traditions.

Arsos has a couple of things to see, as well as being a lovely place to wander around. The Folk Art Museum (see p. 142) gives a good insight into viticulture in days gone by, and children should enjoy the Six Fountains nature trail that follows the valley to the north-west of the village.

A stream runs through this valley, along which six medieval fountains remain, linked by a stone path. These fountains were critical to village life in the days when nobody had running water. Each one has its own story – some were used for watering animals, others for village women to do their laundry (as recently as the 1950s) and others for irrigating the village orchards. Reed beds used to grow along the stream and the village had a thriving basket weaving industry.

Nowadays, the fountains are preserved by the village for tourists to visit. Get children to look for fresh water crabs and frogs in the stream, and try to identify the many types of butterfly flitting around the banks.

Arsos also has a lively cultural scene; there's a traditional music night in June, a village fair in August and a festival on the last Sunday of September. Check the village website for details: **www. arsos.org**.

Natural Wonders & Spectacular Views

Mount Olympus

You'll notice what look like giant golf balls scattered across the mountain tops of Cyprus. These are radar stations belonging to the British and Cypriot armies. You're not supposed to go close to them for security reasons but on a day trip I joined, the driver took great delight in taking his four-wheel drive through a gap in the fence and driving it right up to one of the 'golf balls'. It's not so much the illicit fun in doing this (and there were plenty of other jeeps up there) but the amazing views that make it worth the trip. We could see all the way across the northern plains to Nicosia, and the whole of the northern coast was outlined beneath us. A giant Turkish flag etched into a distant mountain face was a chilling reminder of the political situation.

Across the sea in the distance was a hazy mountain range, which driver said was the Turkish mainland; it puts in perspective just how close Turkey is. It was a strange thought that we were looking down into the northern occupied side of the island, and that such a beautiful, tranquil place could be the subject of such antagonism.

Cedar Valley ★★

Cedar Valley is an area of astonishing natural beauty, located in the far west of the Troodos range on the edge of the Paphos forest. You'll soon see how it gets its name – the valley is populated by thousands of majestic Cypriot cedars (*cedrus brevifolia*), related to the cedar of Lebanon – shapely, graceful trees, many of which are 25 m high.

It's quite tricky to get here and you do feel as though you're in the middle of nowhere; look out for a sign from the main

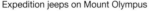

Expedition jeeps on Mount Olympus

road between Kykkos and Stavros tis Psokas. You have to bump down this tiny road for a few kilometres before you're in the valley proper. The E4 European Long-Distance Path goes through Cedar Valley and it's worth walking a little bit of it; take binoculars and get children to look out for mouflon (see p. 138), which live wild around here, usually in small groups. You can follow a trail up the Tripylos Mountain to the forest station, a 2.5 km upward hike – stunningly beautiful and infinitely rewarding with the view at the top, but very tiring!

Caledonia Falls ★★★ ALL AGES

The Caledonia trail in the Troodos Mountains is one of the most fun for families and is great for children as it's downhill all the way, with plenty of opportunity for crossing the Kryos Potamos River on stepping stones. The well-marked path is only 3 km, although the descent takes a couple of hours with children as there's lots of picking your way over rocks and water.

Follow the signs to the Presidential Palace at Troodos and park at the trail head, which is signposted. Take water and a picnic! As you pick your way down through the forest, it's hard to imagine the rather barren slopes of the hills below, as this is an enchanted wood of dappled shade, splashing waterfalls and trees such as horse chestnut and wild plum. Most of the species are labelled and the CTO provides a free leaflet with explanations about the plants.

The trail criss-crosses the river a lot, so you shouldn't expect to do this walk with a buggy, although a baby backpack is fine if you can balance on the stepping stones. There are lots of lovely picnic spots overlooking the river.

Sadly, the day we did this walk included the most torrential thunderstorms I've ever seen in Cyprus and we ended up soaked to the skin, so we passed on the reward at the end of a dip under the Caledonia Falls, a fairly impressive waterfall. Another treat awaits, though: the trail ends at the Psilo Dentron restaurant, a welcoming, establishment next to a trout farm, where you can eat freshly grilled mountain trout straight from a huge outdoor barbecue. Get the restaurant to order a taxi back up to the trail head to pick up your car – unless you fancy the 3 km uphill climb!

Platania Picnic Site

Just off the B9 heading east from Troodos Square is one of the biggest picnic sites, Platania, where Cypriots go at weekends to cook *souvlaki* in the open air and enjoy the scent of the pine trees. There's a playground here, and toilets, as well as several benches and barbecue pits. It gets busy, though, so come early to stake your pitch.

Persephone Trail ALL AGES

Follow this easy, 3 km linear trail from Troodos Square to an amazing lookout point from which you can see a vast expanse of the south coast on a clear day, across the southern slopes of

Troodos and the wine villages as far as Limassol Port and the Akrotiri Salt Lake. The trail can be done with an off-road buggy and takes up to two hours (out and back). Go armed with a trail map from the CTO and look out for various points of interest. Keep children amused by setting them challenges – who can spot the most types of creepy crawlie, for example, or the most varieties of flower.

Aquaria & Animal Parks

Stavros tis Psokas ALL AGES

On a day trip to Kykkos and Cedar Valley, you may as well press on to Stavros tis Psokas, a forest station in a beautiful setting amongst the pines. Here, you can see the extremely rare Cyprus mouflon in a forest enclosure.

Children might think it's just another mountain goat but the mouflon's history is inextricably linked with that of the island. It's thought to have been brought here in Neolithic times, 6000 BC, and to have been hunted throughout history for its flesh and curved horns. In the Middle Ages, tame leopards were used to hunt mouflon, as not many other creatures could match the sheep for agility.

The mouflon is heavily protected nowadays and nobody knows exactly how many are left; normally, helicopters are used to do aerial surveys but the forests of the Troodos are too thick for this to be effective.

Children are guaranteed to see one mouflon at least during their visit – it's the official symbol of Cyprus Airways and is painted on the tailfins of all their planes!

Historic Buildings & Monuments

Trooditissa Monastery

5 km north-west of Platres on the Platres–Prodromos Road.

Sadly, only orthodox pilgrims are allowed into this beautiful monastery but its history is fascinating, nonetheless. The monastery was built in the 13th century above a cave in which two hermits had guarded a priceless icon of the Virgin Mary for decades. The hermits died but locals were alerted to the cave by a ghostly glow being given off by the icon, and the monastery was built to house the precious relic. You can walk up to the cave (although it's not terribly atmospheric nowadays) – it is

Fire: Beware

The Troodos forests are very prone to fire in the hot, dry summer months. Be really careful what you throw away; never leave a glass bottle, for example, where it can catch the sun and never discard cigarettes in the mountains. If you do notice a fire or smoke, dial 1407.

Traditional Village Life

The tranquillity of a Cypriot village is a long way from the sometimes frenetic pace of life in the big resorts. When you visit a village, you'll find an almost archetypal image of old men playing backgammon in the café, or leading donkeys laden with straw or grapes, while old women in black embroider lace in a shady doorway. Villages always have a church at their centre, and usually one or two cafés and tavernas, which form the focal point of village social life. Occasionally, you'll find a bakery and a small post office in the square as well.

Cypriot women rarely spend time in the café. Foreign women aren't necessarily banned; it's just a kind of unwritten rule that the café is for the men, although women will be treated with courtesy if they do go in and ask for a drink. But essentially, the café is where men gossip, make business deals, drink strong, black coffee (and later, brandy or ouzo), play chess, cards and backgammon. In the days before television, the café was the main source of entertainment in a village.

Women work in the fields and look after the home. It may appear that Cypriot men do very little, but the working day does start much earlier for those with agricultural land, with most people taking a lunchtime siesta and then returning to the fields until sunset. Men of retired age may spend the whole day at the café.

Village life may seem very quiet in the heat of the day, although the reality, if you spend a night, is that it's actually quite noisy. Many people keep chickens and dawn can be a cacophony of cockerels crowing, dogs barking and donkeys braying. Village social life perks up at weekends, when young people who work in the towns come back to the family home.

signposted from the road 300 m east of the turnoff for the monastery. The walk only takes a couple of minutes and there are some beautiful views.

Kykkos Monastery
ALL AGES ★★★

If you only take your children to one monastery, make it this one. Built on a mountain peak north west of Troodos, at an altitude of 1,318 m, this 12th-century monastery is staggeringly wealthy, an absolute eye-opener.

I've never seen so much gold and opulence in one place; the main church is absolutely festooned with extravagant chandeliers, candle sticks, goblets and icons, all in rich gold, encrusted with amazing jewels. It's an in-your-face reminder of the wealth and power of the church in Cyprus.

Yet despite the crowds, Kykkos is a peaceful, spiritual place. The first President of Cyprus, Archbishop Makarios III, served as a novice here. He was buried at

Kykkos Monastery

Throni, 3 km to the west and his burial place is signposted from the road up to the monastery, if you're interested.

The monastery was founded during the reign of Emperor Alexios I Komnenos (1081–1118 AD), although the current building is as recent as the early 19th century. The emperor's beloved daughter had been cured of a mysterious illness by a local hermit, Isiah, and when offered a reward, the hermit asked for a precious icon of the Theotokos (Virgin Mary) that was kept at the imperial palace at Constantinople (now known as Istanbul). The emperor sent it to Cyprus together with funds to pay for the construction of a monastery where the sacred relic, which was allegedly painted by St Luke, would be kept.

The icon, covered in silver, is housed in a shrine of tortoise shell and mother-of-pearl that stands in front of the iconostasis.

There are huge queues to see it and it's surrounded by hundreds of other icons, but it's the reason a lot of people come here.

The monastery is also endowed with the most beautiful mosaics and frescoes in amazing colours, the gold gleaming in the shafts of sunlight bouncing off the ancient walls.

There's a wonderful Byzantine museum, too, housing more gold, jewels, religious artefacts and icons. It only takes a little while to go round if you're with children and need the speedy version of the visit, and it's inside the monastery.

Kykkos produces *zivania* and a variety of other alcoholic drinks and holds religious fairs on 8th September (Birth of the Virgin) and 15th August (Dormition of the Virgin).

Open Daily 10am–4pm Nov–May; 10am–6pm June–Oct. **Admission** €2.57 to the museum; entrance to the monastery is free. Dress suitably – no shorts or sleeveless tops. Cloak-like garments are provided at the entrance for anybody not meeting the required dress code. **Amenities** Shop.

Kefelos Venetian Bridge ★★
FIND

Along a track (tarmac, mainly) off the F616 from Mandria to Agios Nikolaos. The bridge is signposted from the road before you enter the village (coming from Troodos towards the coast).

I love this 600-year-old bridge, hidden deep in the forest and leading to nowhere. It's the best known of the surviving medieval bridges, high, elegant and beautifully symmetrical. Find it on the Troodos close-up map (from the CTO) and it gives you a sobering perspective of how long it must have taken to cross the mountains and the island on foot or by donkey or camel.

This bridge is, in fact, along one of the old camel routes, known as Kamilostrata – or Camel Road.

Camels were favoured over donkeys in medieval times as they could carry loads of between 200 and 500 kg and could travel up to 50 km a day, transporting copper from the nearby Pera Pedi mines to Pera Vasa for processing before it was taken on to Paphos for export.

The bridge is in a beautifully shady spot and children can paddle in the river (watching out for the brown and white freshwater crabs that live here). It's a lovely place for a picnic, although it does get busy with 4x4 off road excursions. The good news is they all tend to arrive at once, in the morning (as they all follow a similar itinerary).

INSIDER TIP »

The Venetian bridges of Cyprus are featured on one of the tougher nature trails, Enetika Gefyria. This is a 17-km linear trail that incorporates the medieval bridges of Elia, Kefelos and Roydia, but it's not suitable for small children – stronger teenagers, maybe! It is strikingly beautiful and virtually free of tourists. More details from the Department of Forests, *www.moa.gov.cy*.

Top Museums

Socrates Traditional House FIND ★

In the village of Omodhos.

This is an amazing little place which should be of interest to the whole family as it gives an incredible insight into how Cypriots used to live. When we went, the house was tended by one very old lady who spoke little English, but she beckoned us inside her dusty Aladdin's Cave and showed as old sepia wedding photographs, ancient toys and

Kefelos Venetian Bridge

pieces of furniture that had obviously been handed down through the family. We were the only people there and she pressed glasses of Commanderia wine on us. As there is no entrance fee and she was so helpful and enthusiastic, I felt obliged to buy a bottle!

Admission Free.

Folk Art Museum

At the centre of Arsos village, ☎ 25 943 223.

A small but interesting display in a 19th-century house of the heritage and traditions of one of the principal wine-growing villages of the Troodos. Residents of Arsos led a relatively isolated life right up to the 1960s and there's a collection of old photographs here telling their story, as well as traditional agricultural tools and old wine-making equipment.

Open 8am–1pm Mon–Fri; 3pm–6pm Thurs. **Admission** €0.43.

Child-friendly Tours

Troodos 4x4 excursions ★★★

Ascot Tours uses jeeps and has fun, well-informed drivers, ☎ 25 329 388, **www.ascotrentacar.com**.

There's no end of companies offering jeep safaris to the Troodos from the coastal resorts. I can highly recommend these for families, provided you choose the right company. Some operators use minibuses so the 'off-road' part of the day is no fun at all; choose a company that has jeeps or Land Rovers instead.

A typical tour starts off with a wine tasting and moves on to

the Kefelos Venetian bridge, Kykkos Monastery and Mount Olympus. Most of them stop for lunch in Platres and visit the Milomery Waterfall (less impressive than the Caledonia Fall) in the afternoon. In between these stops are sections off-road, along dirt tracks and with frequent pauses to find out about the island's flowers and herbs or to look at points of interest.

Admission From Limassol, adults €59.85, children €34.20.

For Active Families

Skiing on Mount Olympus

Mount Olympus gets quite a lot of snow some winters and has two short ski lifts and a handful of ski runs. I certainly wouldn't recommend making this a skiing holiday but if you're a keen skiing family, it's fun and gimmicky to say you have been to Cyprus to go skiing. You can rent ski and snowboard equipment at Sun Valley on the north face of the mountain and buy a lift pass, but don't expect anything spectacular. The snow is likely to be pretty slushy too. The season is short, from December to early March. You can also rent snowboards and cross-country skis, or book lessons: **www.cyprusski. com**.

Admission Passes: adults €14 (€ 21 per day with equipment), children €12.

Troodos Hikes ★★★ GREEN

There's no better way to admire the beautiful views and mountain forests than on foot. The whole area is criss-crossed with

Troodos Facts & Figures

- **The mountain range of Troodos is thought to be 92 million years** old. There's a theory that the birth of Aphrodite emerging from the foam of the sea is a metaphor for the geological birth of Cyprus, as it rose from the sea bed millions of years ago.
- The Troodos mountain range is the source of all the main rivers of Cyprus, water from which is trapped in reservoirs by 100 dams.
- The Troodos is home to nearly 800 different plant species, 72 of which are endemic and 12 of which are found nowhere else in the world.

walking trails, many of which are suitable for younger children.

Artemis Trail

A 7-km trail circling the summit of Mount Olympus. The trail meanders through the pine and juniper forests with the occasional dazzling views, particularly south towards Omodhos and Mandria. The walk should take up to three hours, depending on how often you stop. Take a leaflet with you from the CTO, which elaborates on all the signs stuck to trees and rocks.

As well as trees and plants, you'll see interesting rock seams, including chromite, harzburgite (no, I hadn't heard of it, either), and a thick vein of pyroxenite, rich with glittering crystals. There are quite a few exploration pits up here, where prospectors have looked for valuable minerals. You'll also cross a couple of ski runs, although in summer, these just look like fire breaks in the forest.

Trees and plants to look out for include giant 400-year-old pines, dog rose, wild sage and juniper.

There are no facilities around the trail, so take water.

Atalanta Trail AGES 8 AND UP

This is another circular trail around Mount Olympus, lower down than the Artemis Trail and therefore, longer. It's about 9 km and takes up to four hours to walk. The starting point is the Post Office in Troodos Square. Somewhat inconveniently, the trails ends short of a full circle and you have to walk along the road back to Troodos if you've parked there; it's probably a better bet for families with older children, a good picnic lunch packed and time to spare. The flora is a bit more varied than on the Artemis trail as you're lower down; look out for pine, cedar, oak, rock rose, wild plums and pears and blackberries. About 3 km from the start there's a spring from which you can drink. Children will probably be most interested in point 37 on the trail – the entrance to a disused mine. Chrome was mined here from 1950 to 1954 and again from 1973 to 1982.

Snakes in Cyprus

Cyprus has eight species of snake, three of which are poisonous and one of which, the blunt-nosed viper, should be avoided as it's danger-ous. Snakes are very shy and won't attack unless provoked; they're more likely to slither away when they hear you coming. If one rears up and hisses at you, stand completely still – easier said than done. Personally, I think it's an honour to see a live snake in the wild, although anyone who finds them lurking by a swimming pool at night might not agree (keep the pool lights on if you're worried). It is, incidentally, extremely rare to get bitten by a snake in Cyprus.

These are the **venomous** ones:

- Cat snake (*Telescopus tallax cyprianus*) Up to about 80 cm. Has a broad flat head, vertical slit eyes and large scales on the forehead. The snake is beige, brown or green, with a diamond-like pattern along its back.
- Montpellier snake (*Malpolon monspessulanus insignitus*) Has large round, lidded eyes. Markings are yellow stripes or spots on brown in young snakes and plain grey or olive in adults, with a yellowish underbelly. It kills like a cobra does, rising up off the ground and striking quickly. Its bite isn't fatal, but you should get medical help immediately if bitten.
- Blunt-nosed viper (*Macrovipera l.lebetina cypriensis*) A bigger snake, up to 130 cm and as thick as an adult's arm. Sandy in colour

Livadi Trail ALL AGES

This 1.5 km circular trail from a point on the from Troodos Square to Karvounas Road is the only trail on the island that is suitable for wheelchairs. It passes through impressive stands of pine and has lovely views, short as it is. You can take a picnic or have a cook-out at the Kampos tou Livadiou picnic site which forms part of the trail.

Moutti tou Stavrou Trail
ALL AGES

Start point is Selladi tou Stavrou, 3 km above Stavros tis Psokas at the crossroad junction of the roads to Kykkos Monastery, Stavros tis Psokas and Pyrgos.

This short 2.5-km trail is suit-able for children, and heads through the pine trees above the Stavrou tis Psokas forest station, with far-ranging views of the north and west coasts as far as Akamas.

Riding ★ AGES 12 AND UP

📞 *01582 467 468 (UK), www.ridein cyprus.com.*

A British tour operator, Ride in Cyprus, offers riding holidays along the Camel Road over the Venetian bridges of the Troodos. In summer, when it's too hot for long rides, there are shorter itin-eraries. These tours are for expe-rienced riders only but would with a blunt nose. You don't want to get bitten by this one – but the chances of seeing one are extremely slim.

Non-venomous snakes:

- The Large Whip snake (*Coluber jugularis*) Big and alarming-looking, but not harmful and the most common of Cypriot snakes. Olive-brown as a juvenile, turning blue black in maturity with lighter shading under the head. Up to 2.5 m long. This snake eats blunt-nosed vipers! It also climbs trees to raid birds' nests.
- Worm snake (*Typhlops vermicularis*) Pinky-brown in colour, like a big worm, only 30 cm long. Hides under rocks.
- Cyprus Whip snake (*Coluber cypriensis*) The only reptile unique to Cyprus. Starts life beige with a pale pink underside, turning olive green and then black in maturity, with a green tinge.
- Cyprus Grass snake (*Natrix natrix cypriaca*) A more ordinary-looking snake, ranging from light brown to black, with no distinguishing markings. It swims well, eats frogs and fish and can emit an unholy stink if frightened. It's highly endangered so you're unlikely to see one.
- Coin snake (*Coluber nummifer*) The markings of this snake are very similar to the venomous blunt-nosed viper. You can tell the difference by its bigger head with large scales, round pupils and tapering tail. Its body is shinier, too.

certainly suit families with horse-mad teenagers who could ride a horse of 15 hands in height. They're a wonderful way to see the countryside, eating in local tavernas and sleeping in village accommodation. Short rides can be tailored for family groups but these horses are not seaside ponies and you do spend several hours a day in the saddle, so they aren't suitable for small children.

Shopping

The Troodos is a wonderful region in which to shop for traditional handicrafts and products – even such simple things as honey from mountain bees make great gifts.

You could pretty well do all your gift shopping in one village, Agros, which has a fantastic range of sweet shops, deli-butchers and workshops selling rose products. Omodhos is good, too, for general souvenirs, new age items and lace from Lefkara.

Roses in Agros

In the village of Agros, you'll see rose products on sale everywhere – rosewater, rose liqueur, rose brandy, rose perfumes and aromatic rose candles – all made using traditional methods from the locally grown flowers. There's even a rose-flavoured wine. In the tavernas, you can try rosewater-flavoured puddings such as *mahalepi*, a blancmange-like substance that floats in rose-water syrup.

The biggest rose workshop is Chris Tsolakis, 12 Rose Avenue, 4860 Agros. **Credit** *MC V.*

Traditional Sweets

Agros is also famous for its sweets. There are 40 to 50 kinds of sweets in syrup, flavoured with walnut, cherry, water melon, grape, quince and rose. Workshops in the village also produce all manner of jams and marmalades, which make good presents to take home. If you miss the opportunity, buy sweets from Agros online from the mouth-watering mail order site, **www.anemoessa.com.cy**. The actual shop is in Nicosia but they will deliver internationally.

Kafkalia Ltd

Agros village, 📞 *25 521 426.*

Another product for which Agros is famous is its meat, salted or smoked and produced using traditional Cypriot recipes. In the village, look out for *chiromeri*, *lountza* and bacon. These three products are made of pork meat, wine and salt, with coriander added for the *lountza*. If you're on a self-catering holiday or planning a barbecue at one of the forest picnic sites, take some Agros sausages with you – they're delicious, made of pork, wine, salt, coriander and other spices. *Cash only.*

Tsiakkas Winery

Off the E806, before Pelendri village, 📞 *25 992 080.*

One of the most beautifully situated wineries, producing a range of reds, whites and roses, some organic, using cabernet sauvignon, Riesling and chardonnay grapes. You can taste the wine before buying, of course.

Open *Daily 9am–5pm except Sun.* **Credit** *MC V.*

Monastery of the Holy Cross

At the centre of Omodhos.

It shouldn't be the only reason to visit a monastery and I apologise for my shallowness but there's a stall inside the Holy Cross at Omodhos selling beautiful fridge magnets in the form of icons! They make an unusual gift or souvenir. The monastery at Kykkos sells them, too, but the Omodhos stall has more variety.

FAMILY-FRIENDLY ACCOMMODATION

Platres

EXPENSIVE

Forest Park Hotel ★

P.O. Box 59018, CY-4820, Platres, 📞 *25 421 751, www.forestparkhotel. com.cy.*

A local institution and the only four-star hotel in the mountains. The Forest Park has hosted government ministers and celebrities through the ages (author

Daphne du Maurier wrote much of the book *Rebecca* here when she stayed in 1936) and is the place to come if you want a resort rather than a mountain guesthouse. The hotel, which is situated amidst the pine trees outside Pano Platres, caters well for families, with an indoor and outdoor pool, children's pool, video games, table tennis and a pool table. Cycling, angling and horse riding can all be arranged through the reception. There's a bar and restaurant, babysitting and interconnecting rooms for families.

Incidentally, the thing to do here is to have a brandy sour. The drink is said to have been invented by the Forest Park's barman and served to King Farouk of Egypt in the 1940s. Now it's served all over the island.

Rooms *137, including family suites and chalets.* **Rates** *From €63.22 per person per night, B&B.* **Credit** *MC V.*

Amenities *Bar, restaurant, entertainment, babysitting, kosher kitchen (the only one on the island), three pools, sports facilities.*

Kakopetria

MODERATE

The Mill Hotel ★

Milos Street 8, Kakopetria, 📞 *22 922 536,* **www.cymillhotel.com**.

A small, stylish hotel in a former mill, as the name implies. The rooms have exposed beams, stone work and granite bathrooms with jacuzzis and the restaurant is child-friendly – and vegetarian-friendly. There's lots to do in and around the village and the hotel can also arrange mountain bike tours (although these are not suitable for small children).

Rooms *13.* **Rates** *From €41 per person per night, B&B.* **Credit** *MC V.* **Amenities** *Restaurant, bar, mountain bikes.*

Monastery of the Holy Cross, Omodhos

Linos Inn ★

34 Paleo Kakopetria Street, 📞 *22 923 161. www.linos-inn.com.cy*

Pretty inn with a restaurant and taverna attached. Some of the rooms have four-poster beds and jacuzzis – it's strangely decadent for a mountain village! There are three suites suitable for families, and the hotel also has a four-bed-room villa in the village with its own pool and screening room.

Rooms *13 and a four-bedroom villa with pool.* **Rates** *From €55 per person per night, B&B.* **Credit** *MC V.* **Amenities** *Two restaurants, sauna, garden, jacuzzis.*

Spilia

MODERATE

Marjay Inn

Spilia, 📞 *22 922 208, www.marjay. com.*

This tiny guesthouse in the village of Spilia attracts a lot of walkers as it is right on the E4 walking trail. There are only six rooms, two of which are suitable for families, with cots and children's beds on request.

The owners can arrange all sorts of wonderful activities, from guided bike tours to cookery lessons or helping out in the village with fruit picking and wine making.

Rooms *6.* **Rates** *From €27.35 per person per night, B&B.* **Credit** *MC V.* **Amenities** *Restaurant, various activities in the village.*

Omodhos

MODERATE

Stou kir Yianni ★★★ FIND

15 Linou, Omodhos, 📞 *25 422 100, www.omodosvillagecottage.com.*

A real find in the middle of Omodhos – a gorgeous little boutique hotel and funky restaurant in an old stone house, now a listed building. There are three suites in bright, contemporary shades of yellow, terracotta and lime green, with four-poster beds, living areas and kitchens, although you'll probably want to eat in the pretty courtyard restaurant downstairs, which has live music every evening. Staying overnight in Omodhos is a wonderful experience, as the atmosphere in the village is much more authentic (and calm) when all the day trippers have gone.

Rooms *Three suites with space for extra beds.* **Rates** *From €68 per person per night, B&B.* **Credit** *MC V.* **Amenities** *Bar, restaurant, extra beds for children.*

Troodos

MODERATE

Jubilee Hotel

On the E910 just north of Troodos Square, 📞 *25 420 10, www.jubilee hotel.com.*

The highest hotel in Cyprus, up in the Troodos right next to the ski slopes, so the place to be if you plan to ski in winter. The hotel was built in 1935 and has an established following. It's a two-star, with a bar and café, very conveniently located for Troodos Square, where several of the walking trails start. There are tennis courts along the road and the hotel has mountain bikes for hire. If you don't want to drive but want to stay in the Troodos, this could be the ideal base.

The hotel also runs residential summer camps for children, with adventure sports and mountain-based activities; details are on its website.

Rooms 37. **Rates** From €35 per person per night, B&B. **Credit** MC V. **Amenities** Bar, café, bicycle hire, summer camp programme for children.

Agros

MODERATE

Rodon Mount Hotel GREEN ★★

Troodos, 📞 25 420 107.

With 165 rooms, the Rodon is a big hotel for such a small village, but it's a fantastic base from which to explore the region and really family-friendly. It's also to be admired as the hotel was built by local people and is run by the local community.

Children will love it here – there's a pool, children's pool, games room, multipurpose sports court, and even a children's club. In late August/early September there are races organised here by the Cyprus Running Club, including a special 3 km course for children.

As well as a restaurant, there's a *kafenion* (a traditional coffee shop), a taverna and a gift shop selling products made in the village.

Rooms 165, including 15 four-bed family suites and six studios for disabled use. **Rates** From €33–68 per person per night, B&B. **Credit** MC V DC AE. **Amenities** Restaurant, bar, café, taverna, shop, two pools, children's club, gift shop, babysitting.

FAMILY-FRIENDLY DINING

INSIDER TIP ▷

In towns and rural areas, look for tavernas with a Vakhis certificate. Vakhis was a famous chef who lived on the island in 300 AD and these certificates are a sign that the restaurant is deemed by the CTO as being authentic and traditional, using local ingredients to prepare seasonal dishes.

Platres

MODERATE

Psilo Dendro

Off the main road above Platres at the foot of the Caledonia Trail, 📞 25 813 131.

Fancy some fish and chips? This is the place to come. Attached to the restaurant is a trout farm so there's nowhere better for fresh mountain trout, cooked on a big barbecue. The restaurant is cavernous but very friendly and has a big menu of all the usual Cypriot specialities – but the trout is the reason to come here. Book a table for lunch and walk the Caledonia Trail to work up an appetite.

Open Daily 11am–5pm. **Main course** Trout from around €9.90. **Credit** MC V.

Skylight Café

Pano Platres, ☏ *25 422 244.*

A taverna with its own swimming pool, guaranteed to be a hit with children. Serves all the usual Cypriot dishes as well as baked potatoes.

Open *Daily lunch and dinner.* **Meze** *From €11.50.* **Credit** *MC V.*

Kakopetria

Mesostrato Taverna

Palaias Kakopetrias 47, Kakopetria, ☏ *22 924 700.*

Part of the quirky, boutique Linos Inn in Kakopetria village, the restaurant serves a huge meze and a slightly less huge meze using village halloumi and locally smoked sausage, as well as more unusual dishes like ostrich and mountain trout. There's a pizzeria/café on site, too, should your children be tired of Cypriot dishes!

Open *Daily lunch and dinner.* **Meze** *From around €11.50.* **Credit** *MC V.*

Mill Hotel

Milos Street 7, Kakopetrias, ☏ *22 922 536.*

The restaurant at this unusual stone-and-wood village hotel has dining on a shaded deck offering amazing views over the rooftops and in winter, open fires inside. The menu is eclectic, with some fantastic vegetarian dishes like stuffed red peppers with spicy

hot feta cheese, or grated carrots with sesame seeds and yoghurt. In addition, there are burgers, pasta, mountain trout, pancakes and banana splits.

Open *Daily lunch and dinner (closed 20th Nov–20th Dec).* **Main course** *From around €10.* **Credit** *MC V.*

Omodhos

Taverna Ambelothea

☏ *25 421 366.*

This big, friendly taverna just outside the village has a sunny terrace and in winter, log-burning fires inside. The owner's wine is served alongside generous, tasty meze and lots of local meats.

Open *Daily 10am–11pm.* **Main course** *From around €9.* **Credit** *MC V.*

Stou Kir Yianni

15 Linou, Omodhos, ☏ *25 422 100,* **www.omodosvillagecottage.com.**

Seek this out for classy rustic cooking in a gorgeous setting of a pretty stone courtyard, with lots of emphasis on local ingredients – beans, pulses, okra and mountain trout as well as all the usual favourites and fresh fruit from the family's own orchards. There are burgers and omelettes for children who are meze-d out, and there's live music every night.

Open *Daily breakfast, lunch and dinner (separate menu in the evenings).* **Meze** *From around €17.* **Credit** *MC V AE DC*

7 Larnaca

LARNACA

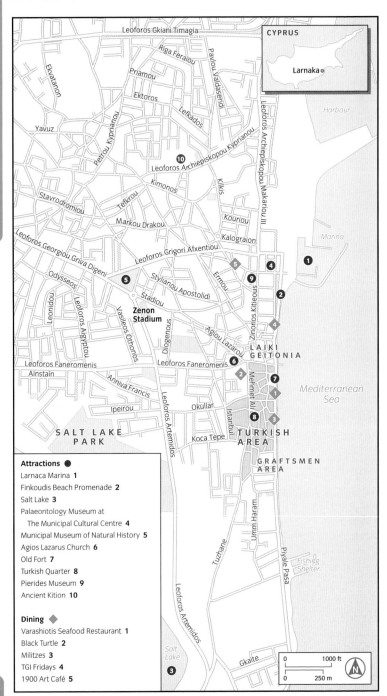

CYPRUS

Larnaka ○

Leoforos Gkiani Timagia

Riga Feraiou

Priamou

Ektoros

Lefkados

Pavlou Valdaserai

Ekvatanon

Yavuz

Petrou Kyprianou

Leoforos Archiepiskopou Kyprianou

10

Leoforos Archiepiskopou Kyprianou

Kimonos

Kilkis

Stavrodromiou

Tefkrou

Markou Drakou

Kouriou

Kalograion

Harbour

Leoforos Archiepiskopou Makariou III

Marina

Leoforos Georgiou Griva Digeni

Leoforos Grigori Afxentiou

5

4

1

Odysseos

Leonidiou

Leoforos Aigyptou

Vasileos Othonos

5

Stylianou Apostolidi

Stadiou

Zenon Stadium

Diogenous

Zinonos Kitieos

Errou

9

2

4

Agiou Lazarou

6

LAIKI GEITONIA

Leoforos Faneromenis

Ainstain

Leoforos Faneromenis

Anniva Francis

Leoforos Artemidos

Ipeirou

Okullar

Mehmet Ali

2

7

1

Mediterranean Sea

SALT LAKE PARK

Koca Tepe

Istanbul

8

3

TURKISH AREA

CRAFTSMEN AREA

Umm Haram

Tuzhane

Piyale Pasa

Fishing Shelter

Salt Lake

Gkaite

3

Attractions ●

Larnaca Marina **1**
Finkoudis Beach Promenade **2**
Salt Lake **3**
Palaeontology Museum at
   The Municipal Cultural Centre **4**
Municipal Museum of Natural History **5**
Agios Lazarus Church **6**
Old Fort **7**
Turkish Quarter **8**
Pierides Museum **9**
Ancient Kition **10**

Dining ◆

Varashiotis Seafood Restaurant **1**
Black Turtle **2**
Militzes **3**
TGI Fridays **4**
1900 Art Café **5**

0   1000 ft
0   250 m

N

The first and sometimes only glimpse people get of Larnaca is from the air, as this is the principal gateway to Cyprus. The town sprawls around a wide bay and has a faintly Middle Eastern feel, dry and dusty in the summer, and its waterfront lined with palm trees and the minarets of mosques piercing the otherwise low-lying skyline.

Larnaca serves many purposes. It has a large expatriate community, not all of them British, although Brits are attracted to the sunny climate and the fact that Larnaca has a slightly more authentically Cypriot feel than places like Paphos. Several foreign consulates are located here, as it's more accessible and a bit cooler than Nicosia, the capital, and quite a few people who work in Nicosia choose to live in and around Larnaca and commute.

Why stay here? Well, there are several excellent family hotels to which people return year after year. The town centre has a certain buzz and a wide sandy beach flanked by a long pedestrian promenade, not dissimilar to something you might find in the south of France. The beaches of Ayia Napa and Protaras are an easy day trip away and inland are some of the most beautiful and unspoilt villages on the island.

There is a certain poignancy about the area. Here, more than anywhere else, you can see the devastation caused by the 1974 Turkish invasion. Whole villages which used to be Turkish have been deserted, their mosques standing lonely and forlorn.

Although Larnaca has an interesting and colourful history, its archaeological sites can't compare to those of Paphos. What's more, its natural attractions are limited.

What you will find, though, are friendly people and a good international mix of tourists. It also has a drier climate than in the west, which can be an advantage if you're travelling with your family outside the main summer season.

ESSENTIALS

Getting There

By Air Larnaca International Airport is the island's main point of entry, served by flights from all over Europe. The airport is situated to the west of the town by the Salt Lake and has a motorway connection to Limassol and on to Paphos and Nicosia. From the airport to the hotels around Larnaca Bay takes about 20 minutes.

By Car All the main car hire companies have representation at Larnaca airport and it's easy to get from here to the downtown area or to the rest of the island. Limassol is about 40 minutes away; Paphos about 80 minutes and Nicosia under an hour. The motorway also goes all the way to Ayia Napa in the other direction and the journey takes about one hour, meaning that Larnaca is well placed for visiting pretty well all of Cyprus.

By Boat Larnaca has its own yacht marina at 34° 55' 05" N / 033° 38' 29" E, which is an official port of entry. There is mooring for 420 yachts but the marina is pretty over-subscribed so book ahead if you plan on arriving by boat.

📞 *24 653 110, telex 4500 CYTMAR. VHF: Listening: Ch16 Working Ch8.*

VISITOR INFORMATION

Orientation

Larnaca town is fairly easy to navigate although there is a cluster of small, winding streets at the centre and some complicated one-way systems. If you get lost, just head for the waterfront. The airport is to the west of the town and the main area of hotels to the east of the bay. The best town beach stretches from the old fort which is by the oldest part of the town to the yacht marina and is called Finikoudes promenade.

Getting Around

Larnaca has a fairly good bus system. Buses 22 and 24 regularly run to the airport and at the eastern end of the main promenade by the yacht marina there is a terminal for the inter-city buses, which serve Limassol and Nicosia. Just a little further from here, past the post office, is the terminal for PEAL buses, which operate into the Troodos

Mountains. Buses to the main hotel area around the bay leave from just opposite the Pierides Museum.

Larnaca also has plenty of service taxis and regular cabs can be hired from taxi ranks. Always make sure the meter is switched on before you start your journey.

It's also possible to arrive at Larnaca by boat if you are in your own yacht.

Child-friendly Events & Entertainment

Anthestiria in Larnaca

The Anthestiria Festival is a celebration of spring and nature's rebirth. A parade of floats and people carrying beautiful, fresh flowers fill Larnaca's seafront promenade and lots of local children take part.

May.

Kataklysmos

Kataklysmos is a uniquely Cypriot Festival celebrated all over the island but nowhere more so than Larnaca. The word actually means 'flood', and the six-day celebration combines the Orthodox holiday of Pentecost with commemoration of the Great Flood described in the book of Genesis in the Bible.

There are all sorts of events related to water from sailing regattas to swimming contests, as well as dance, drama and poetry readings. Fairgrounds set up all along the seafront in Larnaca and there is a general holiday atmosphere, culminating in fireworks in the evenings. It's a great family occasion and you shouldn't miss it if you are on the island.

50 days after Easter, for six days during May or June.

Kypria Festival

Island-wide cultural festival with ballet, opera, cinema, art, theatre and music. In Larnaca, performances are held at the Patticheion Amphitheatre. Some are accessible to children – for example, world-class touring ballet companies. You can see a list of performances online and book tickets in advance.

Sept–Oct. ☏ 24 665 795, www.kypria festival.com.

WHAT TO SEE & DO

Children's Top 10 Attractions

❶ **Riding a camel** at the Camel Park at Mazotos. See p. 159.

❷ **Poking around** ancient Neolithic houses and graves at Chirokitia. See p. 161.

❸ **Learning to make** halloumi and help the villagers harvest oranges and olives with Cyprus Villages. See p. 165.

❹ **Peering close up** at the birds, animals and insects of Cyprus at the Natural History Museum. See p. 163.

❺ **Going wild** at the funfairs at the Kataklysmos festival in summer. See p. 154.

❻ **Cycling** along the seafront of Larnaca. See p. 165.

❼ **Choosing** your own fish from the display in the fish tavernas (for the adventurous child). See p. 170.

❽ **Pedalling** a pedalo or trying a banana boat ride in Larnaca Bay. See p. 156.

❾ **Waking up to the sound of braying donkeys** during a stay in a traditional stone house.

Colourful beach café, Larnaca

⑩ **Trying to count** the flamingos on the Salt Lake. See p. 158.

Beaches & Villages

Larnaca Bay

A cluster of upmarket hotels stands on the bay east of Larnaca in the area called Voroklini. There's nothing as such to do or see here, but if you're staying, the beaches are nice enough – sandy and gently shelving – and there's a handful of tavernas and shops catering to the hotel guests.

The water is clean here but there's one blot on the landscape in the form of a large oil refinery. After a few days, you'll get used to it!

Larnaca Waterfront ★

Larnaca's main promenade, backing Finikoudes Beach, stretches for about 800 m, a strip of wide, sandy beach and gently shelving seabed, ideal for children. You can find pretty well anything on this beach, including sunbeds, umbrellas, banana boat rides, parascending and pedalos for hire. The beach is backed by a long line of restaurants, all of which have outdoor seating. There are also several bars, of varying degrees of trendiness, which come to life in the late afternoon. The best thing about this beach is that it has a real buzz about it in the evenings when locals come here after work to swim, stroll and have pre-dinner drinks. The beach is busy right up until midnight and is perfectly safe to walk around on at night.

Closer to the old fort is a string of fantastic fish restaurants right on the water, a reminder of how Larnaca used to be when it was just a humble fishing port.

McKenzie Beach

This is a sizeable stretch – 1 km – of greyish sand to the west of the town centre, running almost as far as the airport. It's not quite as bad as sitting under the flight path to Heathrow, but there is considerable aircraft noise and, inevitably, pollution. Still, the beach has sunbeds and umbrellas, watersports and a long string of cafés, tavernas and tourist shops. There are lifeguards and despite the proximity of the airport, the water and sand quality are such that the beach has Blue Flag status.

Kiti Beach

Kiti Beach is much quieter, far from the madding crowds of downtown Larnaca, a long strip of pebbles and sand starting a few kilometres beyond the salt lake and extending to the remote lighthouse at Cape Kiti. There's more of the same the other side of the lighthouse. You'll find fewer facilities here but there are tavernas on the beach. Don't be put off by the stones; the seabed is sandy and shelves gently. There are a couple of small hotels here, one of which, the Faros Village, is particularly family friendly (see p. 168).

You'll see a Venetian watchtower, dating back to the 16th century, perched on an outcrop just inland from the lighthouse. It's been restored, although there is nothing inside.

Lefkara ★★★

The lace-making village of Lefkara is one of the most popular day trips from any part of Cyprus. The village is an easy drive from Larnaca on the Nicosia–Limassol motorway, or there's one bus every day (Mon–Sat) from Plateiou Agia Lazarou, by the St Lazarus church.

The village is very pretty (in fact there are two, Pano Lefkara and Kato Lefkara) although packed with tourist buses in summer. A lot of EU funding has gone into renovating the facades of the old buildings and improving the pavements. Wizened old ladies in black sit outside their shops, embroidering intricate lace table cloths (and creating excellent photo opportunities if you ask politely first), and every other shop sells lace made in the village. Those that don't do lace sell silverware, also made in the village.

The story goes that the ladies in the past took up lace-making to supplement their incomes while their husbands were at sea or working in the fields. Those men in the village who couldn't take on heavy manual labour became silversmiths. Local lore claims that Leonardo da Vinci visited and took some Lefkara lace back to Italy, thus starting a fashion for Lefkara lace.

Kalavasos ★

This lovely, whitewashed village is a prime spot for agrotourism development and a lot of houses have been renovated with grants to take paying guests. The village, on the banks of the Vasilikos river about 40 km from Larnaca, made its money from copper mining until 1972 and one of the trains that used to haul the ore is still here, posed on an abandoned stretch of railway and beautifully lit at night – a rare sight in Cyprus, which has no working railways. The Neolithic site of Tenta (see p. 161) is an easy drive from here.

Tochni ★★ FIND

Perched in the hills off the Limassol–Larnaca motorway (and very complicated to find, I might add, from personal experience), Tochni has also been subject to a lot of renovations and is as idyllic as villages come – narrow, cobbled streets, gorgeous old stone houses built around gardens (some with swimming pools), bougainvillea spilling

Lefkara, the famous lace-making village

Bishop Lazarus & the Salt Lake

There is a local legend that the lake was created by the Bishop Lazarus, as a punishment to a local woman who was carrying some grapes. Lazarus asked her if he could have some grapes to eat and when she refused, he turned her vineyard into a useless, salty lagoon in a fit of pique – pretty ungrateful behaviour for someone who had already been raised from the dead!

over stone walls and a couple of sleepy tavernas. If you don't need the facilities of a big hotel, rent a house with a pool and use this tranquil place as your base, with just donkeys braying and cocks crowing to wake you up in the mornings (see p. 169).

Kofinou & Kornos
If you're driving towards Nicosia, it's worth taking a brief detour off the main road to visit these two small villages where pottery is made. Kofinou has rather a sad history as it used to be a Turkish village and the Turkish section is now abandoned and boarded up. The village does, however, have some good tavernas where you can try the local *kleftiko*, very slow cooked lamb or goat baked in a special oven. A few kilometres further along the road, villagers living in Kornos also make pottery out of the local clay, which you can buy at several shops.

Zygi
The little fishing village of Zygi has almost, but not quite, escaped the developers and is relatively unspoiled, famous for its fish tavernas and long ago, as a port from which carob was exported.

If you're doing the Camel Park at Mazotos, drive down here afterwards for lunch or dinner.

Natural Wonders & Spectacular Views

Larnaca Salt Lake
If you arrive in summer, the Salt Lake is nothing but a dust bowl but in winter it's a different story. The lake fills with water and from January onwards, thousands of flamingos arrive from as far away as Turkey and Iran. They are an amazing sight, cutting a swathe of dazzling orangey-pink across the lake as they stand in the shallow water feeding on shrimp.

The flamingos begin to depart at the end of March, the final flocks leaving as late as June. Walking along the Salt Lake is very pleasant in the winter months and you'll find orchids growing under the pine trees.

The salt lake used to be used for commercial salt production but the proximity of the airport and resulting pollution means that the salt is no longer good for human consumption, so the lake is purely decorative nowadays.

Aquaria & Animal Parks

Camel Park ★ ALL AGES

Mazotos village, very well signposted from the B4 coast road between Larnaca and Zygi.

The Camel Park is a great day out for children; I've never seen such plump, friendly camels. This probably stems from the fact that you can buy bags of carob pods at the entrance, which they love – a kind of camel candy.

The camels are kept in a large paddock and you can choose between rides around the paddock or the park, or a ride out on the beach for all the family.

In addition to the camels, there is a playground with bouncy castle and a petting zoo set around a big model of Noah's Ark. Part of the park is a very family-friendly taverna with its own swimming pool surrounded by lawns, so you can easily make a day of it.

Open 9am–5pm winter, 9am–7pm summer. Admission Adults €3, Children €2, which is deducted from the price of camel rides of €9 and €6, respectively. Amenities Swimming pool, restaurant serving Cypriot specialities and burgers/sandwiches, petting zoo, play area.

Drapia Horse Farm ★ FIND
AGES 5 AND UP

Near Kalavasos, west of Larnaca, ☏ 24 332 998, www.cyprusvillages. com.cy.

Excellent riding centre near Kalavasos, offering lessons, one- or two-hour rides out, half-day and full-day treks through the

Resident of the Camel Park, Mazotos

countryside. The horses are in fine condition, some of them beautiful Arabians, and riding is English or Western style.

Children can ride but if you want to go out on a more advanced hack, the farm staff will look after them for up to two hours and teach them about the care of ponies and donkeys, cats and dogs. There are weekly packages, too, for anybody wanting to learn from scratch.

Historic Buildings & Monuments

Hala Sultan Tekke ★
This lonely mosque, which perches on the edge of the Larnaca Salt Lake, is regarded as one of the holiest places in the world of Islam. The mosque was founded in 647 AD when Umm Haram, an aunt of the Prophet Mohammad, broke her neck falling off a mule during an Arab raid on Cyprus and died. She

was buried here and a mosque built in her memory.

The original mosque is no longer here but today's structure stands in a little oasis of date palms, cypress and olive trees and is a peaceful place visited by Cypriots and foreign Muslims as well as the occasional tourist. You can go inside the mosque and see the sarcophagus of the aunt at the back as well as the slabs of rock that marked the original grave. Although it's not of immediate interest to children, most six year olds have begun to study world religions at school and may be familiar with the layout of a mosque.

Ayios Lazaros Church

Town centre, between the original Turkish and bazaar areas.

The church dedicated to Lazarus dates back to the ninth century, when his remains were found on the island of Cyprus and the church built in his honour.

The Bible says that Jesus raised Lazarus from the dead, after which he (Lazarus) was expelled by the Jews and put in a leaking boat, which was washed up on Cyprus, where he became a bishop.

The current structure dates back to the 17th century. There is much to see inside, the main attraction being an icon of Lazarus emerging from his tomb after resurrection. His remains were supposedly housed in the crypt but they were taken to Constantinople in 901 and have since turned up in France.

Open *8am–12.30pm April–Aug; 8am–12.30 pm and 2.30pm–5pm Sept–Mar.*

The Turkish Quarter and the Old Fort

Larnaca once had a sizeable Turkish community and the former Turkish quarter stretches all the way from the Lazarus church to the fort, although the old

Ayios Lazaros Church

town is such a jumble of streets that it's difficult to discern where one neighbourhood ends and another begins.

You'll see the mosque, Cami Kebir, which is much used today; Larnaca still has a large Muslim population. The chunky fort stands at one end of Finikoudes promenade, right on the waterfront. The fort was actually built as the castle by the Lusignans and adapted by the Turks in 1625. There's very little inside now; just a small museum. The inner courtyard is sometimes used the parties in summer.

Open 9am–7.30pm Mon–Fri June–Aug; 9am–5pm Mon–Fri Sept–May.

Kition

It's a great tragedy that Larnaca has been built bang on top of the ancient city of Kition, which dates right back to the 13th century BC. Sporadic excavations are carried out but there is really not very much to see.

Kition was famous its time thanks to its harbour, from which goods from Cyprus were exported all over the Mediterranean.

It was also an important naval base and you can actually see part of the old dockyards (*neoria*), at the foot of Pamboula Hill. It's really quite difficult, though, to figure out what's what and the site will be of limited interest to children. There is one area that is vaguely organised, known as Area II, where you can look down upon the excavations from a raised walkway.

Open 8am–2.30pm Mon, Tues, Wed and Fri; 8am–5pm Thurs. Closed Sat and Sun. Admission €1.71.

Choirokoitia ★ ★ AGES 5 AND UP

Off the E133, near Tochni.

This fascinating excavation of a Neolithic settlement reveals one of the oldest archaeological sites in Cyprus. Children will be intrigued by the strange habits of the Choirokoitians, who lived here in an unusually large community of about 2,000 in 6800 BC. Their huts were made of stone and clay and shaped like beehives and the dead were buried in convenient, underfloor graves beneath the huts, going down several layers for large families. Each corpse was surrounded by gifts and personal effects.

Walkways guide you around the site, which is built into a hillside and surrounded by a defensive wall, and there are some reconstructed 'beehive' houses so you can see how people used to live. Excavations suggest that the village residents were successful goat breeders and also indulged in spinning, weaving and pottery. They worshipped fertility gods and wore necklaces made of shells and cornelian.

Open Daily 9am–5pm Nov–Feb; 9am–6pm Mar, Apr, Sept and Oct; 9am–7.30pm May–Aug. Admission €1.71.

Tenta

Signposted from Tochni and Kalavassos.

Smaller than Choirokoitia, Tenta is another Neolithic village, this time believed to have accommodated about 150 people in circular mud and stone structures, some flat-roofed and some round-roofed. Although the village is close to Choirokoitia, its inhabitants had different burial practices, rather casually leaving their dead outside the houses, where skeletons have been found amidst the household waste.

Open *10am–4pm, Mon–Fri.* **Admission** *€1.28.*

Stavrovouni Monastery

This spectacularly sited monastery, perched high up on a rocky peak 10 km off the Larnaca–Nicosia road, has close ties to the famous Mount Athos monastery in Greece. Stavrovouni, which means 'Mountain of the Cross', was, according to legend, founded in the fourth century by St Helena, mother of Constantine the Great, who donated a fragment of the cross on which Jesus died to the monastery when her ship was wrecked off the Cypriot coast.

Women aren't allowed into Stavrovouni and men and boys who want to visit must be modestly dressed. But if you do want to go and wait outside, the views are stupendous.

There is another monastery, Agia Varvara, at the foot of the hill which is open to all visitors; you can buy icons here painted by the monks.

Open *(Stavrovouni) Daily 8am–12pm and 2pm–5pm Sept–Mar; 8am–12pm and 3pm–6pm Apr–Aug.*

Ayios Minas Monastery

Very close to Lefkara, this monastery is run by nuns who specialise in icon painting. You can see the nuns at work and buy very beautiful reproduction Byzantine icons on the spot.

Top Museums

Pierides Museum ★
AGES 5 AND UP

Zinonos Kitieos, Larnaca, 📞 *24 652 495.*

This is the oldest privately owned museum in Cyprus, set up by local philanthropist, Dimitrios Pierides (1811–1895), in a bid to protect the antiquities of Cyprus from being plundered by archaeologists and foreigners in high office. The collection includes a vast range of objects belonging to the family dating back to prehistory and covering the Iron Age, Roman occupation, Byzantine, Crusader and Ottoman periods. There is a mixture of pottery, glassware and a colourful display of Cypriot folk art.

Open *9am–1pm and 3pm–6pm Mon–Fri 1st Oct–14th June; 9am–1pm and 4pm–7pm Mon–Sat, 9am–1pm Sun 15th June–30th Sept.* **Admission** *€1.71.* **Amenities** *Shop.*

Archaeological Museum
On the seafront promenade, 📞 *24 630 169.*

The Archaeological Museum is pretty similar in content to the Pierides Museum, with a collection of pottery, glassware and folk art. Children may enjoy the

Larnaka Municipal Cultural Centre

reconstructed Neolithic hut and tomb from Choirokoitia.

Open *9am–5pm Mon–Sat; 10am–1pm Sun.* **Admission** *€1.71.*

Larnaka Municipal Cultural Centre

Plateia Evropis-Seafront promenade, 📞 *24 658 848.*

A cultural centre in a series of old warehouses containing the island's only palaeontology museum, where you can see the fossilised remains of pygmy elephants and hippopotami that once lived on the island.

Open *10am–1pm and 5pm–8pm Tues–Fri; 10am–1pm Sat.* **Admission** *€1.71.*

Municipal Museum of Natural History ★ AGES 5 AND UP

Approximately 500 m north-east of the Archaeological Museum, in the Municipal Gardens, 📞 *24 652 569.*

A small but worthwhile introduction to the island's fauna and flora, with displays of rare insects, birds, animals, rocks and plants. Pay a visit here before you venture into the countryside – it'll help you identify species in the fields and mountains. The museum is understandably popular with local schools and children seem to love it.

Open *10am–1pm and 4pm–6pm Tues–Sun 1st June–30th Sept; 10am–1pm and 3pm–5pm Tues–Sun 1st Oct–31st May.* **Admission** *€0.35.*

Traditional Museum of Embroidery and Silver Smithing

Patsalos Residence, Lefkara, 8 km from Skarinou, off the Lefkosia–Lemesos road, 40 km from Larnaca.

This little museum in the lace-making village of Lefkara describes the local history of silversmithing and lace embroidery.

Open *9am–5pm Mon–Thurs; 10am–4pm Fri–Sat.* **Admission** *€1.71.*

Child-friendly Tours

Walking Tours of Larnaca

The CTO offers free guided walks every Wednesday from the CTO office on Vasileos Pavlou Square, leaving at 10am. The walk covers the history of Larnaca and the role the sea has played in the city's development.
☎ 24 654 322 for more information.

Self-Drive Tour of the Central Plain ★

This is one of the routes recommended by *Rural Cyprus*; you can pick up the book with maps in it from the CTO.

The drive, a good day trip covering about 80 km, starts at the village of Kellia, north of Larnaca, and goes through Troulli, Avdellero, Petrofani, Dali, Perachorio, Pyrga, Ayia Anna and Kalo Chorio.

There are several highlights along the way. After Kellia, take a detour to Agios Georgios Monastery, also known as Mavrovouni after the black rock which surrounds it. The village of Athienou is famous for its milk and in the village you'll find various shops selling halloumi and yoghurt. The village bakeries also produce Athienitiko bread, baked on flat stones, so try to get some for a picnic lunch.

At Dali, you can visit the archaeological dig of Ancient Idalion, while in Kornos, there are several pottery shops selling goods made from clay from the area.

In Pyrga, the tiny chapel of Agia Ekaterina has a little slice of Cypriot history inside; there's a

portrait of the Lusignan king, Janus, and Queen Charlotte, and the church itself dates back to 1421.

Ayia Anna is a pretty little village with traditional houses, some of which have been beautifully restored, and a Vakhis taverna – a certificate that means the taverna produces authentic, slow-cooked Cypriot food.

The Old Coast Road ★

This is another self-drive itinerary, heading west from Larnaca along the coast and inland to Tochni. Full details and directions are in the *Rural Cyprus* booklet from the CTO.

The first time I drove this old coast road, I was swept away by its beauty. This is one of the few parts of the island where there is no development on the beach – just kilometres of uninhabited, pebbly beaches on one side of the road and tomatoes, cucumbers and artichokes growing in the fields on the other. Houses are beginning to spring up here, so see this lovely, unspoiled part of the island while you still can.

You can start this tour at the Hala Sultan Tekke Mosque if you haven't already seen it, and admire the flamingos on the salt lake (see p. 158) if you're doing it in winter. Stop for a visit to the Camel Park at Mazotos and take a detour inland to Agios Theodoros, a village that's been partly abandoned. The drive back to the coast from here is through the Pentaschoinos Valley, filled with orange groves, dark cliffs towering over the road.

Zygi is a fantastic place for lunch because of its fish tavernas, right on the beach. The village used to be a trading port and you'll see old stone warehouses where carobs used to be stored after being brought here on camel trains.

Maroni village has some impressive traditional architecture and there's a dig going on outside the village to uncover a 16th-century BC settlement.

Tochni, an inland hill village, is absolutely lovely, with some wonderful agrotourism accommodation – I'd recommend spending a few nights here (see p. 169). Children should also enjoy the nearby Neolithic settlement of Choirokoitia (see p. 161).

Cycling Tours and Village Fun
★ ★ GREEN FIND AGES 5 AND UP

📞 24 332 998, www.cyprusvillages. com.cy.

The wonderful agrotourism company Cyprus Villages has a bike hire centre in Kalavasos with adults' and children's bikes and will arrange family cycle tours combined with traditional village activities, so children can have a go at halloumi-making or assist with the olive or orange harvest, depending on the time of year.

For Active Families

Cycle Ride to Meneou
AGES 8 AND UP

For families with older children, there's an easy, flat cycle ride all the way from the tourist beach to the Hala Sultan Tekke Mosque,

or further if you want to carry on. From the far end of the tourist beach to Meneou, just beyond the mosque, is 18 km. Just follow the coast – there's a cycle path by the road when you get to Larnaca port. Cycle all the way along Finikoudes Promenade (stopping for a swim if you like), past the castle and turn westwards onto the airport road (left at the lights). Go past the airport roundabout and turn right towards the mosque. There is a restaurant and picnic site in the wood here and you can walk around the shore of the salt lake for a bit.

Rock 'n' Bowl Bowling Centre

7081 Pyla, Larnaca, 📞 24 822 777.

Always a good bet on a rainy day! There are 15 bowling lanes, with bumpers for small children (and hopeless adults) and the unusual feature of 'glow bowling' in the dark with fluorescent equipment. Also has fast food, a play area, video games and a bouncy castle.

Open Daily 10am–12am.

Shopping

Larnaca has a decent array of shops, although they're spread all over the town. You'll see labels like Mango, Fendi, Diesel and more prosaically, Marks & Spencer. If there is one main shopping street, it's Zenon Kitieos, which crosses Ermou, another good location. Here, there are masses of jewellery

Tolerance

Racism is an extremely sensitive subject in Cyprus. On an island famed for its hospitality, xenophobia has no place. But Cypriots have enormous national pride and the very essence of the country – the famous Cypriot hospitality – is being undermined in the eyes of many by the need to import foreign workers. Ten years ago, all the workers in a hotel would be Cypriot. Today, they're from Russia, Bulgaria, Romania and any number of other, mainly East European countries, as are labourers on building sites and petrol pump attendants. Now that Cyprus is a member of the EU, the foreign workforce is likely to expand further. Some Cypriots openly express dismay about this – but the jobs need to be filled.

There's also an ongoing problem of the ingrained suspicion and in places, hatred, of Turkey. Having said this, though, Turkish Cypriots do live in the southern part of the island in villages alongside Greek Cypriots. There is a genuine desire to solve the Turkish 'problem'. Visitors should find Cyprus a conservative and patriotic but essentially easygoing, friendly place to visit.

shops and an unusually large array of opticians; as with elsewhere in Cyprus, glasses here are a great buy, so don't pass these by if you need a new pair.

Look out for ceramics in the former Turkish quarter south of the fort on the streets of Akdeniz and Bozkurt; you can buy pretty tiles and other objects straight from the workshops here.

Athos

39 Grigoris Afxentiou Street, Carithers Building, ☏ 24 626 256.

This fascinating shop, an outpost of the ultra-devout Mount Athos Monastery in Greece, sells Byzantine and church music, Greek and English religious books, carvings, incense, jewellery and even wine.

***Open** 9am–7pm.* ***Credit** MC V.*

Emria Pottery

13 Mehmet Ali Street, ☏ 24 623 952.

There's an array of mugs, vases, plaques and reproduction items in this pottery shop. The owner will show you round the workshop, so it's quite interesting for children.

***Open** 9am–6pm.* ***Credit** MC V.*

Koukli

26 Filiou Zanetou Street, ☏ 24 655 627.

This gift shop sells generally very tasteful knick-knacks but is particularly good for scented candles and picture frames.

***Open** 9am–6pm.* ***Credit** MC V.*

Kition Coins & Antiques

9 Gladstone Road, ☏ 24 817 597.

A quirky shop selling old coins, banknotes, stamps, books,

antiques and albums, mostly related to the time when Cyprus was a British colony. A valuation service is offered here, too.

Open 9am–6pm. *Credit* MC V.

Kornos Pottery

2 Agioplaston Street, Kornos, 📞 *22 533 712.*

Pottery made in the village of Kornos from local clay – everyday things for the home as well as reproduction items based on original designs.

Phone to see if it's open. *Credit* MC V.

Physis

Merica Building, 44 Hakket Street, 📞 *24 665 900.*

A brilliant organic and health food shop where you can stock up on baby food, essential oils, herbal remedies, gluten free and soy products – essential shopping if a member of the family is on a special diet.

Open 9am–6pm. *Credit* MC V.

FAMILY-FRIENDLY ACCOMMODATION

Larnaca – Voroklini

EXPENSIVE

Palm Beach Hotel ★★

📞 *24 846 600, www.palmbeach hotel.com.*

The *grande dame* of Larnaca hotels, an institution to which people return year after year. The beach itself may be a thinnish strip but the gardens are shaded by a palm grove and the rooms are spacious and elegant. Families might prefer the Garden Studio Bungalows, which have their own pool and in summer, a separate restaurant. Otherwise, there's a choice of four places to eat and several bars – I had a stupendous fish meze in the taverna here. Children have their own pool, waterslide and playground and there's a children's menu in the restaurant – even children's buffets from time to time.

Rooms 228. *Rates* From €92.71 per person per night. *Credit* MC V DC AE. *Amenities* Children's club, pool, fitness centre, massage, tennis, squash, table tennis, several bars and restaurant, beach with watersports, wedding chapel (that also does christenings).

Golden Bay Hotel ★★

📞 *24 645 444, www.goldenbay.com.*

Large, elegant five-star hotel on the beach, with lawns sloping down towards the sea. Interiors are contemporary. The hotel is popular with families but also attracts a lot of conference groups. Four restaurants (we particularly liked the Yacht Club, outside on a warm wooden deck), various bars, children's club, indoor and outdoor pools, scuba diving.

Rooms 192, several interconnecting. *Rates* From €179.40 per night;. *Credit* MC V DC AE. *Amenities* Children's club, pool, fitness centre, massage, several bars and restaurant, beach with watersports, wedding chapel.

Lordos Beach Hotel

☎ 24 647 444, www.lordosbeach.com.cy

An attractive, if a bit blocky, four-star with spacious grounds and a landscaped pool next to a wide, sandy beach. The whole hotel was refurbished in 2006. The big highlight for young children here is the Treasure Island mini water park with slides and a paddling pool, next to a playground. There are two restaurants, one with children's menus, and three bars.

Rooms 173. *Rates* From €98 per room per night. *Credit* MC V DC AE. *Amenities* Children's club, pool, fitness centre, massage, tennis, several bars and restaurant, beach with watersports.

Larnaca – West

MODERATE

Flamingo Beach Hotel

1523 Piale Pasha St, Larnaca, ☎ 24 828224, www.flamingobeachhotel.com.

A laid-back three-star on McKenzie Beach, handy for the wide, sandy strip and beach facilities. There's a rooftop swimming pool, restaurant, bar and café. All rooms have air conditioning. There are no children's facilities like a club, but the location is great for beach-loving families who prefer to be out of town a bit.

Rooms 64. *Rates* From €51 per person per night. *Credit* MC V DC AE. *Amenities* Pool, bar, restaurant, café, video games.

Larnaca – Pervolia

MODERATE

Faros Village

Faros Avenue, Pervolia, ☎ 24 422 111, www.farosvillage.com.

This holiday village, 15 minutes outside Larnaca on the very tip of Cape Kiti, has a peaceful location right on the beach. Accommodation is in bungalows, in spacious rooms mainly on the ground floor. There's plenty to do – tennis, swimming, watersports, scuba diving and beach volleyball – with a regular activity programme including things like boules contests and archery. Children are entertained in a mini-club and there's also an art studio. Meals are all buffet, with different themes and regular entertainment.

Rooms 134. *Rates* From €45 per person per day, half board, including soft drinks and wine. *Credit* MC V. *Amenities* Various sports, watersports, mini-club, bicycle hire, shop.

Pano Lefkara

MODERATE

Hotel Agora ★

☎ 24 342 901

A small hotel in the village centre set around a leafy garden and pool, with tables in its restaurant overlooking the street. There's a cosy lounge with books and PlayStation. Stay here and soak up the atmosphere of the village after the tour buses have gone.

Rooms 19. *Rates* From around €60 per room per night. *Credit* MC V. *Amenities* Swimming pool, babysitting, restaurant, bar with fireplace.

Lefkarama Village Hotel ⋆

On the street next to the church, ☏ *24 342 154, www.lefkarama.com.*

The friendly British owners of this stone-built hotel can help arrange horse riding, fishing and mountain biking. It has simple but pretty rooms and a large, shaded courtyard for eating and sunbathing.

Rooms *10, including one family suite.* **Rates** *From around €50 per room per night.* **Credit** *MC V.* **Amenities** *Babysitting, restaurant, courtyard.*

Choirokoitia

INEXPENSIVE

Porfyrios Country House ⋆⋆
FIND **GREEN**

☏ *25 366 622, www.filokypros.com.*

The only inn in the village of Choirokoitia, near the Neolithic settlement, is a gorgeous agro-tourism project. An old stone house has been converted into six self-contained suites, big enough to be considered apartments, really, clustered around a decent-sized pool in a pretty courtyard. It's completely private and the suites are amazing, combining traditional features like wooden beams, stone floors, loft rooms and in one, a galleried bedroom, with modern conveniences. They're wonderfully cool inside. I'd recommend this as a real alternative to the coast – perfect for exploring the hill villages and the Troodos and not too far from the bigger towns for day trips. The village is sleepy but beautiful, with tavernas and shops.

Rooms *Six suites, two interconnecting. Each one sleeps three plus cot.* **Rates** *From €60 per studio per night.* **Credit** *MC V.* **Amenities** *Fully equipped kitchens, private bathrooms, pool with towels provided.*

Tochni

INEXPENSIVE

Eveleos Country House ⋆⋆
GREEN

☏ *25 366 622, www.filokypros.com.*

The sister property to Porfyrios (see above) is a similar setup, in a restored stone house with 10

Porfyrios Country House, Choirokoita

studios and apartments grouped around a pool in a sun-drenched courtyard. The village is as pretty as they come, and attracts a lot of artists as well as holidaymakers in search of a more authentic experience – there are a lot of agrotourism projects here.

Rooms 10 suites, from studios to one two-bedroom. Rates From €50 per studio per night. Credit MC V. Amenities Fully equipped kitchens, bathroom, satellite TV, pool, pool towels, balcony or terrace.

Kalavasos

`INEXPENSIVE`

Takis House ★ `GREEN`

📞 *24 332 998, www.cyprusvillages. com.cy.*

Takis House is just one of the properties of Cyprus Villages, all of which are agrotourism projects and range from village apartments in stone houses to villas with pools. This one is good for families as it's bigger than most, with six one-bedroom and three two-bedroom apartments. There are walking, fishing, cycling and riding nearby and Cyprus Villages can arrange village activities – halloumi making, lessons in moussaka preparation, orange and olive picking, or even a boat trip with a fisherman. The company also owns the Tochni Taverna, where its reception is located, and from here, you can book treatments in a small day spa.

Rooms Nine apartments. Rates From €700 for a week for four people in a two-bedroom apartment, including hire car, although you could take a

one-bedroom apartment for €581 and have a child on a sofa bed for free. *Credit MC V. Amenities Fully equipped kitchens, bathrooms, air conditioning, pool and taverna nearby, village activities, day spa in Tochni.*

Agioi Vavatsinias

`INEXPENSIVE`

Pavlis House ★

📞 *23 340 071, www.agrotouism. com.cy.*

A fantastic, stone-built house in a mountain village west of Larnaca famous for its wine and unusually, silk production. Pavlis House comes complete with its own little museum and winery and the owner, Mr Pavlos, makes *zivania*, the local firewater. There are three double bedrooms around a common living area and kitchen and a decent sized pool – perfect for a larger family or a small group of six. Mr Pavlos also owns a taverna in Lefkara, which you will be encouraged to visit!

Rooms Three plus space for cots. Rates From €43 per room per night. Credit MC V. Amenities Kitchen, air conditioning (optional), pool, terrace, suitable for disabled, tavernas and shops nearby, walks from doorstep.

FAMILY-FRIENDLY DINING

Larnaca

`EXPENSIVE`

Varoshiotis Seafood ★

7 Piyale Pasha Street, 📞 *24 655 865.*

Seek out this classy seafood restaurant for a more special occasion rather than a casual lunch, with a huge fish meze, individual fish dishes and some pasta on the extensive menu. I'd come here for dinner, with older children who can sit through a long meze in the evening. It's right on the water and has a romantic, cosy atmosphere.

Open Daily 12pm–11.30pm. Advance reservations essential. **Main course** Around €12–24. **Credit** MC V DC AE.

MODERATE

Black Turtle ★

Mehmet Ali 11, ☎ 24 650 661.

A great choice for vegetarians, with lots of unusual veggie dishes, as well as good fish meze (fortunately not including turtle) and regular Cypriot dishes. There's live music Wednesdays and Saturdays, sometimes with dancing.

Open 8pm–1.30am Tues–Sat. **Credit** Cash only. **Main course** From around €11.

Militzes Restaurant

Piyale Pasha 42, ☎ 24 655 867.

Right on the seafront, this is a typical taverna, with chequered tablecloths and a laid-back feel. Come here for a break from fish meze – the oven-baked stews are fantastic and there was a certain satisfaction to getting a nine year old to try goat (and like it)!

Open 12.30pm–12am Mon–Sun. **Main course** From around €9. **Credit** MC V.

TGI Friday's

Athinon Avenue 38 42, ☎ 24 816 666.

Reserve this for when your children go on meze strike, or when you secretly crave a basic steak or a decent burger. It's fun and funky, like all TGI Friday's, and in a good location right on Finikoudes beach. The puddings are enormous and you can wash down your Sizzling Shrimp with a giant-sized Margarita if you're so inclined.

Open Daily 12.30pm–1.30 am. **Main course** From around €8.03. **Credit** MC V.

INEXPENSIVE

1900 Art Café

Stasinou 6, ☎ 24 653 027, **www.art cafe1900.com.cy**.

This quirky café-restaurant in a renovated old house serves Cypriot favourites and snacks. The walls are adorned with the work of local artists and there's a fire in winter. Children should like some of the more comforting dishes like meatballs, stuffed vegetables and chicken in different sauces.

Open Daily 6pm–1am. Advance reservations essential. **Main course** from €7.69. **Credit** MC V.

Tochni

MODERATE

Tochni Tavern

In Tochni village, ☎ 24 332 998, **www.cyprusvillages.com.cy**.

The agrotourism company Cyprus Villages owns this

The Cyprus Flag

Ironically, the Cypriot flag symbolises peace among the two communities living there (Greeks and Turks). The map of the island is golden/yellow, in honour of the copper mines that gave the island its name. The white background denotes the colour of peace, as do the green olive branches.

traditional taverna. The views are gorgeous, across the village rooftops towards the sea, so try to get a table on the terrace. Food is slow-cooked according to traditional recipes, so make the most of the kebabs, *stifado* or *koubebia* (stuffed vine leaves) as a change from the ubiquitous fish.

Open *Daily, lunch and dinner.* **Main course** *From around €12.* **Credit** *MC V.*

Zygi

MODERATE

Captain's Table

Grigoris Afxentiou 28 ☎ *24 333 737.*

The best of the Zygi fish tavernas, patronised by Cypriots from all around the area. There are plenty of seats right by the water and the fish meze is fabulous, with huge portions.

Open *Daily 11am–11pm. Book ahead.* **Meze** *From around €20.52.* **Credit** *MC V.*

Loizos Koubaris Fish Taverna

Grigori Afxentioui, ☎ *24 332 450.*

You'll find this fish taverna right on the beach in Zygi, ideal for a laid-back lunch and a swim. Plenty of families dine here. Book ahead if you want a table by the sea.

Open *Daily 11am–11pm. Advance reservations recommended.* **Meze** *From around €18.* **Credit** *MC V.*

Kato Drys

MODERATE

Platanos Taverna

Kato Drys, 10 minutes from Lefkara, ☎ *24 342 160.*

Small village taverna in the shade of a huge plane tree. The restaurant is a good alternative to the busier places in more touristy Lefkara and is famous for its lamb and onion stew.

Open *Daily lunch and dinner.* **Main course** *From around €12.* **Credit** *MC V.*

8 Ayia Napa & Protaras

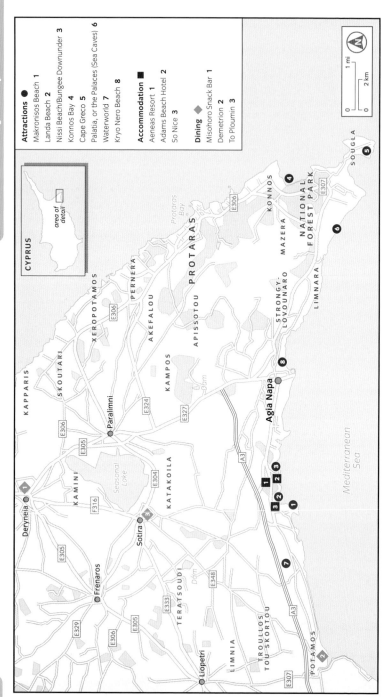

Attractions ●
Makronisos Beach **1**
Landa Beach **2**
Nissi Beach/Bungee Downunder **3**
Konnos Bay **4**
Cape Greco **5**
Palatia, or the Palaces (Sea Caves) **6**
Waterworld **7**
Kryo Nero Beach **8**

Accommodation ■
Aeneas Resort **1**
Adams Beach Hotel **2**
So Nice **3**

Dining ◆
Misohoro Snack Bar **1**
Demetrion **2**
To Ploumin **3**

CYPRUS

area of
detail

The eastern end of the island is a stark contrast to the forested mountains and more peaceful resorts of the west, although it does have a beauty of its own, with a rather arid landscape of deep red soil dotted with windmills, and soft, sandy beaches fringing bays of amazingly aquamarine water.

People come here for sun and fun, packing out the hundreds of nightclubs and bars, dancing till dawn and sleeping off their hangovers on the beach for most of the next day. In fact, early morning is the best time to get a spot on any of the beaches as most visitors under 30 are still in bed.

The area was really only developed for tourism after the Turkish invasion of 1974, when the much nicer beaches of Famagusta to the north were suddenly cut off, depriving the island of its main resort. The small fishing village of Ayia Napa grew and grew, sprawling as far as the British military base to the west and the beautiful and remote Cape Greco to the east. Meanwhile, the inland town of Paralimni began to extend its own tentacles to the coast as the beach resort of Protaras began to grow.

The explosion in cheap package holidays and the rise of the clubbing scene of the late 1990s, combined with a string of TV reality shows starring Ayia Napa and its excesses all led to the rise of the resort's fame. Unfortunately, the publicity wasn't all good and Ayia Napa developed a reputation as a place dragged down by lager louts, assisted by the bad behaviour of some British squaddies, who were eventually banned from the bars and clubs. Nowadays, things are marginally quieter, and the scandals are fewer and further between, partly due to the Cypriot government's zero tolerance of drugs.

In my opinion, the best time for families to come to this area is early and late season, so April/May and September/October, when it's less crowded, the locals are in a better mood and you can still enjoy fantastic sunshine and make the most of the beautiful beaches.

If you've got very young children and want nothing more than to splash around in the shallows, you probably won't stray very far, but if you're feeling slightly more adventurous, you can enjoy the best of both worlds and have plenty of beach time combined with a few forays inland towards the Troodos, Nicosia, Larnaca and some of the hill villages.

ESSENTIALS

Getting There

By Air The nearest airport is Larnaca, served by a wide variety of international airlines and from airports all over the UK. The drive takes about one hour. Flying into Paphos is not really an option if you are staying in the east unless you are prepared for a transfer time of nearly two hours.

By Car The drive from Larnaca is easy. Leave the airport and join the A3 motorway which goes around the outskirts of the town and heads east straight through the British military base. The motorway ends at Ayia Napa but if you are carrying on to Paralimni and Protaras, both are clearly signposted along the E327.

VISITOR INFORMATION

The CTO office in Ayia Napa is at Leoforos Kryou Nerou 12, ☎ 23 721 796. There's also an office in Protaras, at Leoforos Protara, Kavo Gkreko 356, ☎ 23 832 865. If you've got time, pick up maps first at Larnaca airport – there's a booth there and you will need a local map if you're renting a car.

Orientation

Getting around Ayia Napa is fairly easy as there are only three or four main roads. You could argue that the old monastery forms the centre of the town and indeed, this is where the main pedestrianised area is, its heart known as the Square. Much of the action, however, is along the roads where the hotels are.

The E309, Leoforos Nissi, runs east–west while Leoforos Archbishop Makariou runs north–south from the monastery and Square to the port. A lot more hotels are along Leoforos Kryou Nero, which runs from the centre to the east and the beach of the same name.

Paralimni is actually located inland; its beach area merges into Protaras and is strung out along the east coast that begins around the point of Cape Greco from Ayia Napa.

A little way to the north of this is the town of Deryneia, which has little of interest other than serving as a viewing point into the occupied north and the 'ghost town' area of Famagusta, controlled by the United Nations and frozen in time from the day of the invasion in 1974. Now that Cypriots can freely cross the border, however, this is of less interest than it used to be.

INSIDER TIP ▶▶

Don't be surprised to see the area referred to as 'Ammokhostos' – this is the Greek-Cypriot word for 'Famagusta' and although Famagusta itself is occupied by Turkey, the east of the Republic is still referred to as the 'Famagusta area'.

Getting Around

Public transport in Ayia Napa is not very good, although you can use local buses. There are regular direct buses to and from Larnaca and one a day to Nicosia, although its timings are not great for a day trip as the return bus leaves mid-afternoon. Buses (☎ 23 821 318) run on the hour to Protaras and Paralimni and all of them leave from the bus stop between the square and the harbour at Leoforos Makariou III

32A. In Paralimni, the bus stop is at Agiou Georgiou 12.

There is a taxi rank close to the Square but there are no service taxis in this area. Most people get around by motorbike, although this is obviously not ideal when you have children in tow. Your best bet is to hire a car if you intend to explore the area.

Child-friendly Events & Entertainment

Kataklysmos

Kataklysmos, or Festival of the Flood, marks the day of Pentecost, 50 days from Greek Easter. It's an excuse for rock bands, partying, food stalls and water sports around Ayia Napa harbour. If you're here for the festival, a water pistol for your child is an essential accessory!

Ayia Napa puts on a three-day celebration over a long weekend that includes traditional dances, poetry and singing at the harbour.

Pentecost, during May or June.

Beach Volleyball National Tournament

Organised by the Cyprus Volleyball Federation at Protaras, this is a fairly glamorous and action-packed sport, well worth watching.

June. ☎ 22 663 603, www.volleyball.org.cy.

Ayia Napa Cultural Winter

The Cyprus Tourism Organisation is keen to promote Ayia Napa as a year-round resort (which it currently isn't) and lays on cultural events every Thursday in winter, from dance to concerts.

See the CTO for details.

Ayia Napa Festival

Ayia Napa throws a big cultural festival in the last week of September every year, with all the action in the Square in front of the monastery. There's folk dancing, classical and pop music, opera, drama, art exhibitions and stalls selling traditional Cypriot folk art. It's a great time to be here – a real reminder that there's more to Ayia Napa than clubs and pubs.

Last week of Sept.

WHAT TO SEE & DO

Children's Top 10 Attractions

❶ **Hanging on tight** for a high-speed RIB Safari around Cape Greco with cliff jumping. See p. 189.

❷ **Trying out** or just watching the madcap activities on the Slingshot and the Skycoaster. See p. 188.

❸ **Cooling off** at the waterpark. See p. 188.

❹ **Getting up close to the** marine life at the Marine Life Museum. See p. 186.

❺ **Riding a donkey** in the hills. See p. 187.

6 Paddling in the shallow water of Nissi Beach. See p. 179.

7 Learning to snorkel in the clear water off Konnas Beach. See p. 180.

8 Taking a day trip to the north to see how Turkish people live. See p. 184.

9 Cycling to Cape Greco to admire the view. See p. 184.

10 Walking on the sea floor with Undersea Walkers. See p. 189.

Beaches & Resorts

Ayia Napa

Ayia Napa. What can I say? Famed as Europe's second clubbing capital after Ibiza, the whole resort is dedicated to decadence and excess. Your teenagers will no doubt thank you for bringing them here, although whether you want to let them out at night unattended is another matter.

What are the good points of Ayia Napa? Well, there's no shortage of entertainment, from people-watching to cooling off in the waterpark to the extreme Luna Park where thrill-seekers flock to the expensive but amazing rides. The beaches around here are some of the best in Cyprus – and also some of the most crowded.

The tourist office offers a couple of guided walks which are worth doing if you can persuade your children. Each takes about three hours. 'The Ayia Napa You Don't Know' visits the old aqueduct, the monastery, a couple of churches, the Museum of Marine Life and a traditional coffee shop, and includes a ride on an old wooden bus.

'Ayia Napa and the Sea' is a walk around Cape Greco, a coffee stop at the fishing harbour (there's a wooden bus involved in this tour, too) and a visit to the Roman tombs at Makronissos. Book either tour in advance through the CTO.

Harbour, Ayia Napa

Nissi Beach

The main *raison d'être* for Ayia Napa is, of course, the beaches. Starting west of the town and heading eastwards, the best family beaches are described below.

Makronissos Beach

Makronissos beach is 5 km west from the centre of Ayia Napa, connected to the resort by a cycle path and road. It's more a string of bays than one long beach, with soft yellow sand, watersports galore, cafés and lifeguards on duty. The beach itself is nice enough but it is popular for beach parties at night and may be strewn with bodies sleeping off the excesses for most of the morning. It is, however, quieter than Nissi Beach down the road.

For a break from the beach, explore the Makronissos Tombs, an excavation of 19 rock-cut tombs, used during the Roman period. Archaeologists believe the dead were placed in clay sarcophagi that were originally covered with three flat tiles. The tombs had a rectangular entrance originally closed with one or two slabs. There's not a huge amount to see but it's an interesting site, nonetheless.

Landa Beach

The next beach along heading towards Ayia Napa, Landa is fringed by smart hotels and although it's a decent size, still gets very busy. Still, if you're staying here, it's quieter than next door Nissi Beach, the heart of the action. Expect the usual array of sunloungers, umbrellas and watersports.

Nissi Beach

Nissi Beach takes its name from the little island offshore (Nissi means island) and is one of the finest and most popular beaches in the area. There is a cluster of large hotels here, which means it is almost always crowded but there are plenty of distractions. As well as enjoying the soft sand and a gently shelving seafloor, you can sit and watch the antics of the Bungee Downunder customers for hours, speculating about which victim is going to be dunked head first in the sea.

This is also the best beach for people-watching, if you're so inclined, and seems to attract the better-looking tourists. One thing to remember is that the beach is never quiet; a line of beach bars thumps out music all day long and the afternoon may be punctuated by a foam party. It's not the place to go if your baby needs a nap after lunch.

Ayia Thekla

A small Blue Flag beach about 3 km west of Ayia Napa, with golden sand and lifeguards on duty. Watersports are available on the beach and you can walk there from the road. It's a little quieter than Nissi Beach.

Sandy Bay

Between Nissi and Ayia Napa there's a string of smaller, sandy beaches in an area broadly known as Sandy Bay. Vathia Gonia is about 500 m east of Nissi Bay, followed by Pernara

beach as you head further east towards the town centre, and the rocky Katsarka, which extends to the fishing harbour. All of these are backed by large hotels and apartments, and all get busy, but the sand is nice enough and the water shallow and calm.

Kryo Nero

This is the main town beach, stretching about 1 km east from the centre towards Cape Greco. Although it's sandy, it's nothing special for families and it tends to be packed with people who are staying in the centre, here for the nightlife and not inclined to stray much further than their own front door. Needless to say, there is no shortage of facilities including snack bars, watersports and shops.

Konnos Bay ★ ★ ☆

Konnos Bay is one of the finest beaches in the east of the island, quiet, relatively undeveloped and only accessible to people who can be bothered to make the

Konnos Bay

Fig Tree Bay

journey out of town. It does, of course, get busy, especially from mid-morning when the day tripper boats tend to arrive, but there is usually space for everybody. The beach has a small café where you can get lunch and a watersports centre. The sea, a dazzling shade of turquoise, is very sheltered here and a really good place to start teaching children to snorkel.

Protaras

Protaras is supposed to be the upmarket side of Ayia Napa and it's true that the clubbing scene is less frenetic here, making the resort more suitable for families. This does not mean it's quiet, though; development here has not been especially sensitive and the resort seems to have very little greenery and far too much concrete.

Although it has plenty of facilities and things to do, I find it quite stressful with the endless cacophony of bars showing English television, shops selling tacky souvenirs and plastic

things on the beach and restaurants serving 'international' cuisine with little concession to the fact that you're on the island of Cyprus.

Having said this, the beaches are good, the sea is clean and you can't fault the climate. If you're just looking for an undemanding beach holiday and are not that bothered about seeing the real Cyprus, Protaras should fulfil your needs.

Fig Tree Bay

Fig Tree Bay is the main beach area of Protaras and you can imagine how lovely the beach must have been before the rash of development that has largely scarred this landscape. Pretty well at the centre of Protaras, it's worth a visit, though, for the idyllic setting – a stretch of golden sand, clear, calm water, shade from one ancient fig tree and a little island offshore to which you can swim. There are lifeguards and plenty of facilities. In peak season, the setting is marred somewhat by ranks of sunloungers.

Ayia Triada

This is the northernmost beach before you get close to the Turkish occupied zone. It's relatively quiet, small and stony with shallow water and gently shelving seabed, making it good for children provided they have jelly shoes. There are a couple of tavernas and the usual water-sports facilities.

Louma

The main beach of Pernera Bay, Louma is sheltered by rocky cliffs. The beach is fairly quiet as it is a little out of town, away from the main action of Protaras. There's actually some shade here, at the northern end of the beach and if you clamber around the southern end, there are a few more sheltered coves and quieter places. The sand here is lovely, soft and fine, and the water clear and shallow, so it's perfect for small children.

Green Bay

This small beach is less crowded than some of the others due to its lack of facilities. Get there early to bag a spot – the northern end is sandy, and to the south there sandstone rocks on which you can bask and climb around.

Kokkinokhoria ★

These so-called red villages in the hinterland of Ayia Napa get their name from the rich, red earth that surrounds them, prime potato-growing country.

It is from here that Cyprus exports potatoes, particularly to the UK. There isn't a huge amount to see, although it is a pleasant contrast to the coast. The red landscape is gently rolling, punctuated by windmills and the occasional stone-built village. As well as potatoes, you'll see carrots, citrus fruits and *kolocassi*, a strange root vegetable with huge elephant-ear leaves.

There are five villages to explore, Xylofagou, Avgorou, Frenaros, Liopetri and Sotira. They are all reasonably pretty and each one has a café and a least one taverna as well as a church, although there isn't anything of particular interest to children who are generally more focused on the beaches in this part of Cyprus.

The Cave of the 40 Martyrs

Near the village of Xylofagou, a cave set into the cliff east of Cape Pyla has an interesting local legend attached to it. The story goes that 40 martyrs of the Orthodox church were buried here in the 16th century, Christian soldiers in the Roman army who chose to die rather than renounce their faith when the Ottomans invaded the island. Bones have actually been found in a cave, but not belonging to human beings – just long-extinct animals. You can't go into the cave because it's dangerous but you can see it in the cliff face as it's a huge space, some 40 m high.

Living in Cyprus

Have you fallen in love with Cyprus? Some 50,000 Brits love the island so much that they have made it their permanent home. They represent a sizeable chunk of the overall population, which is only 788,000.

It's not just retired people who move to Cyprus. Plenty of young families emigrate to start a new life in the sun, attracted by the climate, the friendly people, the healthier lifestyle and the property prices, which are lower than those in the UK (although higher than in some other sunny destinations).

Popular enclaves where Brits buy houses include Pissouri, Tala, Mandria and Oroklini as well as the suburbs of the main resort towns. There are international schools in Larnaca, Nicoisa, Limassol and Paphos, all of a good standard, and plenty of local schools if you want to try immersing your children in the Greek language.

A property purchase is a big impulse buy, though! If you are serious about buying and moving to Cyprus, there are several golden rules.
Come back several times to see the island at different times of year. Shop around extensively. Do not be sucked into the estate agents' hosted 'inspection trips', where your expenses are paid but there's a very heavy sell. Think about where you want to live – urban or rural? Do you want a pool? Modern house or stone-built villa?

Talk to local expats, look at schools and think about what you might do to earn a living. With the right permits, you can certainly work here but make sure your skills would be needed.

Finally, *never* buy property in the north without a thorough understanding of title deeds and sound legal advice to go with it. There are huge legal implications concerning land ownership prior to the Turkish invasion of 1974 and when the island is eventually reunified, you could have a battle on your hands to prove that your dream home actually belongs to you.

Dherinia

This sad place is a stark reminder that Cyprus is still a divided island. The main reason for visiting here is to use the hilltop location as a vantage point from which to stare into the so-called dead zone, the area towards Famagusta, a resort that was once the pride and joy of all Cypriots. The UN-controlled suburb of Varosha is a spooky sight, frozen in time from 1974, the construction cranes untouched for more than 30 years.

There are several cafés and tavernas here with viewing platforms and binoculars for hire.

This is not to say Dherinia itself is a ghost town; you'll see hoardings from property

Ayia Napa Monastery

developers all over the place and clusters of white holiday villas under construction.

Dhekelia Base

The British sovereign base area in the east of Cyprus at Dhekelia occupies a large area from the east of Larnaca all the way up to the western fringes of Ayia Napa, extending north to the Attila line. The base isn't just occupied by the British military; several thousand Cypriots also live here and quite a lot of the land is farmland.

Before the motorway was built, it was easy to go and drive around for a sneaky look, but most people now bypass the area as the motorway skirts around the outside.

What's interesting about the eastern sovereign base area is that it abuts the Green Line and there is no UN buffer zone here,

so its inhabitants stare straight into the occupied North. Turkish Cypriots from the North can move freely across two border points, although these crossings are not available to tourists. Despite the more relaxed atmosphere nowadays, you should still only use the official crossings.

Sites of Natural Beauty

Cape Greco ★★★

The far south-eastern tip of the island, Cape Greco is undeniably beautiful and a real escape from the crowds of the big resorts. You should definitely make a trip here, either driving, cycling (for which you will need bikes with good tyres as the track is fairly rough) or with older children, walking the 7 km from

Ayia Napa or 4 km from Protaras.

The coastline here is studded with sea caves, rock platforms and tiny coves and the sea is astonishingly clear. Paddling is fine but swimming is not always safe because of high winds. You can't actually get right down to the Cape because of a lighthouse and a British military installation, but the views are stunning. If you want to spend the afternoon here and need more facilities, head a little distance north towards Konnos Bay.

Palatia ★★

The Palaces, as it's known in English, is a dramatic stretch of coastline to the east of downtown Ayia Napa heading towards the point that ends in Cape Greco. There are no beaches here as such but impressive stacks and arches, sea caves and slabs of white, flat rock, dazzling against aquamarine sea. The best way to enjoy the scenery with children is to take a boat trip.

Historic Buildings & Monuments

Ayia Napa Monastery
AGES 5 AND UP

Historic monuments are thin on the ground in this area but if you are in Ayia Napa, do take a look at the old monastery, which dates from the Venetian era of 1489 to 1571. The monastery is a tiny haven of tranquillity amidst the mayhem and was actually built around an old

church dating back to the eighth or ninth century. It's cut into the rock and is partly underground. You can see the original well inside, which still contains water.

The monastery hasn't been used for many years but there is a small chapel in the gatehouse, used by various local religious communities as a place of worship, the building itself serving as a conference centre.

Children may be interested to know that the two trees in front of the monastery, sycamore figs, a species mentioned in the Bible, are supposedly more than 600 years old.

Open Winter 9.30am–3pm, summer 9.30am–9pm. **Admission** Free.

Top Museums

Thalassa Museum ★★ FIND
AGES 5 AND UP

Leoforos Kryou Nerou 14, Ayia Napa, 📞 23 721 179.

This is a worthwhile museum situated in the centre of Ayia Napa, in a striking building of marble, onyx, wood and metal. It's not an aquarium, but rather an exhibition of the marine environment and its relationship to the island, on six levels including audio-visual displays depicting the history of Cyprus. There's also a life-sized replica of a 4th-century Greek trading ship, *Kyrenia II*, that sunk off the coast of Kyrenia.

Open 9am–1pm Mon, 9am–5pm Tues–Sat, Oct–May; 9am–1pm Mon, 9am–1pm, 6pm–10pm Tues–Sun

June–Sept. **Admission** Adults €3, children €1. **Amenities** Gift shop, cafeteria, amphitheatre for presentations.

Marine Life Museum

Town Hall, central Ayia Napa, trying to find out www.pieridesfoundation. com.cy.

A small, privately-run museum in the Town Hall, owned by the philanthropic Pierides Foundation and sponsored by Hellenic Bank.

The museum includes a reconstruction of the sea bed from prehistoric times, with fossils of shells, sponges, corals, ammonites of the late Cretaceous period, 65 to 130 million years ago. There are also displays of shells, sea and lake birds, and underwater life, as well as stuffed fish and turtles (all of which died naturally – nothing was removed live from its environment for the museum). There are also some aquaria with living fish.

Open 9am–2pm Mon–Fri, 9am–1pm Sat. **Admission** Adults €1.71, children €0.85. **Amenities** Gift shop.

The Farm House AGES 5 AND UP

Monastery Square, Ayia Napa.

Completely incongruous in the middle of the resort, this recreation of an old farmhouse is built from mud bricks, with traditional arches inside. The rooms are a step back in time, with antique furniture, old tools, a weaving loom and outside, a tread-wheel, plough and a traditional oven.

Child-friendly Tours

Essentially, you can get anywhere from the east, including Paphos and Akamas (see chapter 3), but it's quite a long way. With children, the best bet is tours to Nicosia, the Troodos, the north and maybe Larnaca. I wouldn't suggest Paphos from here unless you want to start your day with a two-hour transfer.

Thalassa Museum, Aiya Napa

Troodos Excursions

Eman Tours, 32A Makarios Avenue, Ayia Napa, 📞 *23 721 321, www. emantravel.com.*

This tour makes a day trip to Nicosia, the Troodos Mountains and the wine-growing town of Omodhos. It's quite a long journey on the bus but there are several stops for children to run around and explore.

Admission From Ayia Napa, adults €26, children €13, excluding lunch.

Famagusta Half-Day

Eman Tours, 32A Makarios Avenue, Ayia Napa, 📞 *23 721 321, www. emantravel.com.*

A full day to the north might be a bit much for small children but Eman Tours offers half-days to Famagusta to see the magnificent Venetian walls, the historic centre, the main mosque (formerly an orthodox church) and the UN-controlled 'ghost town'. There's time for a swim, too.

Admission From Ayia Napa, adults €29, children €14.50.

Catamaran Cruises ⭐

Interyachting, Protaras, 📞 *25 811 900, www.interyachting.com.cy.*

Relaxing family-themed catamaran cruises from Protaras make a great day out away from the beach. You cruise towards Famagusta Bay, stopping for swimming before lunch, coming back late afternoon under sail, wind permitting. There are evening cruises and family day cruises, too, with a magician to entertain children. Buffet lunch is included and the wine flows. The price includes a coach pickup from most of the big hotels.

Admission Full day: adults €75, children €36, family €179.

Argonaftis Animal Park Donkey Safaris ⭐

📞 *25 586 333, www.argonaftis.com.*

This scenic farm-park is about 20 minutes from Ayia Napa amidst the 'red villages', on a hill right by the side of the Achna Dam reservoir, with a wonderful view of the lake.

The place combines a donkey sanctuary (except the donkeys work here as well as being cared for) with a mini-zoo, housing horses, goats, sheep, mouflon (see p. 138), pigs, rabbits, squirrels, snakes and ostriches.

The excursion includes samples of Cypriot specialities like halloumi and village bread, followed by a gentle trek on donkeys (children can have a lead rein) to a 14th-century church dedicated to Agios Giorgios. The trek is followed by dinner and festivities, with bouzouki music and dancing. In winter, it's a daytime activity with lunch, and in summer, an evening event – really worth it, despite fairly large numbers.

Admission Adults €69, children €38, including transfer, snacks, donkey trek, dinner or lunch with wine, and musical entertainment.

For Active Families

Bungee Downunder
AGES 13 AND UP

Nissi Beach, 📞 *99 605 248.*

A great spectator sport at Nissi Beach, where a 60 m crane towers above the blue Mediterranean, just inviting you to be hoisted to the stop, trussed up in a rubber rope and encouraged to leap off... Teenagers can't get enough of it, of course, and there's a barbecue and bar at the bottom, creating a party atmosphere. The operation is Australian-run and has an excellent safety record.

Open *9am–6 pm in summer; night-time jumps in peak season.* **Admission** *€76.92 per jump.*

Thrill Rides **AGES 13 AND UP**

Luna Park, centre of Ayia Napa.

My children can't wait till they're old enough to try this thrill-seekers' paradise on the waterfront in Ayia Napa, although nothing on earth would get me on the Skycoaster, a kind of giant bungee/trapeze/swing that allegedly makes you feel like Superman flying.

Its neighbour, the Slingshot, is even more terrifying, and pretty well does what it suggests, resembling a backwards bungee jump. There's also an Aerodium, which is slightly more bearable and gives you the impression of free-falling as you bounce around like a boiling egg on a huge upward jet of air. Needless to say, all children love this place and as a spectator attraction, I find it mesmerising.

There are tamer rides for smaller children, including a ferris wheel and bumper cars.

Skycoaster 📞 *99 891 251,* **admission** *€20.51 per ride.* **Slingshot** 📞 *99 640 608,* **admission** *€20.51 per ride.* **Aerodium admission** *€34.18 per ride.*

WaterWorld ⭐

18 Ayia Thekla, Ayia Napa, 📞 *23 724 444.*

Ayia Napa's WaterWorld claims to be the biggest themed waterpark in Europe and without doubt is a great place to cool off on a hot day. You'll find all the usual attractions here, from terrifying slides to watery flumes and a giant wave pool, all designed around a theme of ancient Greece.

There are some really good things for small children, including the Minotaur's Labyrinth, a totally dry attraction, essentially a giant soft play area. There's a huge family raft ride and Trojan Adventure, a children's mini-waterpark.

The whole family can play in the Atlantis activity pool, in which you have to make your way across the water on a series of rolling logs and slippery lily pads.

There are plenty of places to eat, including a fast-food outlet, a self-service restaurant, a creperie, ice-cream parlour and a fish and chip shop.

Open *Daily 10am–6pm May–Oct.* **Admission** *Adults €17.09, children €10.25; entrance price varies according to where you buy the ticket.*

Protaras Fun Park

In the heart of Protaras next to Paschalia Hotel, ☏ *23 833 889.*

A smaller effort than WaterWorld in Ayia Napa but still good for cooling off, with the usual array of flumes, lazy river rides and pools.

Raptor Sea Safari AGES 4 AND UP

☏ *96 596 938, www.manic-ribs.com.*

Yet another thrill ride, this time on the water, clinging to a powerful RIB (rigid inflatable boat). There's a three-hour safari, suitable for four year olds upwards, which is actually rather nice, passing all the best beaches, the sea caves, Cape Greco lighthouse, Konnos Bay and up to the Famagusta area.

Speeds on this one are not too terrifying and there are lots of stops for swimming, cliff-jumping, fish feeding and watching the undersea 'walkers' at De Costa Bay. A drink and snack are included and snorkel equipment is provided.

There's also a 'speed ride' of just 20 minutes (all most people can take), up to 100 kph with terrifying turns and wave-jumping, suitable for teens but not small children.

Departures *Daily 10am and 1.30pm, in season.* **Admission** *Three-hour trip: adults €39, children under 12 €19.*

Undersea Walk AGES 8 AND UP

Da Costa Bay, ☏ *96 537 613, www.underseawalkers.com.*

A gimmicky and somewhat expensive experience but one that has a certain allure... if you've never dived before, this is a great way of experiencing the undersea world, walking on the sea bed 3 m down wearing a self-contained helmet, into which air is pumped.

Children over eight or taller than 1.20m can participate and you don't need to be able to swim. There's a bit of marine life in De Costa Bay and fish usually approach the 'divers'.

A new addition is the underwater BOB, a scooter with attached helmet. A trip on this lasts 30 minutes in the company of an instructor, so anybody over 13 can have a go and play James Bond.

Admission *Adults €52, children under 16 €42; BOB costs €70. 15% discount for booking online.*

Cycle Hire

Rainbow Rentals, 46 Nisiou Avenue, Tequila Block A, Shop 3 Ayia Napa, ☏ *23 721 878.*

Several of the hotels rent bikes but this rental company has decent quality children's bikes, road bikes and mountain bikes. Most people ride scooters round here but there is pleasant cycling on the flat. If you want to go to Cape Greco, get mountain bikes with proper rugged tyres.
Open *9am–6pm.*

Shopping

Ayia Napa and Protaras are packed with shops but it tends to be lots of the same. Endless jewellery stores sell gold and watches at good prices, while there's a fair amount of fashion and clubbing gear on sale in small boutiques, particularly around the Square in Ayia Napa. Shops open until 11pm every night except Sundays.

The best time for browsing is after sunset in the Square, when stalls appear selling jewellery, pottery, leather goods and Lefkara lace. I've found that this is a really nice time to take children out for an early supper and stroll, to sit and have a drink or ice cream, people-watch a bit, shop and then retire.

FAMILY-FRIENDLY ACCOMMODATION

Practically all the accommodation in the Famagusta area is sewn up by tour operators, who will offer inclusive packages, the best way to get a reasonable deal. Having said this, hotels do accept individual bookings and you might pick up a bargain in the low season. Some properties close in winter.

There is barely any agro-tourism on offer in this part of the island – the main reason for being here is the beach, so villages houses offering accommodation are few and far between.

A lot of the hotels are fairly luxurious. Staying in a four- or five-star hotel in Cyprus is pretty standard for many holidaymakers as the prices are so reasonable. There are barely any one- or two-star hotels, which is

why 'inexpensive' options don't tend to appear below.

Ayia Napa

EXPENSIVE

Grecian Bay Hotel ★ ★ ★

Kryou Nero 32, CY-5340 Ayia Napa, ☎ *23 842 000, www.grecian.com.cy.*

A five-star beach hotel about 10 minutes' walk east of the port and set around an impressive lagoon pool. This is a good place to come with a baby – the gardens are wonderfully shady and there are plenty of places to set up camp for the day under a tree and dip in and out of the pool. There's an open-air taverna right by the wide, sandy beach, and a beach bar, as well as the main restaurant and an à la carte restaurant. Four to 12 year olds can join the children's club in summer, while adults chill in the spa, which offers treatments outdoors, weather permitting.

Rooms 271, including family suites and 28 interconnecting rooms. Rates From €43–90 per person per night, B&B. Credit MC V DC AE. Amenities Indoor and outdoor pools, several restaurants, theme nights, spa, gym, tennis, squash, golf driving range, table tennis, games room, beach with water sports, shuttle to Cape Greco and into Ayia Napa.

Atlantica Aeneas Resort ★★

Nissi Avenue, Ayia Napa 5344, ☎ *22 724 000, www.aeneas.com.cy.*

Although the Aeneas is the 'wrong' side of the road, opposite Nissi Beach, it makes up for it by having the most enormous swimming pool (a breathtaking 4,000 sq m), a free-form lagoon complete with bridges, fountains, underwater jets and shallow play areas, as well as a children's pool and indoor pool. The whole resort is low-rise and very popular with families. There's a daily entertainment programme and a children's club. A new wing of very stylish suites is up and running, some of them literally opening into a separate lagoon-pool – great for swimmers, less so if you have toddlers.

Rooms *326, many of which can take a family.* **Rates** *From €100 per room per night, B&B.* **Credit** *MC V DC AE.* **Amenities** *Indoor and outdoor pools, several restaurants with children's menus, theme nights, free WiFi, gym, shops, bicycle hire.*

Adams Beach Hotel ★ ★ ★

Nissi Beach, Ayia Napa, ☏ *22 840 000, www.adams.com.cy.*

I like the Adams Beach a lot – it's one of the classiest of the upscale hotels at this end of the island and it has good family suites with a screened-off area containing bunk beds. The hotel is right on Nissi Beach and has shaded gardens with a children's playground and children's club (four to 12). In addition, there are waterslides, children's menus and babysitting. There's a choice of restaurants and a romantic taverna on the beach. It's a good choice if you want the climate and the sandy beaches of Ayia Napa but feel the need for a cocoon from the excesses of the resort in high season.

Rooms *296.* **Rates** *from €50 per person per night, B&B and €110 in a family suite.* **Credit** *MC V DC AE.* **Amenities** *Indoor and outdoor pools, several restaurants with children's menus, theme nights, gym, shops, tennis, beach, beach volleyball, squash, waterslides.*

MODERATE

So Nice ★ ★ ★

103 Nissi Avenue, ☏ *23 723 010, www.sonice.com.cy.*

Despite its cheesy name, this low-rise bungalow complex is actually rather, well, nice. The accommodation is in white-washed houses absolutely festooned with jasmine, hibiscus and bougainvillea and the property is in vast gardens, right on Landa Beach, which although crowded in summer, has a very gently shelving seafloor, so it's ideal for children. The bungalows are set around a lagoon-shaped pool and there are useful features for families: a 'healthy infant' menu, a decent playground, free satellite TV, kitchenettes in the apartments (as well as a restaurant on site) and the water park is within walking distance.

Rooms *44.* **Rates** *From €50 to €101 per room per night.* **Credit** *MC V DC AE.* **Amenities** *Restaurant, bar, lagoon pool, beach with watersports, playground, children's meals, children's pool, gardens.*

Napa Mermaid Hotel ★ ★ ★
FIND

Kryou Nero 45, ☏ *23 721 606, www. napamermaidhotel.com.cy.*

Ayia Napa's answer to the gorgeous Londa in Limassol or the Almyra in Paphos – yummy mummies, look no further! This lovely four-star beach hotel has been renovated into a smart boutique property with minimalist interiors, white sun loungers, stripped wood floors and a zen-like calm inside. Despite this, it's family-friendly, with a children's pool, babysitting, children's meals and high chairs. There are two bars (one in the pool) and two restaurants, with regular theme buffets and a touch of fusion cuisine.

Rooms 144 (a family of four can fit into a junior suite). **Rates** From €105 per room per night, B&B. **Credit** MC V DC AE. **Amenities** Two bars, two restaurants, pool, children's pool, children's meals, sauna, gym, tennis, table tennis, beach with watersports, babysitting.

Protaras

EXPENSIVE

Grecian Park ★ ★ ★

📞 23 844 000, www.grecianpark. com.cy.

The setting here is really special, next to the national park of Cape Greco, with wonderful views. This lavish five-star hotel, sister of the Grecian Bay in Ayia Napa, has some great touches for adults as well as being child-friendly – I love the Cliff Bar, with rattan furniture on a dark wood deck, overlooking the sea from a clifftop position, and the romantic Umi restaurant on the

fourth floor (see p. 193). For children, there's a separate pool, a playground and mini-club for ages three to 12. You can walk along the coast from here around the national park, or take the free shuttle into Ayia Napa.

Rooms 240, including five family suites. **Rates** €43–90 per person per night, B&B. **Credit** MC V DC AE. **Amenities** Indoor and outdoor pools, several restaurants, theme nights, spa, gym, tennis, squash, golf driving range, table tennis, games room, beach with water sports, shuttle to Cape Greco and into Ayia Napa.

MODERATE

Mimosa Beach Hotel ★

📞 23 832 797, www.mimosabeach. com.

A small, 57-room hotel, more traditional in style than some of the behemoths in the main resort. The hotel is in a lovely position, around the headland from Fig Tree Bay, right on a sandy beach in pretty gardens. It's quite simple – there's a pool, children's pool, playground, watersports centre, a couple of bars and a child-friendly restaurant. Rooms are spacious with balconies and air-conditioning.

Rooms 57. **Rates** from €58.11 per room per night, B&B. **Credit** MC V DC AE. **Amenities** Pool, beach, play area, restaurant, bar, watersports, tennis, gym, sauna.

Marlita Hotel Apartments

PO Box 33199, Protaras, 📞 23 831 420, www.marlitahotelapartments. com.

A largish block on Marlita Bay, in a relatively peaceful spot in the middle of Protaras. There's a children's pool, playroom and playground and the restaurant does children's meals.

Rooms 140. **Rates** from €111 per apartment sleeping four per night. **Credit** MC V DC AE. **Amenities** Pool, beach, play area, restaurant, bar, watersports, children's club, tennis, volleyball, entertainment programme.

FAMILY-FRIENDLY DINING

EXPENSIVE

Umi ★ ★ FIND

Grecian Park Hotel, Cape Greco, ☎ 23 844 000.

If you're staying at the Grecian Park and can get a babysitter, this romantic Japanese fusion restaurant is worth a try for the gorgeous views (it's on the fourth floor with huge picture windows) and the sushi and sashimi. There are big deckchairs outside and you can eat under the stars in summer.

Open Daily 7pm–11pm. **Main course** Around €16–45. **Credit** MC V DC AE.

MODERATE

Los Bandidos ★

Aris Velouchiotis 2, ☎ 23 723 258, www.losbandidosmexican.com.

Reputed to be the best Mexican on the island. Service is slow so take colouring pencils or activities

for children – and prepare for fantastic sizzling fajitas and huge vats of frozen strawberry margaritas. There's a huge choice and a decent children's menu with mini-portions of fajitas, ribs and tacos. Book ahead as it's always busy.

Open Daily 5.30pm–11pm. **Main course** From €8.55. **Credit** MC V.

Vassos Fish Harbour Taverna ★

Archbishop Makarios III Ave 51, ☎ 23 721 884, www.vassosfishrest.com.

Big, busy and long-established, this fish taverna is right on the harbour and turns out excellent meze, meat and fish, all day long, with superb octopus, grilled with a squeeze of lemon. Lots of locals eat here, which is always a good sign. Children will love the two pelicans that hang around waiting for fish. Book ahead, especially for Sundays.

Open Daily 9am–10.30pm. **Meze** Around €20. **Credit** MC V. **Amenities** High chairs, children's play area.

INEXPENSIVE

Cappuccino Inn ★ FIND

Limanaki (the harbour), Ayia Napa, ☎ 23 725 980, www.inhostage.com/cappuccino.

A great little café on the harbour with over 30 different types of coffee. Children will love the crepes, waffles and smoothies, while adults might go for the honey-drenched baklava. The owner, Thiakos Zissis, is a bit of a local celeb thanks to his very poignant book, Famagusta, A

Town In Hostage, a haunting photographic essay about Varosi, the 'ghost town' of Famagusta.

Open *Daily from 9am till late.* **Credit** *MC V.*

Potamos

Demetrion ☆

Liopetri river, at Potamos on the beach, ☎ *23 991 010, www.marjay.com.*

Lovely, family-friendly taverna in a fantastic location on the mouth of the Liopetri river, right on the beach. The restaurant is very friendly and the staff love children. The menu is pretty well all fish, changing seasonally. Play on the beach or swim before lunch or dinner.

Open *Daily* 12pm–11pm **Meze** *€20.* **Credit** *MC V.* **Amenities** *Beach.*

Protaras

Il Cavaliere ☆

Pernera 6, ☎ *23 831 022.*

For Italian dishes, this is the perfect family restaurant – child-friendly with a children's menu, fresh-baked pizza, play area and cartoons showing. It's not just pizza and pasta – there are regional Italian meat dishes, too, and plenty for vegetarians.

Open *Daily 6pm–11pm.* **Main course** *Around €10.* **Credit** *MC V.* **Amenities** *Children's menu, play area.*

Sotira

To Ploumin ☆

28 October 3, Sotira, ☎ *23 730 444.*

A fantastic taverna serving mainly organic food in the setting of an old farmhouse. You eat surrounded by antiques and family memorabilia and ancient farming equipment, and this is a great chance for the more adventurous to try some of Cyprus's unusual dishes (game or garlicky snails, for example, or wonderful vegetable dishes with beans, rich sauces or halloumi cheese) while the meze is perfect for children.

Open *Daily 5pm–midnight; closed Mon Nov–May.* **Meze** *From €12.* **Credit** *MC V.*

Dherynia

Misohoro Snack Bar Taverna ☆

Democratias 21, Dherynia, ☎ *23 743 943.*

A very friendly, cosy little taverna opposite the church in Dherynia, welcoming to children and priding itself on its local specialities. The meze is fantastic value but the taverna also does excellent grills and a fine traditional *kleftiko*, with lamb that falls off the bone.

Open *Daily 11am–11pm except Tues.* **Main course** *From around €7.* **Credit** *MC V.*

ΤΗϛ ΘΕΟΤΟΚΥ

ΜΡ ΘΥ

ΧΕΙΡ
Γ. ΚΕΠΟΛΑ
2005

NICOSIA

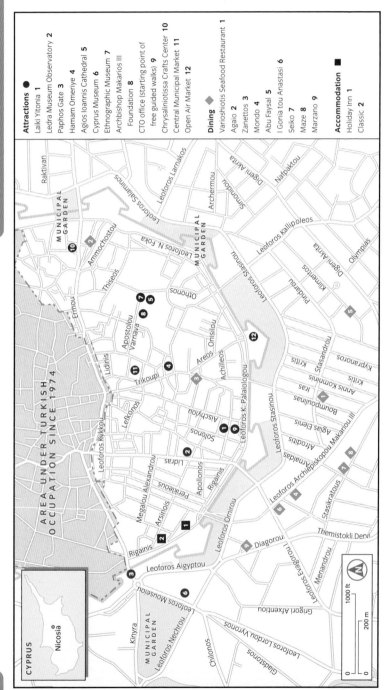

Attractions ●
Laiki Yitonia **1**
Ledra Museum Observatory **2**
Paphos Gate **3**
Hamam Omeriye **4**
Agios Ioannis Cathedral **5**
Cyprus Museum **6**
Ethnographic Museum **7**
Archbishop Makarios III
Foundation **8**
CTO office (starting point of
free guided walks) **9**
Chrysaliniotissa Crafts Center **10**
Central Municipal Market **11**
Open Air Market **12**

Dining ◆
Varioshiotis Seafood Restaurant **1**
Agaio **2**
Zanettos **3**
Mondo **4**
Abu Faysal **5**
I Gonia tou Anastasi **6**
Seiko **7**
Maze **8**
Marzano **9**

Accommodation ■
Holiday Inn **1**
Classic **2**

Nicosia enjoys the dubious distinction of being the world's last divided capital, a situation many Cypriots hope will change.

A lot of visitors bypass the capital altogether – after all, it gets stiflingly hot in summer and the beaches are a long way away. There is, however, a rich cultural heritage here and some excellent museums. The restaurants are better than in the tourist resorts, as they're aimed at the local and business market, and the shopping is reasonable. For most, the reason to visit is to nip across into the north, which although easily accessible nowadays, still has an air of mystery about it and a sense of a different culture, with minarets piercing the skyline, Turkish coffee shops and bustling street markets as well as fine Ottoman and Lusignan architecture.

Nicosia at first glance is a sprawling, dusty city, its inner sector enclosed by a fine sandstone ramparts built by the Venetians in the 16th century. It's here that you are most likely to spend a day with your family, and all the main sights are fairly close together.

If you do stay in the capital longer or are here on business with your family, there is an increasing amount of green space for citizens to play in. The Acropolis Park at the junction of Akropoleos and Athalassis is being developed and has picnic areas, while the green space along the Pedaios River, which flows south–north along the western flank of the old city, is being turned into cycle and walking paths.

ESSENTIALS

Getting There

By Air The nearest airport is Larnaca, served by a wide variety of international airlines and from airports all over the UK. The drive takes about 40 minutes. Flying into Paphos is not really an option if you are staying in the east unless you are prepared for a transfer time of nearly two hours.

By Car The drive from Larnaca is easy. Nicosia is connected by motorway and is well signposted. Traffic in the city can be pretty chaotic and parking somewhat random, free in some places and metered in others. Nicosia is not really a driving city. If you are spending a night here, leave the car and do as much as you can on foot.

VISITOR INFORMATION

The CTO office in Nicosia is at Aristokyprou 11, in Laiki Yitonia, just east of Plateia Eleftherias, ☎ *22 674 264*. If you've got time, however, pick up maps at Larnaca airport – there's a CTO booth there and you will need a local map if you're renting a car.

Orientation

You'll enter Nicosia (coming from Larnaca) through the new city, along wide boulevards lined with trees and low-rise office blocks. The old city is encircled by huge ramparts, bisected in many places by roads. Its epicentre is Plateia Eleftherias in the south-west, behind which is the pedestrian zone. Gardens and the occasional car park line the outside of the walls. You can, of course, drive inside the walls and there is parking here, but I'd recommend walking as much as your children will tolerate because there's lots of one-way roads and it's very confusing. The car parks outside the walls are the most convenient.

The Green Line (known outside the city as the Attila Line) effectively chops Nicosia in half, a long string of sheet-metal barriers, coiled barbed wire and oil drums. You can walk its length through the old city (see p. 204) although I only recommend this with older children as young

ones might find it both tiring and boring!

Getting Around

Within the old walled city, walking is the best way to get around. There are urban buses but these tend to radiate out towards the suburbs and it's not likely that a family on a regular holiday would use them. Inter-urban buses operate from different bus stations around the bastions. ALEPA buses to Limassol and Paphos leave from the Tripoli bastion, while EMAN buses for Ayia Napa go from the Constanza bastion. Buses for Larnaca go from Platiou Solomou.

Nicosia has plenty of taxis; you can even book airport transfers online through *www.cyprus taxireservations.com*.

Private taxis don't come in any particular colour or make but they always have a number plate starting with T and some have a yellow TAXI sign. Make

Balloons for sale in Nicosia

sure the meter is switched on only once you're in the car.

INSIDER TIP »
Nicosia is nowadays referred to as Lefkosia, the Greek Cypriot name for the city.

Child-friendly Events & Entertainment

Urban Soul Festival

Check the website for details and dates: www.urbansoulfestival.com.

An all-day festival celebrating reggae, hip-hop, electronic music, dance, art and performance art. It's a family affair, with music and art workshops for children and a lot of participation from local schools as well as internationally known bands and DJs. The event takes place in the open air, in the heart of the old city.

End of Sept.

Horse Racing

☎ 22 782 727, www.nicosiarace club.com.cy.

Held at the Nicosia race track on Wednesdays at 3pm and Sundays at 2pm. Horse racing is a special interest activity, of course, but Cypriots take their children anywhere, so if you're keen, you can go as a family.

Kypria Festival

www.kypriafestival.com.

A big annual music and dance festival staging anything from jazz to ballet and opera. Get a programme and you may find something of interest to children.

Sept–Oct at venues all over the city.

Summer Cultural Nights

Get a list of what's on from the tourist office, ☎ 22 674 264.

Nicosia has a regular programme of evening cultural events, some of which are fun for children if you're mooching around the city's squares on a hot summer's night, enjoying a drink or ice cream. Look out for Greek and Cypriot folk singers and local rock bands in squares such as Ayia Varvara, Faneromeni and Palouriotissa.

Independence Day

A military parade through the city centre and various celebrations around it.

1st Oct.

Archangel Michael Day

This annual celebration at the Archangel Michael Monastery commemorates the monastery's namesake with stalls selling local food and wine.

7th–8th Nov.

WHAT TO SEE & DO

Children's Top 10 Attractions

❶ **Watching** the craftsmen at work in Laiki Yitonia. See p. 201.

❷ **Eating your way** through a real Cypriot meze. See p. 213.

❸ **Imagining** how Cypriots used to live in the deserted village of Fikardou. See p. 203.

❹ **Sampling** an ostrich burger at Ostrich Wonderland! See p. 200.

5 Cycling around Athalassa National Forest Park. See p. 204.

6 Walking the Venetian walls and imagining how it once felt to defend the city. See p. 205.

7 Admiring the gold jewellery in the Cyprus Museum. See p. 206.

8 Exploring the open-air market and seeing how many strange fruits you can name. See p. 210.

9 Visiting the north of the city and learning some Turkish words. See p. 202.

10 Climbing up to the Ledra Museum Observatory and seeing how many differences you can spot between the north and the south. See p. 205.

Attractions with Animals

Ostrich Wonderland Theme Park ALL AGES

Agios Ioannis Malountas, 25 minutes' drive from Nicosia, ☏ *22 991008.*

A huge ostrich farm, dressed up as a 'park', where you can see the ostriches, learn about their breeding and products and sample the goods in the shop and café. It's similar to the ostrich park near Pissouri (see p. 55) – worth it if your children need an animal fix but less good for the sensitive or vegetarian child as there are ostrich burgers on offer!

Open *Daily, 9am–7pm May–Oct; 9am–5pm Nov–April.* **Admission** *€1.71.* **Amenities** *Restaurant, shop.*

Melios Pet Centre ★ ALL AGES

Korinthou, Ayioi Trimithias, 2671 Nicosia, ☏ *22 835 920,* **www.melios petpark.eu**

What started as a private collection of birds is now a sizeable animal park, with a large pet shop attached. The eclectic collection includes deer, monkeys, skunks, racoons, wallabies, sheep, goats and porcupines, as well as hundreds of varieties of birds, housed in reasonable enclosures along tree-lined walkways. There are no big cats; the focus is mainly on the birds. Children can play in the playground after the visit while parents relax in the café.

Reunification

The one thing all Cypriots have in common, which will crop up again and again in conversation, is the conflict with Turkey over the northern part of the island. Every family is affected by this, having either lost land or relatives through the Turkish invasion 30 years ago. Everybody wants to see the island reunified, but as far as Greek Cypriots are concerned, it must be on their terms. In a UN referendum held in April 2004 concerning reunification of the island, 76 % of Greek Cypriots voted against, while 65 % of Turkish Cypriots were for an undivided island. The debate continues.

Laiki Yitonia

Open *9am–7pm Tues–Sun.* **Admission** *Free.* **Amenities** *Café, playground, shop.*

Nicosia Districts

Laiki Yitonia ALL AGES

Laiki Yitonia means 'the neighbourhood of the people' and every big town in Cyprus has one – a prettily refurbished old area of shops and restaurants. In Nicosia, the Laiki Yitonia, which starts just behind Plateia Eleftherias, is very small, only 10 minutes or so to traverse, but it's the place to go for lunch or a drink. Tavernas and restaurants nestle in a tangle of pedestrianised streets and old houses, and you'll find all the inevitable souvenir shops here, as well as craft workshops. Local businesspeople and tourists come for lunch and there's always a buzzing atmosphere. Cynics may call it tacky but I think it's one of the nicest parts of the capital, especially some of the vine-covered terraces outside the tavernas, which are cool and shaded on a hot day.

Tahtakale District ALL AGES

Just north of a cluster of museums in the old town, including the **National Struggle Museum** and the Makarios Cultural Centre, is a small district called Tahtakale in which lots of old houses have been sensitively renovated in the traditional style; it's worth a wander if the weather's not too hot. North of

201

The Legend of Adonis <<

Local legend has it that Adonis, lover of Aphrodite, was killed by a crazed wild boar in the area around Dhali. The poppies which splash scarlet across the fields in spring are said to have sprung from his blood.

here, the other side of Ermou Street, is the Chrysaliniotissa church and district, where Greek Cypriots live in the shadow of the Green Line, Turkish flags fluttering in the breeze across the barricades at the end of the roads. The architecture here has a real Ottoman feel and the district was once home to several artisans, including candle and cabinet makers. (Note that if you walk the length of the Green Line through the old city, you'll pass through this area anyway, so don't duplicate when you're planning your day!)

North Nicosia ALL AGES

While you're in Nicosia, don't miss the opportunity to visit the north. Getting across the border is relatively easy now that the Ledra Crossing has reopened (in April 2008) and that tensions seem to be easing. You can go on foot, as part of a tour, or in a hire car. Cars cross at the Metehan crossing point or at the Ledra Palace checkpoint. Assuming you have a UK or EU passport or a visa to enter the north, you simply show your documents and buy some additional car insurance at the border.

Things to see on the northern side include the **Selimiye Mosque**, which was a cathedral until 1570, when the Ottomans added two tall minarets; and nearby **Buyuk Han**, a former caravanserai in the 16th century, now a collection of cafés, shops

Buyuk Han, North Nicosia

and a hamam (Turkish bath). If your children are in the mood for walking, make your way to the **Abrahmet** district, where there are some lovely old 19th-century mansions and some good places to eat.

Surrounding Villages

The villages in the Nicosia district clinging to the southwestern slopes of the Troodos give a real insight into Cypriot village life as they're virtually undiscovered by tourists, who rarely venture here. More settlements are scattered across the **Mesaoria** plain south of the city; winter and spring are the best time to visit, when the almond trees are in blossom and the landscape more gentle-looking and green.

Tamassos

Tamassos is an ancient city-kingdom located about 21 km southwest of Nicosia. It's mentioned in Homer's *Odyssey* as a copper-producing place and you can still see the ancient copper workshops dating back to the sixth or seventh century BC. Other than that, Tamassos is a sprawling archaeological site with the remains of a temple dedicated to Aphrodite, two royal tombs and several smaller ones and the remains of the citadel. It's not wildly exciting for children but of interest for keen historians and archaeologists.

Open 8.30am–4pm Nov–Mar, 9.30am–5pm Apr–Oct. *Admission* €1.71.

Pera

Combine a visit to Tamassos with the pretty village of Pera, packed with scenes you might find on a Cypriot postcard – narrow cobbled streets, a traditional café, stone walls festooned with bougainvillea.

Dhali Village and Idalion

Dhali Village lies south of Nicosia, just east of the A1 motorway, close to the Attila Line. Its main attraction is the ancient hillside site of Idalion, currently under excavation and believed to date back to 1200 BC. There isn't too much to see here but it's worth dropping in if you are passing, particularly as the dig is still going on and some impressive urns and figurines of Aphrodite have been uncovered.

Fikardou

Fikardou is a 'ghost' village in the eastern foothills of the Troodos, abandoned early in the 19th century and today, preserved as a kind of living museum. Only one or two people live here now, although the village is well ensconced on the tourist trail and the taverna is always busy.

The houses are made of stone, some with impressive woodwork features and tiled roofs. Two are open to the public, displaying features like an old loom, spinning wheel, 19th-century furniture, an olive press and *zivania* (grape spirit) stills. It's of some interest to children and makes a good day out in combination with some of the other Troodos villages.

Walking the Green Line

There isn't a vast amount to see but some people are fascinated by Nicosia's division and you can walk across the old town pretty close to the 'line'. The advantage of doing this walk is that it takes in residential neighbourhoods you may otherwise miss.

Start at the Flatro bastion on the eastern ramparts and set off westwards along Agiou Georgiou. Stop at the lovely old 15th-century church on Chrysaliniotissis.

Keeping the barriers on your right, head towards the corner of Ermou and Pentadaktylou, where Greek and Turkish soldiers stare at each other across sandbags.

Carry on west and you will pass through the revitalised Faneromeni district to Lidras Street, where a crossing has recently opened. There's a lookout here from which children can peer across into No Man's Land, a dusty street with buildings pockmarked with bullet holes. Some of the buildings are rumoured to be seeded with land mines. You can then walk along Pafou, right up against the border, and leave the old town at the Pafos Gate.

You are only allowed to cross the Green Line at the official checkpoints.

Open 8am–4pm Nov-Mar, 9am– 5pm Apr–Oct. *Admission* €1.71. *Amenities* Taverna.

Sites of Natural Beauty

Athalassa National Forest Park

The Athalassa Park is the 'green lung' of Nicosia, south-east of the city centre, with 840 hectares of nature trails, picnic sites, a playground, botanical gardens and sports facilities. You'll find over 20 km of easy cycling and walking trails and a large lake which attracts migratory birds; the walking trail around the lake takes about one hour. The park has 500 types of tree, as well as herbs and indigenous flowers. At the Park of Nations (part of the main development) you can see where foreign heads of state plant trees in remembrance of their visits to Cyprus.

Historic Buildings & Monuments

The Green Line AGES 5 AND UP

Neither a building nor a monument, the Green Line is nonetheless the reason, sadly, a lot of people come to Nicosia. It refers to the line that effectively splits the island in two, between the Turkish north and the Greek south. The name comes from a humble green pencil with which Major-General Peter Young marked a cease-fire line on a map of Nicosia during hostilities in 1964. Since the 1974 Turkish invasion it has actually separated the city. It's a strange phenomenon, (reminiscent of old Berlin for anybody who's been there prior to the Wall coming down). Streets come to an abrupt end with sheet metal, coiled wire, watchtowers and police blocking off the road. On one side, there are fast food restaurants and Marks & Spencer; on the other, minarets, dusty, unkempt buildings and Turkish coffee shops.

You can walk along the Green Line for a bit (see p. 204) or, if you've got very small children and simply want to have a look, you can check out the view to the 'other side' from the **Ledra Museum Observatory** on top of Woolworths (on the corner of Lidras and Arsinois streets). There are telescopes up here from which you can view the northern half of the city, right across to the huge Turkish flag carved into the **Kyrenia Mountains** to the north (you can see this flag from the top of Mount Olympus, too).

Open Daily 9.30am–5pm. **Admission** €1.28 (to the observatory).

Venetian Walls ALL AGES

Encircling the old city, the walls built by the Venetians were fortified by 11 heart-shaped bastions and protected by a deep moat. The entrances to the old city are named after other cities on the island in whose direction they face, hence the Paphos Gate, Famagusta Gate and so on. The Venetian walls actually replace an even older structure built by the Franks in the 14th century; the Venetians demolished them as they were too weak, too big for the Venetian army to man and too close to the hills in the east and south-east, where the enemy might have been lurking. Today, you can walk around part of the walls, looking at the views from the top or relaxing in the

Venetian Walls

parks that occupy the space where the moat would have been.

Hamam Omeriye ★ FIND
AGES 13 AND UP

Tyllirias Square 8, www.hamam baths.com.

The gorgeous Omeriye Hamam is in the old town of Lefkosia, next to the Omeriye Mosque and not far from the Archbishop's Palace. The hamam was built in 1570 as a gift to the city from Lala Mustafa Pasha to after the island fell to the Ottomans.

This isn't really a place to take children but it's a great treat for, say, a mum and teenage daughter for a pampering day. As well as the traditional steam rooms, the hamam offers hot stone massage, aromatherapy and various other popular treatments, in an amazingly atmospheric setting of vaulted ceilings and ancient walls. In 2006, the building received the Europa Nostra prize for the Conservation of Architectural Heritage.

Open 9am–9pm Mon (couples only); 9am–9pm Tues, Thurs, Sat (men only); 9am–9pm Wed, Fri, Sun (women only).

Agios Ioannis Cathedral
Near the Archbishop's Palace, Agios Ioannis, the city's official cathedral, is built on the site of the 14th-century chapel of the Benedictine Abbey of Agios Ioannis the Evangelist of Bibi. The cathedral itself is not huge (the Ottomans ruled that Christian buildings of worship were kept small and modest) but the interior is beautiful, a riot of

Biblical painting. Agios Ioannis Cathedral

intricately carved woodwork coated in gold leaf, lit by crystal chandeliers. The four large icons are by Cretan John Kornaris and were painted between 1795 and 1797. The 18th-century wall paintings depict scenes from the Bible and the discovery of the tomb of Agios Varnavas near Salamis. It's in this cathedral that new archbishops of Nicosia are consecrated. While it's not likely to appeal to children, it's worth a quick look inside if you are passing.

Open 8am–12pm and 2pm–4pm Mon–Fri; 8am–12pm and during Mass Sun.

Top Museums

Cyprus Museum ★★ FIND
AGES 5 AND UP

Mouseiou 1, Lefkosia.

If you only visit one museum in Cyprus, make it this one, which

The Military Presence in Cyprus

There are British military bases (Sovereign Base Areas, or SBAs) at Akrotiri/Episkopi and Dhekelia covering 98 square miles, or 2.74 % of the country's territory. The bases were retained by Britain under the 1960 treaty, which gave Cyprus its independence. The bases enable the UK to maintain a permanent military presence at a strategic point in the Eastern Mediterranean. The Army presence includes the Joint Service Signals Unit at Akrotiri and 62 Cyprus Support Squadron Royal Engineers and 16 Flight Army Air Corps at Dhekelia, alongside a variety of supporting arms.

RAF Akrotiri is an important staging post for military aircraft and the communication facilities are an important element of the UK's worldwide links. Either base can be used for a variety of both military and humanitarian operations.

A UN peacekeeping force, UNFICYP, comprising 1,209 military personnel, has been on the island since 1964. It arrived after the outbreak of fighting in December 1963 and Turkish threats to invade. Its chief task is to supervise the buffer zone between the Republic of Cyprus in the south and the area in the north occupied by Turkey. The peacekeeping force is also present to maintain the ceasefire and is an important reassurance to Greek Cypriots, given that 35,000 Turkish troops occupy the north of the island.

It is also possible to find up to a regiment's worth of British soldiers serving with these UN Forces in Cyprus, although there is no operational link between British soldiers serving in the Sovereign Base Areas and UNFICYP. These soldiers serve on an unaccompanied six-month tour of duty as UN soldiers, during which they wear UN berets and receive the UN medal for their efforts.

houses an impressive collection of artefacts from prehistoric Cyprus to the early Christian period. Pottery, jewellery, sculptures, statues and coins are all on display, highlights being the famous Aphrodite of Soloi statue, the face of which appeared on the old Cyprus pound banknotes and is used as an emblem for the island. There's also an amazing set of terracotta figures from Agia Irini in the north, believed to date back to the sixth or seventh century BC and to have been created by a tribe embracing a fertility cult. You'll also see beautiful gold jewellery and a display of the island's mining heritage.

Open 8am–4pm Tues, Wed, Fri; 8am–5pm Thurs; 9am– pm Sat; 10am–1pm Sun. *Admission* €3.42. *Amenities* Café, museum shop.

Ethnographic Museum ★
AGES 5 AND UP

Plateia Archiepiskopou Kyprianou, Lefkosia (within the old Archbishopric)

Statue of Archbishop Makarios III

A small museum in the old Archbishopric housing a collection of 19th- and early 20th-century Cypriot folk art including wood carvings, tapestry, embroidery, pottery, national costumes and hand-woven materials. The quality of the workmanship is amazing; you won't want to buy tat from souvenir stalls after visiting here!

Open *9.30am–4pm Mon–Fri.*
Admission €1.71.

Archbishop Makarios III Foundation

Plateia Archiepiskopou Kyprianou.

A complex housing art galleries with work from various eras of the island's history.

There's a Western Europe section (15th to 19th centuries) with mainly religious and mythological themes as well as portraits and landscapes by Sebastino del Piombo, Francesco Vanni, Nicolas Poussin, Theodore Gericault and Eugene Delacroix. A second gallery houses Greek military art, engravings and maps, while a third is dedicated to Greek paintings from 1830 to the present day. There's another section housing contemporary Cypriot art, too.

Open *8.30am–1pm, 3pm–5.30pm Mon–Sat; closed Wed and Sat afternoons.*

Child-friendly Tours

Because Nicosia is a destination for tours rather than a base for tourists, the usual tour companies don't tend to operate from here. If you want to join a tour to, say, Limassol or Akamas for the day and you are staying in Nicosia, you are best off driving the short distance to Larnaca and picking up a tour there.

Larnaca is centrally located and tour operators offer days out from here to the Troodos, Limassol, the wine villages and the west, although the latter would make a long day for young children.

For Active Families

Kykko Bowling ALL AGES

15-19 Archimidous, ☎ *22 350 085.*

Have a go at tenpin bowling for a rainy day, or a day following museum overload! It has lanes with side barriers for children, loud music and fast food.

Open Daily 10am–12am.

Extreme Park AGES UP TO 10

Strovolos Avenue, ☎ *22 424 681, www.extremepark.com.cy.*

Indoor-outdoor play centre with a giant bouncy castle and slides as well as ball pool and other play equipment.

Open Daily 4pm–10pm. Admission €5.12.

CTO Guided Walking Tours

☎ *22 674 264.*

The Cyprus Tourism Organisation offers two guided tours, both free, on Fridays, starting from the CTO office in Laiki Yitonia at 10am. **Old Lefkosia** concentrates on the area inside the walls while **Lefkosia Outside the Walls** extends a bit further and includes some bus transport.

Shopping

As you might expect, Nicosia's shopping is relatively good, although if you come from a big city, you still won't find it particularly special. There's Debenhams (big in Cyprus) containing a lot of brands like Oasis, Morgan and Miss Sixty; Marks & Spencer; and a big range of individual stores including Fendi, Gucci, Mango, Max Mara, Max & Co and Marina Rinaldi. For something a little different, look out for the following:

Chrysaliniotissa Crafts Centre

Dimonaktos 2 (corner of Ipponaktos and Dimonaktos Streets), ☎ *22 348 050.*

A cluster of workshops around a courtyard in the style of an old-fashioned inn, housing some talented craftsmen and women; you can buy stunning icons here, painted by Taliadorou Kalliopi, one of Cyprus's leading iconographers.

Open 9am–1pm, 3pm–6pm (4pm–7pm May–Sept) Mon–Fri; 10am–1pm Sat.

Cyprus Handicraft Centre

Athalassas Avenue 186, Strovolos.

The Cyprus Handicraft Centre was set up to provide work for

people displaced by the Turkish invasion and also to preserve traditional arts and crafts. Children will enjoy seeing artisans practising traditional crafts such as weaving, basket making, wood carving, pottery and the production of leather and traditional copper items. There are shops in Limassol, Larnaca and Paphos, too.

Workshops 7.30am–2.30pm Mon–Fri; 3pm–6pm Thurs (closed Thurs afternoons July–Aug).

Five Senses
Lydras Street 43.

Natural cosmetics and organic beauty products.

Open 9am–1pm and 3pm–6pm.
Credit MC V.

Art Orange
Soufouli Street 6.

Handmade accessories, clutch bags and handbags –teenagers will enjoy it here.

Open 9am–1pm and 3pm–6pm.
Credit MC V.

Maja
Solonos 26.

Handmade jewellery in Greek and Cypriot style.

Open 9am–1pm and 3pm–6pm.
Credit MC V.

Anemoessa
23 Pindarou Street and K. Skokou, Shop 2A, www.anemoessa.com.cy.

There's a fantastic array of Cypriot food and herbal products here – honey, jams, sweets, olive oils, dried fruits, quince, grapes,

figs. Buy gift products in beautiful boxes and baskets. I'd challenge anyone to leave empty handed!

Open 9am–1pm and 3pm–6pm.
Credit MC V.

Central Municipal Market
Although it has an unassuming entrance, Nicosia's covered market provides a fascinating insight into where locals shop and is a good place to pick up a cheap picnic lunch or some goodies to take home. Look out for piles of fresh fruit and vegetables as well as breads, buckets of olives, herbal teas, halloumi and other village cheeses and an array of Cyprus sausages and salamis.

Open 6am–3pm Mon, Tues, Thurs, Fri.

Ochi Square Open-Air Market
Held every Wednesday, near the Bayraktar Mosque, on one of the 11 bastions of the Venetian walls of Lefkosia. This is a weekly farmers' market, packed with fruit, veg, halloumi, sausages and other goodies, a good place for a bit local colour.

Open 6am–5pm Wed. Cash only.

FAMILY-FRIENDLY ACCOMMODATION

Nicosia is a business city rather than a holiday resort so tour operators don't tend to feature it. Hotel rates therefore seem rather expensive, but these are the rack rates the hotels are obliged to quote to the Cyprus Tourism Organisation for the annual official hotel guide. You'll find

Pick up your picnic at the local market

much better deals, especially for the big chain hotels, if you book online. Most also offer promotions for families, such as children staying free when sharing a room with their parents.

Nicosia

EXPENSIVE

Cyprus Hilton ★ ★

Archbishop Makarios III Avenue, 📞 *22 377 777,* **www.hilton.com**.

Essentially a business hotel but with a resort feel thanks to the big pool area and gardens. If you stay here, you will often be in the company of conference guests, although the hotel says it welcomes families and even operates a children's club for five weeks over the summer holiday.

There are indoor and outdoor pools, a decent playground, a spa, fitness centre, tennis, squash and an outlet of Kykko Bowling. Acropolis Park is a short drive away for picnics and play areas. The hotel has four places to eat.

The Paddock Bar serves all-day snacks and international dishes, and the Lobby Lounge serves cakes and snacks, while the other two restaurants are more formal.

*Rooms 298, including family suites and 28 interconnecting rooms. **Rates** From €321 per room, B&B. **Credit** MC V AE DC. **Amenities** Indoor and outdoor pools, several restaurants, children's menus, theme nights, spa, gym, tennis, squash, bowling, playground, babysitting, children's pool, room service, high chairs, cots, promotional rates for families.*

Hilton Park Nicosia ★

Griva Dhigeni, 📞 *22 695 111,* **www. hilton.com**.

Hilton's second hotel in the capital is still marked as the Forum hotel on many maps. The hotel is 10 minutes' drive from the old city in a relatively quiet residential area and is good for families thanks to its pleasant lagoon-shaped pool and gardens shaded by palm trees. There's a fitness centre and four restaurants, including the very pretty

Sorrento Pool Bar and Grill, where you can dine outdoors. The Olympia Restaurant is a bit formal for most families.

Rooms 140. **Rates** From €258 per room, B&B. **Credit** MC V AE DC. **Amenities** Outdoor pool, gardens, several restaurants, health club, babysitting, high chairs.

Holiday Inn Nicosia ★

7 Regaena Street, ☎ 22 712 712, **www.ichotelsgroup.com**.

Another big business hotel, this one located inside the old city, so useful if you are planning to explore on foot. There's an indoor pool and spa and several restaurants, including a Japanese one and fast sushi bar on the ground floor and the very romantic Marco Polo on the roof (summer only) where you eat al fresco with views across the old city.

Rooms 140. **Rates** From €294 per room, B&B. **Credit** MC V AE DC. **Amenities** Indoor pool, several restaurants, spa, babysitting, room service, high chairs.

MODERATE

Classic ★

94 Rigenis Street, ☎ 22 670 072, **www.classic.com.cy**.

A recently opened boutique hotel located within the city walls. The minimalist decor is a stark contrast with the jumbled streets and alleys outside and the hotel has a feeling of calm. It's aimed at the business market but this being Cyprus, takes children. There's all-day dining in the lobby bar and a more formal restaurant, the curiously named 59 Knives,

which is more for business power lunches than families, but there are plenty of places to eat out in the surrounding area.

Rooms 57. **Rates** From €125 per room, B&B. **Credit** MC V AE DC. **Amenities** Fitness room, all-day dining, restaurant.

INEXPENSIVE

Avli House ★

3 Markos Drakos, 2565 Lythrodontas, ☎ 23 842 000, **www.agrotourism. com.cy**.

A 10-bed guesthouse in a village 25 km south of Nicosia, in the midst of a pretty agricultural region of olives, citrus, vines and vegetable cultivation. The village has a riding school and several nature trails and the house is recommended for artists because of its beautiful situation (the owner is an artist and his work is displayed, along with the work of past guests). The property itself comprises three old houses joined together and has been declared an 'ancient monument'; all the materials in its construction and renovation are indigenous to the area. There are five studios, each with bathroom and TV, kitchen and air conditioning. All five share a pretty garden and two have fireplaces. Lefkara and Choirokitia are nearby; the village is a convenient halfway point between Nicosia and the coast.

Rooms 5. **Rates** From €45 per person per night, B&B. **Credit** MC V. **Amenities** Garden, kitchen, fireplaces, cots, art gallery, riding, mini-football pitch, hiking nearby. Village festival on 30th July.

FAMILY-FRIENDLY DINING

Nicosia has a wide array of excellent restaurants catering to the international and business community rather than tourists, as well as some cool lounge bars if you have teenagers or if you've got a babysitter for the evening. All the usual fast-food outlets are present if you're having trouble getting any more meze down your children; there's a **Nando's** on Solomou Square and a **TGI Fridays** on Diagorou. I've also recommended a couple of pizza places as Nicosia has them in abundance.

EXPENSIVE

Varoshiotis Seafood ★★ FIND

Stasandrou 29, 📞 *77 772 040.*

This offshoot of the popular seafood restaurant of Larnaca does a fine line in fish meze and other dishes such as prawns or lobster, as well as tempting puddings – children will love the chocolate fudge cake.

Open *Daily 12pm–12am.* **Main course** *Around €12–24.* **Credit** *MC V DC AE.*

MODERATE

Aigaio ★

Ektoros 40, 📞 *22 433 297.*

Local institution in Old Nicosia producing a fine meze which is very popular with locals. Good, friendly service and a mix of Cypriot and Greek dishes.

Open *Daily 7pm–12am.* **Meze** *From €17.* **Credit** *MC V.*

Zanettos ★

Trikoupi 65, 📞 *22 765 501.*

One of the oldest tavernas on the island, established in 1938 and still going strong. There are some adventurous dishes like snails but plenty for the more conservative palate in a huge and impressive meze.

Open *Daily 8pm–12am.* **Meze** *Around €17.* **Credit** *MC V.*

Mondo ★

Archbishop Makarios III Avenue 9a, 📞 *77 778 044*

Hip modern café, laid back enough to be welcoming to families and located on the main shopping street. Good for coffee, juices and international dishes. The mezzanine bar takes on a cocktail lounge feel in the evenings.

Open *Daily 9am–12am.* **Meze** *Around €17.* **Credit** *MC V.*

Syrian Arab Friendship Club ★★ FIND

Vasilissis Amalias 27, 📞 *22 776 246.*

Nicosia has a lot of Middle Eastern restaurants and this is one of the best. Syrian meze has similarities to Greek Cypriot so it's good for children to pick through and you can always find things like little cheesy pastries, chicken kebabs and dips for bread – hummous and tahini – as well as more adventurous dishes. There's a vegetarian selection, too. What's nice about this place is that you eat dinner in a greenery-filled courtyard under a white tent, giving the experience a desert feel. There are hubble bubble pipes on offer for added atmosphere.

Open *Daily 11am–12am.* **Meze** *From €17.* **Credit** *MC V DC AE.*

Abu Faysal ★

Klementos 31, ☎ 22 760 353.

Popular Lebanese restaurant with a brilliant meze and a superb vegetarian offering, all set in a pretty garden. There's belly dancing at weekends and the whole place doubles up as an art gallery. Puddings and ice creams are all home-made.

Open *12.30pm–3pm, 7pm–11pm Tues–Sun.* **Meze** *Around €17.* **Credit** *MC V.*

I Gonia tou Anastasi ★

Archbishop Makarios III Avenue 3, ☎ 22 384 884.

Authentic Cypriot restaurant serving meze, awarded a Vakhis certificate for its use of local ingredients and 'slow cooking'. Everything is home-made and as usual, the meze is overwhelmingly filling.

Open *7.30pm–10.30pm Mon–Sat.* **Meze** *Around €15.39.* **Credit** *MC V.*

Seiko ★

Stasikratous 26-28, ☎ 77 777 375.

Japanese, which is adventurous for small children, but this hip restaurant has two bonuses: a glass wall behind which you can watch the chefs at work at lightning-fast speeds, and a pool of koi carp. There are over 100 dishes on the menu and even the fussiest child

should enjoy light, crunchy vegetable tempura.

Open *Daily 12pm–3pm, 7pm–12am (except Sun lunchtime).* **Main course** *From €9.91.* **Credit** *MC V DC AE.*

Maze ★

Stasikratous 42, ☎ 22 447 447.

A tasty but uncomplicated range of international cuisine – steaks, fish, grills and salads. The menu changes at night to become more sophisticated and the café takes on the air of a chic lounge and gourmet restaurant after dark, but it's a good place for lunch with children in tow.

Open *Daily 10am–12pm.* **Main course** *From €8.55.* **Credit** *MC V DC AE.*

INEXPENSIVE

Marzano ★

Diagorou 27, ☎ 22 663 240, www. pizzaexpress.com.cy.

An offshoot of Pizza Express but more, with a good range of grills, salads, burgers and pasta as well as the usual fare. There are some tempting antipasti and decadent puddings, too. There's live music on Fridays and Saturdays, and Saturday and Sunday afternoons are devoted to children, with a magician and face painting on Saturdays (1pm–4pm) and a clown on Sundays. There are also pizza-making opportunities!

Open *Daily 12pm–12am.* **Pizza** *From €5.81.* **Credit** *MC V.* **Amenities** *Children's menu, high chairs, entertainment.*

10 History

To put Cyprus in perspective, a basic understanding of its history helps. Historical relics are dotted all over the island and there are many different eras and influences from the last 9,000 years that children can have fun spotting.

The First Settlers

The earliest structures you'll find date from the Neolithic Age, from about 7000 to 3900 BC, although people lived here for many thousands of years before then. The Neolithic, or the 'new stone age', was when people started farming for the first time and built permanent homes for themselves rather than moving from place to place as nomads. Remains of the oldest known settlement in Cyprus dating from this period can be seen in Chirokitia and Kalavassos (Tenta), off the Nicosia–Limassol road. A civilisation had developed along the north and south coasts, using stone tools and later, after 5000 BC, clay pots.

By about 2500 BC, the inhabitants of the island had discovered its copper reserves (the name Cyprus is thought to come from the ancient Greek word for copper) and were mining the metal. If you drive to the very top of the Troodos, where the huge radar 'golf balls' are, you'll see some of these ancient quarries in the hills from where the copper was extracted.

By the Bronze Age, which lasted from around 2500 BC to 1050 BC, Cyprus was getting rich from exporting its copper and had started to trade with Arabia, Egypt and the Aegean region. By around 1400 BC, Mycenaeans from the Greek islands reached the country and liked it so much they stayed, followed by more waves of immigrants. This is how Cyprus acquired the Greek language, religion and habits. It was also the time that cities like Paphos and Kourion were founded. Kourion today is a ruin and makes a very interesting visit but looking at the bright lights, shops and bars of Paphos, it's hard to believe that it is more than 3,000 years old!

Cyprus became richer and more prosperous over the centuries. The island consisted of 10 kingdoms, some of which began to fall prey to waves of invaders. Assyrians, Egyptians and Persians all had a go at taking over. King Evagoras (who ruled from 411–374 BC), of the northern town of Salamis, rebelled against the Persians and briefly unified the island but was forced to give in after a long siege. Help arrived between 333 and 325 BC, when Alexander the Great defeated the Persians and made Cyprus part of his empire.

But Alexander's generals squabbled amongst themselves and Cyprus was eventually handed over to the Hellenistic state of the Ptolemies of Egypt. Paphos became the capital and the island continued to prosper.

Romans, Byzantines & the Ottoman Empire

From 58 BC to 330 AD, Cyprus was part of the powerful Roman Empire. First, it was a province of Syria and later, a separate, independent province governed by a proconsul.

Two missionaries, St Paul and St Barnabas, arrived on the island and converted the proconsul, Sergius Paulus, to Christianity. Cyprus thus became the first country in the world to be governed by a Christian.

A series of disasters characterised the next few decades, with huge earthquakes during the first century BC and the first century AD, followed by an outbreak of plague in 164 AD.

The next significant period was the Byzantine era, which gets its name from Byzantium, the eastern part of the Roman Empire, into which Cyprus fell. The capital of Byzantium was Constantinople, now Istanbul.

Constantine the Great's mother, Helena, is said to have stopped in Cyprus on her journey from the Holy Land, bringing with her remnants of the Holy Cross on which Jesus died, and founded the monastery of Stavrovouni.

The main cities of the island were virtually wiped out in the fourth century AD by massive earthquakes. The cities weren't rebuilt and lay in ruins. New ones were built in different locations, often with huge basilicas.

By now, the Islamic religion was spreading and in 647 AD Arabs invaded the island and wrecked the city of Salamis. For the next few decades, the Cypriot people suffered terribly, moving away from the coast and the constant raids. In 688, Emperor Justinian II and Caliph al-Malik signed a treaty neutralising Cyprus, but the island continued to be attacked by pirates until 965 when Emperor Nikiforos II Fokas regained Cyprus as a Byzantine province and expelled the Arab invaders.

Things went well for a few decades until the self-proclaimed Governor Isaak Komninos mistakenly took on the might of King Richard the Lionheart of England (Richard I). Richard was on his way to the Third Crusade and was shipwrecked on Cyprus, where Komninos was allegedly inhospitable to him. Richard took on the governor and won, and gained possession of the island, later marrying Berengaria of Navarre at Kolossi Castle in Limassol, where she was crowned Queen of England. Richard then sold the island to the Knights Templar for 100,000 dinars, but the knights couldn't afford the upkeep of Cyprus and in 1192, sold it on at the same price to Guy de Lusignan, a French-speaking Crusader Knight, at the time, also King of Jerusalem.

The Catholic church soon replaced the Greek Orthodox church that was so well established, although the Greek Orthodox religion survived, mainly thanks to the orthodox monks who retreated to the Troodos Mountains and built churches and monasteries, decorated with the most beautiful frescoes imaginable. In the 13th century, meanwhile, many impressive gothic buildings were erected by the Catholics, some of which survive today, including the cathedrals of Ayia Sophia in Nicosia, Saint Nicholas in Famagusta and Bellapais Abbey. Famagusta, today in the Turkish occupied zone, was one of the richest cities in the Near East. Nicosia became capital of Cyprus and the seat of the Lusignan kings. The Lusignan dynasty ended when the last queen Catherina Cornaro gave up Cyprus to Venice in 1489; the powerful Venetians had long since been eyeing up the island as a worthy candidate for invasion and had made several attempts.

The Venetians, however, did not bring prosperity to the island. They ruled from 1489 to 1571 but turned out to be both inefficient and corrupt. The Venetians knew that an attack from the expanding Ottoman Empire was imminent and built huge fortifications around Nicosia and Famagusta. But this couldn't stop the Ottomans, and in 1570 the Turks successfully invaded. A

long siege followed, during which the whole population of Nicosia was slaughtered – 20,000 people. Cyprus was now part of the Ottoman Empire. The Catholic rulers were either expelled or converted to Islam and the Greek Orthodox faith was restored. Some 20,000 Turks were settled on the island, but the Greek population's sympathies lay with nearby Greece.

Into Modern Times

At the time, the Turks couldn't be much bothered with their impoverished colony and in 1878, reached an agreement with Britain that Turkey would retain sovereignty of Cyprus and Britain would administer it. This suited the British, who wanted a listening post close to the Middle East. The other half of the deal was that Britain would help protect Turkey's Asian territories from the Russians.

By 1914, World War I had broken out and Britain took overall control of Cyprus when Turkey sided with Germany. In 1923 under the Treaty of Lausanne, Turkey renounced any claim to Cyprus. In 1925 Cyprus

The Church

The church is extremely powerful in Cyprus and until the Turkish invasion of 1974 was the biggest landowner. It still owns large tracts of land today, much of it prime seafront plots devoted to agriculture.

Young people are encouraged to go to church and almost all marriages take place in church. Church attendance is, however, in decline among younger Cypriots.

Cypriots & Ties with the UK

The majority of the population of Cyprus (84.1 %) is Greek Cypriot and Christian Orthodox. Turkish Cypriots, who make up 11.7 % of the population, are Sunnite Muslims. However the island still has strong links with the UK, which administered Cyprus as a colony from 1878 until independence in 1960. The UK then retained two Sovereign Base Areas (SBAs) for its own defence purposes. So Britain still has strong ties with the island and has left its legacy, including driving on the left, a similar legal system to that of the UK, and a widespread understanding of English.

There are currently some 270,000 Cypriots living in the UK, out of an estimated half a million living overseas. Around 30,000 live in the USA and 22,000 in Canada, but the British Cypriot expat population is by far the largest. So every Cypriot you will meet will know someone in the UK, have lived in the UK, have a business connection with the UK or at least have some understanding of where you come from and what it's like there.

was declared a Crown colony and in World War II, Cypriots served in the British forces.

The Greek Cypriots were desperate for independence and some kind of union with Greece. The Turkish Cypriots, however, wanted the island to be part of Turkey, or at least to be divided. An Armed Liberation Struggle (**enosis**) broke out in 1955 and lasted until 1959. During this time, Archbishop Makarios, head of the enosis campaign, was deported to the Seychelles, although he returned in 1959 and was elected president.

Cyprus finally gained independence in 1960 after the Greek and Turkish communities reached agreement on a constitution. A Treaty of Guarantee gave Britain, Greece and Turkey the right to intervene in the island's affairs if it were thought that either side was breaching the terms of the agreement. Part of the deal was that Britain would retain sovereignty over two military bases, which are still occupied today.

The two sides coexisted unhappily until 1963 when violence erupted, stirred up by Makarios and further dividing the Greek and Turkish communities.

More and more powers had an interest in Cyprus around this time. The Cold War was at its peak and the island was vital to Britain and the USA for monitoring Soviet activity in Central Asia, particularly missile testing. The British base at Akrotiri at that time contained nuclear weapons.

Makarios, meanwhile, played a dangerous game between the Russians, Greece and Turkey and the USA, Britain and Greece cooperated in staging a coup in July 1974 to get rid of him and install a government more friendly to the West. Makarios escaped and five days later, Turkey invaded the island, quickly occupying 37 % of the land. The Greek Cypriots immediately lost some of their most beautiful scenery, two important cities, the bulk of their citrus industry and much of their growing tourism infrastructure.

Since then, peace talks have started, collapsed and finished, over and over again. In 1983, Turkey proclaimed the occupied North the 'Turkish Republic of Northern Cyprus' but this is recognised only by Turkey, not by the United Nations or any other country. Some 2,400 United Nations peacekeepers still patrol the buffer zone that separates the two sectors of the island.

One of the biggest incentives for change is Turkey's strong desire to join the EU, something it cannot do while it occupies a chunk of Cyprus. In 2002, UN Secretary General Kofi Annan presented a peace plan for the island, suggesting a federation with a rotating presidency. The plan, however, failed.

Despite this, the EU invited Cyprus, or at least, the Greek Cypriot part of the island, to join by 2004. Plans to reunify the island accelerated and in 2003, Turkish and Greek Cypriots were allowed to cross the Green Line for the first time since the invasion when the Turks eased the border controls. Things were looking hopeful until two referendums were held in 2004 on whether the island could be reunified. The Turkish Cypriots voted 'yes' and the Greek Cypriots an overwhelming 'no', feeling that the sacrifices they would have to make were way too much. The Republic of Cyprus (the Greek Cypriot part) joined the EU in 2004.

Although the two sides now have virtually free movement across the Green Line and new crossing points continue to open, the animosity isn't getting any less. Greek Cypriots are still furious about their land being taken in 1974 and many people still have relatives who have been 'missing' since the invasion. You only have to pick up an English-language newspaper like the *Cyprus Weekly* to see how strongly people feel. In Nicosia, around the Green Line, the walls are peppered with bullet holes and some of the buildings on the Turkish side are believed to be booby trapped with land mines. Although tourism is flourishing in the south and taking off impressively in the north, Nicosia remains the world's last divided capital city and the 'Cypriot problem' remains unresolved.

The Insider

Cypriots speak excellent English and it is unlikely you will need to learn a lot of Greek, although it is, of course, courteous to learn some words and phrases! Learning the language is fun for children, too, and Cypriots will be charmed by their attempts to speak the language.

GREEK PHRASES

If you are serious about learning, there are numerous websites. I like *www.ilearngreek.com* as it has a section for children, with flash cards, and a piece on mythology. You can do a more in-depth, free course at *www. kypros.org/LearnGreek/*, a site associated with CyBC, the Cyprus Broadcasting Association, or pick up some basic phrases for free at *www.bbc.co.uk/languages/ greek/*.

There are plenty of books and CDs on *www.amazon.co.uk*; I've tried (being a lazy sort) *Teach Yourself One-Day Greek* by Elisabeth Smith (£4.19) and have picked up a few phrases.

For children, visit the brilliant site, *www.omega-kids.co.uk* for Greek alphabet sponges, magnetic letters, flash cards, picture and word books, learning mats and games.

If all else fails for adults, *Learn Greek in 25 Years: A Crash Course for the Linguistically Challenged* (£6) by Athens-based journalist Brian Church is a witty, dry book about the intricacies of the Greek language based on the author's newspaper columns (although the book is not specifically about Cyprus).

When Greek is written in an Anglicised, phonetic interpretation, as below, there are bound to be some discrepancies so don't worry if these phrases differ slightly from those in your phrase book; it's more important to read them out loud.

We have hours of idle fun in Cyprus trying to learn the alphabet and read Greek words on road signs and passing lorries, even if we don't know what they mean. It's a great way of passing a car journey.

OK, let's face it – most of us aren't going to become fluent in Greek before setting off on holiday. But it's really worth making an effort to learn at least the basics: Cypriots are proud of their country and their language, and they'll be delighted with any effort that you make to learn about either. And believe it or not, there are some pluses with the language:

● Pronunciation, especially if you've learned the Greek alphabet, is regular and unchanging. Letters and letter combinations are always pronounced the same.

● Pronunciation is made even easier by the fact that the stressed syllable in each word is marked by an accent – though only, alas, in lower case. So where all the letters are capitals – on many road signs, for instance – you're on your own when it comes to deciding which syllable to emphasise.

● Because Modern Greek is descended from Ancient Greek, and because Ancient Greek is the root of lots of other European languages (including English), it's easy to make reasonable guesses at the meaning of Greek words because of their similarity to English. For example, the Greek for menu is *Katalogo* – just like the English word catalogue.

To get ahead:

● Learn a few general greetings – they always go down well (see below).

● Learn some general-purpose phrases which you can adapt to a variety of situations. Then, with a small pocket English/Greek dictionary and phrasebook, you're armed for most holiday situations.

● Speak English. Don't be overwhelmed by the Greek language – with a few general phrases and greetings the vast majority of Cypriots involved in the tourist trade speak English and will be happy to converse in it.

USEFUL TERMS & PHRASES

Alphabet	Transliterated as	Pronounced as in
A α	álfa	a father
B β	víta	v *v*iper
Γ γ	gámma	g before α, o, ω, and *g*et consonants
		y before αι, ε, *y*es ει, η, ι, οι, υ
		ng before κ, γ, χ, or ξsi*ng*er
Δ δ	thélta	th *the* (not as the *th-* in "thin")
E ε	épsilon	e s*e*t
Z ζ	zíta	z la*z*y
H η	íta	i maga*zi*ne
Θ θ	thíta	th *thin* (not as the *th-* in "the")
I ι	ióta	i maga*zi*ne
		y before a, o *y*ard, *y*ore
K κ	káppa	k *k*eep
Λ λ	lámtha	l *l*eap
M μ	mi	m *m*arry

Alphabet	Transliterated as	Pronounced as in
N ν	ni	n *never*
Ξ ξ	ksi	ks taxi
O o	ómicron	o bought
Π π	pi	p *pet*
P ρ	ro	r *round*
Σ σ/ς	sígma	s before vowels or θ, κ, π, τ, φ, χ, ψ *say* z before β, γ, δ, ζ y before λ, μ, ν, ρ laz
T τ	taf	t *take*
Υ υ	ípsilon	i magaz*i*ne
Φ φ	fi	f *fee*
X χ	chi	h *h*ero (before e and i sounds; like the *ch-* in Scottish "loch" otherwise
Ψ ψ	psi	ps colla*ps*e
Ω ω	ómega	o bought

Combinations	Transliterated As	Pronounced As In
αι	e	g*e*t
αϊ	ai	*ai*sle
αυ before vowels or β, γ, δ, ζ, λ, μ, ν, ρ	av	*Av*e Maria
αυ before θ, κ, ξ, π, σ, τ, φ, χ, ψ	af	pil*af*
ει	i	magaz*i*ne
ευ before vowels or β, γ, δ, ζ, λ, μ, ν, ρ	ev	*ev*er
ευ before θ, κ, ξ, π, σ, τ, φ, χ, ψ	ef	l*ef*t
μπ at beginning of word	b	*b*ane
μπ in middle of word	mb	lu*mb*er
ντ at beginning of word	d	*d*umb
ντ in middle of word	nd	sle*nd*er
Οι	i	magaz*i*ne
Οϊ	oi	*oi*l
Ου	ou	s*ou*p
τζ	dz	roa*ds*
τσ	ts	ge*ts*
υι	i	magaz*i*ne

Useful Words & Phrases

When you're asking for or about something and have to rely on single words or short phrases, it's an excellent idea to use *sas parakaló* (if you please) to introduce or conclude almost anything you say.

Airport	Aerothrómio
Avenue	Leofóros
Bad	Kakós, -kí, -kó*
Bank	Trápeza
The bill, please	Tón logaryazmó(n), parakaló
Breakfast	Proinó
Bus	Leoforío
Can you tell me?	Boríte ná moú píte?
Car	Amáxi/ aftokinito
Cheap	Ft(h)inó
Church	Ekklissía
Closed	Klistós, stí, stó*
Coast	Aktí
Café	Kafenío
Cold	Kríos, -a, -o*
Dinner	Vrathinó
Do you speak English?	Miláte Angliká?
Excuse me	Signómi(n)
Expensive	Akrivós, -í, -ó*
Farewell!	Stó ka-ló! *(to person leaving)*
Glad to meet you	Chéro polí**
Good	Kalós, lí, ló*
Goodbye	Adío *or* chérete**
Good health (cheers)!	Stín (i)yá sas *or* Yá-mas!
Good morning *or* Good day	Kaliméra
Good evening	Kalispéra
Good night	Kaliníchta**
Hello!	Yássas *or* chérete!**
Here	Ethó
Highchair	*Psiló karekláki*
Hot	Zestós, -stí, -stó*
Hotel	Xenothochío**
How are you?	Tí kánete *or* Pós íst(h)e?
How far?	Pósso makriá?

How long?	Póssi óra *or* Pósso(n) keró?
How much does it cost?	Póso káni?
I am a vegetarian	Íme hortophágos
I am from London	Íme apó to Londino
I am lost *or* I have lost the way	Écho chathí *or* Écho chási tón drómo(n)**
I'm sorry	Singnómi
I'm sorry, but I don't speak Greek (well)	Lipoúme, allá thén miláo elliniká (kalá)
I don't understand	Thén katalavéno
I don't understand, please repeat it	Thén katalavéno, péste to páli, sásarakaló
I want to go to the airport	Thélo ná páo stó aerothrómio
I want a glass of beer	Thélo éna potíri bíra
I would like a room	Tha íthela ena thomátio
It's (not) all right	(Dén) íne en dáxi
Internet	*Diadiktio*
Left (direction)	Aristerá
Ladies' room	Ghinekón
Lunch	Messimerianó
Map	Chártis**
Market (place)	Agorá
Men's room	Andrón
Mr	Kírios
Mrs	Kiría
Miss	Despinís
My name is . . .	Onomázome . . .
New	Kenoúryos, -ya, -yo*
No	Óchi**
Old	Paleós, -leá, -leó* (*pronounce* palyós, -lyá, -lyó)
Open	Anichtós, -chtí, -chtó*
Pâtisserie	Zacharoplastío**
Pharmacy	Pharmakío
Please *or* You're welcome	Parakaló
Please call a taxi (for me)	Parakaló, fonáxte éna taxi (yá ména)
Point out to me, please . . .	Thíkste mou, sas parakaló . . .
Post office	Tachidromío**
Restaurant	Estiatório
Toilet	Tó méros *or* I toualétta
Right (direction)	Dexiá

Saint	Áyios, ayía, *(plural)* áyi-i *(abbreviated* ay.)
Shore	Paralía
Square	Plateía
Street	Odós
Show me on the map	Díxte mou stó(n) chárti**
Station (bus, train)	Stathmos (leoforíou, trénou)
Stop (bus)	Stási(s) (leoforíou)
Telephone	Tiléfono
Temple (of Athena, Zeus)	Naós (Athinás, Diós)
Thank you (very much)	Efcharistó (polí)**
Today	Símera
Tomorrow	Ávrio
Traveller's cheques	*Taxidiotikí epitagí*
Very nice	Polí oréos, -a, -o*
Very well	Polí kalá *or* En dáxi
What?	Tí?
What time is it?	Tí ôra íne?
What's your name?	Pós onomázest(h)e?
Where is . . . ?	Poú íne . . . ?
Where am I?	Pou íme?
Why?	Yatí?

* Masculine ending -os, feminine ending -a or -i, neuter ending -o.
** Remember, *ch* should be pronounced as in Scottish *loch* or German *ich,* not as in the word *church.*

As a rough guide, pronunciation is as follows:

ai – as in **e**gg
oi, ei, y – as in **I**ndia
ou – as in t**ou**r
ch – as in **h**ome
d – as in **th**ere

General Greetings

Kali**me**ra	good morning. Used both when coming to and going away from a place.
Kali**spe**ra	good afternoon. Used only when coming to a place or meeting someone in the evening or at night.
Kalini**h**ta	good night. Used only as a goodbye greeting in the evening or at night.
herete (e as in egg)	hello, used between 10am and 2pm.
Yassou	hello or goodbye (greeting to one person or a friend).

Yassas	hello or goodbye (greeting to more persons or a more formal and polite way to greet an unknown person).
Adio	goodbye
Yassou file mou Niko	Hello my friend Niko, an easy way to please a Greek friend of yours.
Ela	Come here (although this is often used as a general exclamation and has many meanings).
Opa!	Watch out!
Po-po-po! – an expression of amazement of dismay – the closest translation is the French, Oo la la!	
Oriste!	What can I do for you? (A shopkeeper or waiter might say this).
Kalo taxhidi	bon voyage.
Parakalo	please.
Efharisto	thank you.
Ne	yes.
Ohi	no.
Sighnomi	sorry.
Ti kanete?	How are you?
Kala efharisto	I'm well thanks.
Pos sas lene?	What's your name?
Me lene....	My name is...
Milate anglika?	Do you speak English?
Katalaveno	I understand.
Dhen katalaveno	I don't understand.
Pou ine...?	Where is...?
Pote?	When?

Getting Around

Ti ora fevyi/ ftani to?	What time does the ... leave/arrive?	Proti thesi	first class
Aeroplano	plane	Pos tha pao sto/sti?	How do I get to?
Karavi	boat	Pou ine..?	Where is...?
Leoforio	bus	Ine konda?	Is it near?
Taxi	taxi	Efthia	straight ahead
Tha ithela	I'd like	Aristera	left
Isitirio me epistrofi	a return ticket	Dexia	right
		Piso	behind

Common Road & Place Names

Agia	Saint (female)
Agios	Saint (male)
Kato	Lower
Leoforos	Avenue
Panagia	The Blessed Virgin Mary
Pano	Upper
Petra	Stone
Plateia	Square
Stavros	Cross

Accommodation

Pou ine...?	Where is...?
Thelo ena	I'd like
Kalo xenodohio	A good hotel
Mono	Single
Dhiplo	Double
Dhomatio	Room
Poso kani?	How much is it?
Boro na to dho?	May I see it?

Numbers

1	enas (m) mia (f) ena (n)
2	dhio
3	tris (m&f) tria (n)
4	teseris (m&f) tesera (n)
5	pende
6	exi
7	epta
8	ohto
9	enea
10	dheka

Telling the Time

Ti ora ine?	What time is it?
Ine	It's
Mia i ora	1 o'clock

Efta ke misi	7.30
Simera	today
Appose	tonight
Tora	now
Avrio	tomorrow
Kyriaki	Sunday
Dheftera	Monday
Triti	Tuesday
Tetarti	Wednesday
Pempti	Thursday
Paraskevi	Friday
Savato	Saturday

Eating Out

Pro-ino	breakfast
Mesimvrino	lunch
Vradhyno	dinner
Psomi	bread
Tyri	cheese
Eleoladho	olive oil
Kotopoulo	chicken
Ghala	milk
Nero	water
Tsai	tea
Thelo ena kafe	I want a coffee
Thelo ena tsai	I want a tea
Thelo mia byra	I want a beer
Thelo ena poto	I want a drink

Emergencies

Pharmako	medicine
Pharmakeio	pharmacy
Iatros	doctor
Nosokomeio	hospital
Voithya!	Emergency!
Fonaxte ena iatro!	Call a doctor!
Fonaxte tin astynomia!	Call the police!
Sta andiviotika	antibiotics
Andisiptiko	antiseptic
Dheearea	diarrhoea
Andieeliaki	sunblock

Cypriot Candy

You'll see boxes of Loukoumi for sale all over the island. Its preparation is complicated, so do try it!

The method involves several steps. First, a huge cauldron of water is placed over a hot fire. When the water boils, sugar is added and this mixture is boiled for another hour. The mixture is stirred continuously using an electric paddle. This is followed by adding starch, and the mixture is further boiled for five to six hours, till it becomes shiny and smooth.

After allowing it to cool for some time, different flavours are added to the mixture – maybe almond, cherry, chocolate, lemon or rose (which is made locally). The flavoured mixture is poured into huge wooden trays for setting.

It takes almost five hours to set and then the mixture is cut into squares, dusted generously with icing sugar and packed into small boxes lined with greaseproof paper.

Cyprus also produces more-ish sugared almonds, grown locally, freshly roasted and covered with a creamy coloured sugar coating.

The almonds are first washed, roasted slowly and then put into a copper cauldron. Sugar syrup is used to baste the nuts. Once they are evenly coated with the syrup, the nuts are cooled slightly. The process is repeated a few times so there are several layers of sugar, and then the nuts are cooled properly and boxed.

FOOD & DRINK

You can find pretty well any type of food you want in Cyprus from Chinese to chips, but no visit is complete without a decent exploration of the wonderful Cypriot cuisine, which includes elements of Greek, Arabic and Mediterranean dishes.

There are British influences, too. Cypriots enjoy a good fry-up for breakfast but instead of bacon and baked beans, include delicious, melt-in-the-mouth fried halloumi cheese with olives, cucumber, tomatoes and hot pitta bread, sometimes served with a spiced sausage and eggs.

Lunches tend to be lighter because of the heat but you should take it easy during the day anyway if you're going to tackle a meze in the evening. Meze, or mezedes, is either a starter or an entire meal. Typically, it will include a range of dips like hummous, tahini, taramasalata and smoked aubergine, as well as cubes of cheese, dolmades (stuffed vine leaves), meatballs, beans, sausages, fish, a huge salad with feta cheese, little pastries and more. Children love meze – there is always something they can eat.

A main course follows all the nibbles, often meaty and slow-cooked in a wine sauce, although the less adventurous will enjoy the traditional *sou-vlakia* – cubed chicken, lamb, beef or pork on a big skewer served with fries, salad and a squeeze of lemon.

Pudding is either fresh fruit – the watermelon, figs, peaches, cherries, pomegranate and melon that are grown on the island – or Middle Eastern-style sweets like *baklava*, dripping with honey and scattered with nuts, or *loukmadhes*, little balls of dough fried and dipped in syrup.

Cypriots drink wine with dinner. It's hardly worth buying imported wine as it's much more expensive and besides, Cypriot wine in Cyprus tastes great, with some serious growers nowadays producing excellent vintages compared to the rather rough stuff of a decade ago. The island's own grapes include Mavro, Xinisteri, Opthalmo and Muscat, which make rich, strong wines. Growers have softened these with the introduction of Cabernet Sauvignon, Cabernet Franc, Grenache and Palomino grapes, too.

Some prefer beer, mainly the fizzy lager Keo that is brewed on the island, most refreshing on a hot day. All manner of soft drinks are available for children. Get them to try Airani, a refreshing drink made with live yoghurt and salt, very good for rehydration in the heat.

There are a couple of liqueurs produced for after dinner. Commandaria is actually a sweet dessert wine (it also makes a great marinade for fruit salad if you bring any home). Filfar is a sickly-sweet orange liqueur best avoided unless you like an ultra-sugary Cointreau-type drink.

If you want to be a 'real' Cypriot, you should drink ouzo with water as an aperitif (or better still, with your morning coffee) and zivania, the local schnapps, up to 99% proof, with your meze.

Typical mezedes dishes

Pitta bread for dunking

Halloumi, kaskavalli or feta cheese

Fresh or sun-dried tomatoes

Olives

Sliced artichokes

Kapari (caper stalks)

Lountza (traditional smoked ham)

Loukanika (smoked sausage)

Tzatziki (cucumber, yoghurt and garlic dip)

Houmous (ground chick peas with olive oil, lemon and garlic)

Taramasalata (bright pink fish roe dip)

Octopus, usually fried

Calamari (battered squid rings)

Giant prawns

Barbouni (red mullet) and tsipoura (sea bream)

Sheftalia (sausage)

Koupepia (vine leaves stuffed with rice and spices, sometimes with lamb)

Souvla/souvlakia (cubes of marinated lamb, chicken or pork on the spit, also served as a main course. Good for children as it's fairly plain)

Village salad – a Cypriot term for Greek salad, cucumber, olives, tomatoes and olive oil with cubes of feta sprinkled over the top

Main courses

Kleftiko – knuckle of lamb with herbs and slow roasted at a low heat in a clay oven until the meat falls away from the bone.

Moussaka – traditional Greek dish made from minced lamb or beef and herbs covered with layers of sliced potatoes, aubergine and courgette and sometimes topped with a béchamel sauce.

Pastitsio – a rich bake of meat, macaroni and béchamel sauce – similar to lasagne.

Tavas – a veal, onion and cumin infused dish served straight from the oven.

Afelia – cubes of pork soaked in wine, sautéed with oil, coriander and wine.

Stifado – winter stew made with beef and onions (sometimes made with goat, too).

Keftedes – fried spiced pork and/or beef meatballs.

Fasolia – white bean stew, good for vegetarians.

Louvi me lahana – swiss chard and black-eyed bean stew, another good veggie dish.

Avgolemono – chicken, lemon and egg soup, often eaten at lunch time.

A fish meze would feature only fish dishes, with a mixture of types of fish and shellfish, grilled and fried, usually fairly simply served with a squeeze of lemon.

Children's Menus

A lot of places offer a children's menu to cater to English tastes but it's usually fairly unimaginative – burgers, pasta and pizza. If you're having meze, try ordering two for a family of four so the children can try things, and experiment with chicken souvlaki and chips as a main course, or white fish off the bone. Cypriots are so obliging and child-friendly that they'll go to a special effort to provide child-sized portions of their local dishes.

Puddings

Galatoboureko – custard filo pie.

Kataifi – nut-filled shredded pastries.

Baklava – Pastry filled with nuts and drenched in honey or syrup.

Melomakarona – honey biscuits.

Kourabiedes –white sweet biscuits.

Loukoumades – deep-fried pastry fritters soaked in honey syrup.

Ice cream is available everywhere, either big-name brands or local makes.

If you want coffee after dinner (or in the morning), specify whether you want Cypriot coffee or 'Nescafé', instant coffee drunk by tourists. Cypriot coffee is very strong, served black in a small cup accompanied by a glass of water. Specify when you order how much sugar you would like, as it's brewed with the sugar already added. *Gliko* means sweet, *metrio* medium and *sketo*

with no sugar. Don't make the gaffe of asking for Turkish coffee (which is the same). Similarly, you'll see boxes of Cyprus Delight for sale, which is like Turkish Delight but should not be referred to as such.

Decaffeinated Nescafé is available, as are herb teas in the smarter establishments. If a taverna says it doesn't have herb tea, simply ask for a pot of hot water and a bunch of fresh mint and infuse your own.

The Youth Card 'Euro <26'

Euro <26 is a special card worth investing in if you have teenagers over the age of 13 (11 in some countries - and under the age of 26). It's valid in 41 countries in Europe, including Cyprus, and secures discounts in more than 500 different places in Cyprus alone and more than 100,000 across the continent on items like clothes, sports gear, books, air tickets, theatres and cinemas.

The card costs around £7 for a year, depending on where you buy it (they can be obtained in England, Scotland, Ireland - Northern and the Republic - and Wales). Simply apply by sending a passport sized photograph, the card fee and proof of age to your nearest organisation. Full details are on www.euro26.org and there are regional websites for all the different countries.

If you don't live in Europe, you can still get a card by buying it online. When in Cyprus, simply look for the card logo in different shops and ask for your discount inside!

Index

See also Accommodations and Restaurant indexes, below.

General

A

Abrahmet district (Nicosia), 203
Accommodation. *See also*
 Accommodations Index
  best, 7–10
  types of, 31–32
  useful phrases, 229
Active families, activities for
  Ayia Napa and Protaras, 188–189
  Larnaca, 165
  Limassol, 113–115
  Nicosia, 209
  Paphos, 60–62
  Polis, Latchi, and the West, 84–87
  Troodos Mountains, 142–145
Adonis, legend of, 202
Afelia, 232
Agia Napa. *See* Ayia Napa
Agiasma Trail, 86
Agios Georgios, 48
Agios Ioannis cathedral (Nicosia), 206
Agros, 134, 145–146, 149
Agrotourism, 3, 8, 32
Airports, 26
Akamas (Akamas Peninsula), 5, 11, 28, 75, 80–81
Akamas Jeep Safari, 111
Akrotiri Environmental Information Centre (Limassol), 101
Akrotiri Salt Lake, 100–102
Alcohol, 17, 30, 32, 33, 231
Amathous, 109
Animal attractions, best, 4
Anthestiria Festival, 154
Apartments, 32
Aphrodite Hills (Pissouri), 49
Aphrodite's Birthplace (Petra tou Romiou) (Paphos), 7, 54
Aphrodite Trail (Latchi), 85
Aphrodite Water Park (Paphos), 6, 60
Aquaria and animal parks
  Larnaca, 159
  Limassol, 102–104
  Nicosia, 200
  Paphos, 54–55
  Troodos Mountains, 138
Archaeological Museum (Larnaca), 162–163
Archaeological sites
  Amathous, 109
  Kourion, 104–105
  Larnaca, 161–162
Archangel Michael Day, 199
Archbishop Makarios III Foundation (Nicosia), 208

Argonaftis Animal Park donkey safaris (Ayia Napa), 187
Arodes, 79
Arsos, 135–136, 142
Artemis Trail (Mount Olympus), 143
Ascot Jeep Safari, 59
Atalanta Trail (Mount Olympus), 143
Athalassa National Forest Park (Nicosia), 204
ATMs, 18
Avakas Gorge, 3–4, 81–82
Avdimou, 125–126
Avgolemono, 232
Ayia Napa, 175–194
  accommodations, 190–193
  for active families, 188–189
  beaches and resorts, 178–184
  events and entertainment, child-friendly, 177
  map, 174
  museums, 185–186
  natural wonders and spectacular views, 184–185
  as resort, 178–179
  restaurants, 193–194
  shopping, 189–190
  top 10 attractions, 177–178
  tours, child-friendly, 186–187
Ayia Napa Festival, 177
Ayia Napa monastery, 185
Ayia Thekla, 180
Ayia Triada, 182
Ayios Lazaros church (Larnaca), 160
Ayios Minas monastery (Lefkara), 162

B

Baby, travelling with a, 20, 33, 37
Babysitters, 33
Baklava, 231, 232
Balloon flights, 61
Baths of Adonis, 52–53
Baths of Aphrodite, 82
Beaches
  Ayia Napa and Protaras, 178–184
  best, 4–5
  Larnaca, 156–157
  Limassol, 99–100
  Paphos, 50–52
  Polis, Latchi and the West, 77–80
Beach Volleyball National Tournament, 177
Bicycle rentals, 31, 62, 189
Bicycling tours, 165. *See also* Bicycle rentals
Blue Flag Beaches, 34
Boat trips
  Latchi, 83–84
  Limassol, 111

Accommodations

Restaurants